THE SOCIAL PSYCHOLOGY
OF
TELECOMMUNICATIONS

The Social Psychology of Telecommunications

JOHN SHORT

EDERYN WILLIAMS

BRUCE CHRISTIE

Communications Studies Group,
School of Environmental Studies,
University College, London

JOHN WILEY & SONS
London · New York · Sydney · Toronto

Library of Congress Cataloging in Publication Data:

Short, John.
    The social psychology of telecommunications.

    1. Telecommunication—Social aspects.
I. Williams, Ederyn, joint author. II. Christie,
Bruce, joint author. III. Title.
HE7651.S48   301.16'1   75-44335
ISBN 0 471 01581 4

Printed in Great Britain by Pitman Press, Bath

Preface

Hitherto, the fact that face-to-face contact has almost always been the most satisfactory form of communication has been a fundamental constraint on society. It may be something of an oversimplification to suggest that cities evolved in order to facilitate human communication but there is wide agreement that the physical and social environments of modern man have been conditioned to a very large extent by his apparent need to travel to acquire information. This supposedly fundamental constraint may be undermined by developments in technology, for no longer need all communication involve physical movement. It is within the scope of foreseeable technology to reconstitute by electronic means a virtual three-dimensional representation of an individual who is hundreds of miles distant. Dazzled by such technological marvels, enthusiastic futurists have speculated about possibilities ranging from education at home, to working by audio-video links from homes no longer located in overcrowded cities. The potential significance of such developments for a range of disciplines from sociology and psychology to urban and transportation planning needs little elaboration.

From the initial design of the systems, through the question of how to make the most effective use of the system, to the evaluation of the consequences of more extensive use of the systems, social psychologists can make a significant contribution to the effective planning of these developments. These issues touch on important theoretical questions in many different branches of social psychology.

The book is thus written by and for social psychologists. However, in illustrating the contribution that an integrated range of social psychological studies can make to an 'applied' issue (the substitution of telecommunication for travel) we hope also to interest groups other than psychologists. Inevitably this means that the text may run a danger of being incomplete to different readers for different reasons. This can best be resolved by referring readers who wish to follow up a particular aspect to other sources:

for a popular description of new telecommunications devices, Martin (1971) or Maddox (1972);
for introductions to social psychology, Brown (1965) or Aronson (1973).

More detailed references for specific issues are to be found in the bibliography.

Acknowledgements

We are glad of this opportunity to express our thanks to the Civil Service Department (MSOR) and the Post Office Corporation (Long Range Studies) for their support of the research which gave rise to this book. To the best of our knowledge they were the first two organisations to commission a systematic programme of research on the effectiveness and impact of person-to-person telecommunications systems.

Although the majority of the financial support for the work came from the two original sponsors, research undertaken under contracts and grants from other sources has made a significant contribution to our present understanding. We would therefore like to thank:

The Department of Communication in Ottawa,
The Department of Transportation in Washington,
The Department of Housing and Urban Development in Washington,
The General Electric Research and Development Headquarters in Schenectady,
The Social Science Research Council.

Finally we must acknowledge the intellectual debt owed to several colleagues and collaborators: Hugh Collins, Stephen Connel, Martin Davies, Martin Elton, Roger Pye, Art Schulman, Barry Stapley, Ian Young and in particular Alex Reid the first director of the Communications Studies Group and Brian Champness who coordinated the psychological research.

Contents

1
Issues and Impacts

AN INTRODUCTION TO PERSON-TO-PERSON TELECOMMUNICATIONS

Person-to-person telecommunications are hardly a new phenomenon. Even ignoring the earlier telegraph, telecommunications has been with us for a hundred years—since the invention of the telephone by Bell in 1876. Telephones have entered most business premises, and the homes of a substantial number of us (about 50% of homes in the UK, but nearer 90% in Canada, the USA and Sweden). Why, then, should we suddenly consider that the study of the social psychology of telecommunications is of interest?

One could, perhaps, best answer this question by reversing it. Why, considering its pervasiveness, has telecommunications been so long neglected as a proper subject for study by social scientists? Unlike most of our other technological playthings, the telephone is actually interposed in the communications network between people, between groups and between organizations. Without communication between individuals and groups, one could hardly expect that there would be social organization or culture, yet we have accepted the interposition within our communication networks of a mechanical device, which may alter the form or nature of our communications in various unidentified ways, without as much as a second thought.

When one considers this lack of interest in person-to-person telecommunications, it stands in stark contrast to the plethora of interest in the mass communications, even those of recent origin such as radio or television (Himmelweit, Oppenheim and Vince, 1958, Hovland, Lumsdaine and Sheffield, 1949, Halloran, 1970). Such systems are intrinsically one-way, with none of the possibilities for feedback or interplay between the participants which are the essence of social phenomena. Compared to the more flexible two-way media, mass communications are limited in both the interconnections that can be made and in the purposes for which they can be used (little more than entertainment, transmission of information and propaganda). Furthermore, there are more telephones than televisions in the world as a whole (*UN Statistical Review*, 1973, estimated figures 313 million telephones and 297 million televisions in the world) this difference being especially large for the more advanced countries like the USA (the same source gives 131 million telephones and 99 million televisions in the USA). In the United Kingdom there are approximately equal numbers of telephones and televisions (1973, telephones 17.3 millions, televisions 17.2 millions, *Post Office Telecommunications Journal* and *Monthly Digest of Statistics*) but the television is approaching saturation and growth rate for telephones is about twice that for televisions.

Here then, we have a situation where over 300,000 millions of person-to-person conversations per annum (AT&T estimate, 1971) are being held over the telephone. Yet despite the magnitude of this phenomenon, there has been very little informed speculation about the effect of the use of telecommunications (notable exceptions to this general trend are McLuhan, 1964, Cherry, 1971 and Aronson, 1971, whose work will be discussed later), let alone systematic empirical investigation.

NEW TECHNOLOGICAL ADVANCES

For the reader not already convinced that the study of the social and psychological effects of telecommunications is justified simply in terms of the 'plain old telephone service', we point to the veritable explosion of new telecommunications devices presently being designed, tested or marketed. We are not here discussing peripheral frills such as push-button dialling or simple extensions of qualitatively similar service such as international STD (subscriber trunk dialling), but completely new media, which bear as little resemblance to the telephone as the telephone does to the telegraph. Some of the new media, such as telex or fast facsimile machines (a sort of remote photocopier) will not be discussed since, although of potentially great impact, these media fall outside our prime area of concern—person-to-person telecommunications. However, even excluding such non-interactive media, and considering only those in which both parties can talk to the other, there are still four different types of new telecommunications devices now available. These are:

(a) *Group audio systems*. The normal telephone is a one-to-one medium of communication, which is often felt to be a limitation. However, if one wishes to hold a multiperson meeting it is not necessary to meet face-to-face, despite common practice to the contrary. There is presently available within most telephone systems the possibility for conference calls, by which several people, each at separate locations with their own telephone, can be connected together for a multiperson conversation. The line is completely open, so any participant can speak at any time, and the only limitation as to the distance between the participants is the costs that they are prepared to bear. This system does, however, have serious limitations which have prevented its widespread acceptance. Calls usually take an hour or two to set up, and there is a limit of about half-a-dozen in the number of participants who can take part (due to the cumulative addition of background noise with each further participant).

Figure 1.1   A loudspeaking telephone (British Post Office LST4). Reproduced by courtesy of the Post Office.

Other systems allow satisfactory interaction between groups at separate locations. For example, loudspeaking telephones, such as the British Post Office LST4 (see Figure 1.1) or the Bell Speakerphone, are now to be found in many offices. While loudspeaking telephones are usually advertised as executive aids, allowing handsfree use so that documents can be handled during the conversation, they can be used for multiperson conferences. Unlike conference calls, several of the conferees can be in one location, and the combination of loudspeaking telephones and conference calls can allow very flexible patterns of audio conferences with several locations and several participants at each location. Little is known about whether such media allow normal group processes to occur or whether some distortion results.

Obviously such audio conferences differ from face-to-face conferences in many ways, we shall leave discussion of most of these effects until later chapters, but two defects of audio conferences which can be overcome technically will be discussed here. One of these is the inability to refer to documents or other graphic material: this can often be overcome by the use of remote facsimile machines or other systems which can transmit graphic information over normal telephone lines. The other problem relates to speaker identification: during face-to-face

Figure 1.2   The Remote Meeting Table at Dover House, London. Reproduced by kind permission of the Civil Service Department

conversations, unless the group is very large, there is never any difficulty in identifying who is speaking. One would suppose that this need to identify the speaker serves some purpose; probably that of relating a particular statement to the previous perceptions by the listeners of the speaker's expertise, trustworthiness, credibility, etc. With most audio communications systems, speaker identification is very difficult if there are more than two or three speakers at remote locations. It is not, however, necessary to show a full visual image of the distant participants (as in the conference television systems) for speaker identification, simpler systems will suffice. One such system is the Remote Meeting Table (see Figure 1.2), which is at present in use in several parts of the British Civil Service. Each of a pair of interconnected tables has six microphones, one at each participant's position, and six loudspeakers interspersed with the microphones. As a participant speaks, his microphone is activated by the differential loudness between the various microphones, he captures the transmission line (a normal telephone line) and his voice is switched to his own loudspeaker, which is personalized with his name and lights up as it is activated, at the other end. Thus both the positional information and the flashing light give a clear indication to the participants of the identity of the speaker at the other end. The device raises a number of questions of a psychological nature: is this a satisfactory substitute for physical presence or are the flashing lights just a distraction, and what is the connection between identification and identity?

(b) *Videotelephones*. The use of closed-circuit television for person-to-person communication is not a new idea; such a system was demonstrated by Bell Laboratories over the 250 miles between Washington and New York, in 1927 (Ives, 1927). The videophone, as presently conceived, is a unit comprising camera, cathode-ray tube, microphone and loudspeaker, which can contact similar devices on a switched network by dialling. It is thus essentially a telephone with vision, and in its original conception was seen as a replacement for the telephone to allow one-to-one conversations with vision as well as sound.

Videophone experiments have been proceeding in a number of countries; Dickson and Bowers (1973) list 16 business and government institutions in eight countries who are researching this device. Trial videophone networks have been operating in Sweden, the United Kingdom and the Netherlands; the most ambitious effort in this direction has been by AT&T in the USA with their Picturephone, (viz. Bell System, 1971). As presently designed, the picturephone has a 5 by 5½ inch, black-and-white picture with 250 lines per frame (about the same quality picture as a medium-sized domestic television). The camera can be zoomed, but in its normal position it gives a head and shoulders view of one person. It is intended as a desk-top device and should be viewed from about two feet. There is an associated handset

6

telephone for dialling, and various controls, particularly a 'privacy' control which cuts out the picture. Graphic material can be sent by using a small mirror so that the camera is directed at the desk top but resolution is not sufficient for a full page of normal typescript. There is, in addition, a self-view mode, so that users can view the picture that they are sending. The British Post Office version is shown in Figure 1.3, (further details in Hillen, 1972).

Figure 1.3   An experimental Viewphone (British Post Office). Reproduced by courtesy of the Post Office.

It is by no means clear that the visual channel provided by this device is useful, but the Picturephone is already being marketed in the USA. While sales are not going as well as hoped, due partly to the high rental (over £20 per month), it is still thought that the videophone has a wide range of applications in business, government, health services and other organizations. The AT&T prediction that 3% of business and 1% of domestic telephones in the USA will be Picturephones by 1980 now seems over-optimistic. However, if the costs of transmission of signals drop as much as is suggested by some writers (e.g. Martin, 1971), videophones may still come into general use this century.

(c) *Conference television systems.* The telephone is limited in the sense of being primarily a device for one-to-one communication. The viewphone would be similarly limited. For this reason there has been a certain amount of development work on video teleconference facilities. One such system would be the video equivalent of the conference call, that is, several videophones in two or more locations would be linked together at once. In the USA, AT&T have experimented with such systems, solving the problem as to which participants should be 'on-screen' at any one time by voice-activated circuits which switch views so that the speaker is shown on the screen of all the other participants, while on the speaker's own screen is shown the view of the previous speaker (since self-view might be rather distracting). This set-up, however, deprives the speaker of visual feedback of the audience response and no-one knows what effect this may have on interaction.

Figure 1.4   The Confravision studio at Euston Tower, London. Reproduced by courtesy of the Post Office.

Perhaps the best-known conference television system is the British Post Office Confravision (see Figure 1.4, further details in Haworth, 1972). This system has five studios (London, Bristol, Manchester, Birmingham and Glasgow) which are usually connected in pairs. The video monitors are very similar to domestic television receivers, being 625-line monochrome. One monitor is used for self-view, the other to view the conferees at the distant end; exceptionally in multilocational conferences both may show participants at other studios. In each studio there are two cameras, one of which shows a view of the conferees, the other being used for documents. This system is presently being marketed, being available to any user willing to pay the cost.

Similar systems are on more limited trial in Canada (Bell), Australia (the Post Office), USA (General Electric) and elsewhere. These systems differ in several details from Confravision; some of these differences having possible implications for social interaction and small group processes. For example, the Australian system has a split screen, so that the view of the other participants is an 8 x 1½ rectangle rather than a 4 x 3 rectangle. This allows a substantially bigger picture of the other participants to be shown (since the configuration of the chairs forms the conferees into a long straight line). The Bell Canada system is using projection monitors giving a 14 foot by 2½ foot picture. It seems unlikely that conversing with someone who appears 6 inches high will be exactly equivalent to conversation with a life-sized image.

(d) *Computer mediated conferencing systems*. These are even more advanced in their conception than the previously described systems. Such systems have been much discussed recently (Turoff, 1973) and the Institute for the Future have designed one such system, FORUM, which is widely used (Amara and Vallée, 1974). Each participant in a FORUM conference takes part using a teletype terminal connected via telephone lines and data links to a central computer. Comments are typed in, stored in the computer, and can subsequently be read out from the computer.

This type of system has particular advantages and disadvantages compared to other media that make it unique in its applications. The storage of the messages in the computer means that conferences can be asynchronous—it really doesn't matter whether only a few of the conferees are 'on-line' at any one time; they can always catch up later. Thus conferences can stretch over several weeks, and individuals can choose when to participate without being in danger of missing anything. Furthermore, since all the contributions are on computer store, they can be searched by instructing the computer to output all contributions on a certain topic, from a certain participant, or from a certain date. Input in the typewritten mode has some disadvantages; most people find typing slow and tedious. However, this slowness of input is compensated for by speed of output (reading can be several times faster than listening).

This medium is really too new to have been properly assessed. Whether it genuinely is a new form, which will allow conferences of a novel sort which would otherwise have been impossible, or too expensive in time and money, or whether it is no better than a combination of conference telephony, recorded message devices and the mails, remains to be seen.

TECHNOLOGY ASSESSMENT

The research discussed in this book could be described as technology assessment.

' "Technology Assessment" is the phrase that is currently being applied to the activity of anticipating the broad consequences of technological change. A technological assessment begins with the recognition that the ultimate uses of any technology are frequently much more diverse than envisioned by the original innovators and goes on to seek understanding of the interrelationships among the various consequences of technological change' (Dickson and Bowers, 1973).

Not only is technological advance progressing at an accelerating rate (Jones, 1971) but it seems likely that the scale of the impacts is becoming progressively greater. Methesne (1970) said 'The rifle wiped out the buffalo, but nuclear weapons can wipe out man'. One could add that the telephone and telegraph speeded business and altered our urban way of life, but, as we shall see, future telecommunications could abolish the office, and even the city.

Technological assessment can no longer be a part-time amateur activity for politicians and science-fiction writers. Such assessment requires the development of more objective methods. At present, two of the major methods used are computer modelling (Meadows *et al.*, 1972) and the interaction of experts as in the Delphi technique (Brown and Helmer, 1964); both depend crucially upon the quality of the data fed into the process. As the computer men say: 'garbage in—garbage out'. The first essential is objective data.

Unless there has been some fundamental research on the way in which the new technologies might affect individuals and groups, and the ways in which those individuals and groups will react to and use the new technology, any forecasting process must be extremely hazardous. This then is where we see our place. In studying the way in which people react to and use new telecommunications equipment, we are providing some of the information basic to any clear view of the way in which such systems will or should develop and the impact that they are likely to have upon our society.

Only later can one make any predictions as to what these impacts might be. Until the fundamental questions as to the use of new telecommunications by individuals or small groups have been answered, it seems unlikely that gross predictions relating to the society as a whole will be valid. However, in order to indicate to the reader the potential importance of person-to-person communications, we will briefly discuss a few of the possibilities which have done most to stimulate interest in the area, namely:

the relationship between telecommunications and economic development;
the impact of telecommunications upon transportation;
the impact of telecommunications on energy usage and the environment;

the impact of telecommunications upon urban structure;
the impact of telecommunications upon social organization;
the impact of telecommunications on human relations;
the impact of telecommunications on the individual.

THE RELATIONSHIP BETWEEN TELECOMMUNICATIONS AND ECONOMIC DEVELOPMENT

The wealth of the economically developed countries is obviously dependent upon many factors, but there are reasons for considering communications, particularly the person-to-person media, with their primarily organizing function, to be fundamental in the process of economic growth. Cherry (1971) has shown that, when one makes international comparisons of statistics, the correlation between telephones *per capita* and Gross National Product *per capita* is remarkably high. Other data quoted by Cherry suggests that this relationship holds for less developed countries, or even for an area within one country (states of the USA).

One could argue that this correlation can be accounted for by the use of the excess wealth created as a means to purchase luxury items such as the telephone. However, the alternative explanation, that telecommunications, having an important organizing function, are in some way necessary for economic advancement, is supported by the observations that, (a) the adoption of the telephone has been primarily within the economic sphere (the producers of wealth) rather than the domestic sphere (the consumers of wealth). In the UK, virtually all offices and other workplaces have telephones, but only about half of private homes do (1975). This distribution would contrast strongly with the distribution of, for example, television. (b) The extremely rapid acceptance of the telephone by the business community (see Aronson, 1971, Cherry, 1971) suggests that there was a powerful latent need for it.

The importance of the telephone in business, which suggests that new telecommunications devices will also be adopted first in the economic sphere, is one of the reasons why our research has concentrated initially upon the use of telecommunications in business and government, rather than the home.

TELECOMMUNICATION-TRANSPORTATION TRADE-OFFS

Nearly all transportation has one of two purposes: the movement of goods or the movement of people. While it is unlikely that telecommunications would have any effect upon the movement of goods, there has been widespread speculation (e.g. Harkness, 1973, Dickson and Bowers, 1973, Cowan, 1973) as to the effects of advances in telecommunications upon the transportation of people. It is argued that, apart from a small residue of pleasure travel, a large amount of travel is for the purposes of meeting face-to-face. This would apply not only to travel within work hours, but even to travel to work.

If then new telecommunications devices were developed which were adequate substitutes for face-to-face meetings, there should be a corresponding reduction in the amount of travel to such meetings. The adequacy of telecommunications as a substitute is fundamental, and will be discussed at length in the later chapters of the book.

If the substitution of travel by telecommunications were substantial, this could clearly have a massive effect upon the demand for transportation facilities. Projects with heavy capital investment which are based upon assumptions of rapidly growing transportation needs (such as new airports), could be obsolete even before they were built—particularly since equally heavy investment is simultaneously taking place in new telecommunications facilities.

One must beware, however, of assuming that substitution will be the only effect of improved telecommunications upon the demand for transportation; a synergistic effect, by which the increased possibility for contact by one medium stimulates demand for contact by other media, should not be ignored. Clearly, the telephone, which must be a substitute for *some* face-to-face meetings which would otherwise have occurred, has not caused a marked decrease in the demand for travel—over the same historic period the demand for transport has increased manyfold. We must all have had the experience of contacting someone by telephone and finding, on the basis of that conversation, that a face-to-face meeting is possible and justifiable. The reverse effect also appears; having met someone face-to-face, we keep in contact subsequently via the telephone. Opportunities to telecommunicate may stimulate travel, and opportunities to travel may stimulate telecommunication. The opening of the Severn Bridge, a road bridge linking South-West England with South Wales, was soon followed by the jamming of the telephone trunk routes between those areas. Such synergistic effects are clearly important, and a great deal of work in the field situation is needed before the balance between substitution and stimulation can be delineated with any confidence.

IMPACT ON ENERGY USAGE AND THE ENVIRONMENT

Whether the 'energy crisis' is temporary or permanent, there will always be some cost, financial and ecological, in the use of energy. It is interesting, therefore, to consider the energy usage of telecommunications, particularly as compared to travel. Dickson and Bowers (1973) in comparing the videophone with travel to face-to-face meetings, make the following points:

Communication by videophone telephone requires less energy than communication achieved through physical travel.

The production of the infrastructure for videotelephone systems appears to require less energy and material resources than for transportation facilities.

Videotelephone systems create far less air pollution and extraneous noise than transportation modes.

Underground video telephone systems promise to be aesthetically more satisfactory than airports and highways.

The same authors calculate that for the energy used in travelling by air from New York to Los Angeles and back, one could have 64 hours of videophone conversation between the same locations, and that one (American) gallon of petrol has the energy content sufficient to power 66 hours of local videophone conversation. Clearly, if one were choosing between travel and videophone usage merely on the consideration of minimum energy expenditure, there would be very few occasions in which travel would be more economic. If this is true for video systems, it must be even more true of audio systems. A complete telephone exchange, together with all the local lines, uses only about as much energy as one car running continuously (about 6-100 kW for telephone exchanges, 25 kW for cars). Furthermore, it has been estimated that in the UK in 1970, only 0.03% of national energy consumption was taken up by telecommunications, as compared to 18.4% by transportation. More detailed studies of the energy savings possible by a more extensive use of telecommunications would obviously be worthwhile, but such studies seem unlikely to overturn the basic conclusion; if such systems could act as effective substitutes for travel by the users, energy savings would be considerable, and there would be a correspondingly large reduction in the damage to our environment.

TELECOMMUNICATIONS AND THE URBAN STRUCTURE

Meier (1962) argues in his book *A Communications Theory of Urban Growth* that cities cannot be considered unconnected to the communications processes which take place between the inhabitants of the cities. Thus he says '... interdependencies will result from a sequence of transactions that tend to bring people together in space so as to renew the contacts. Face-to-face interaction, which is most efficient by far in creating and maintaining groups, requires proximity', and elsewhere, 'Proximity, it seems, led to an accumulation of shared experiences and inter-household communications were therefore accelerated. Within a span of only a few generations some sites were enabled to grow into towns ...' His argument is that 'Cities were evolved primarily for the facilitation of human communication'.

How, then, might this situation be changed by the recent developments in telecommunications, whereby face-to-face interaction of a sort can take place at any distance via videophones or conference television? One would predict that the reasons for locating a business or a home in a city would diminish, and might soon become less than the reasons for getting out of the city as quickly as possible (such as high rents, transport difficulties, dirt and noise, crime in the streets). The recent trend away from urban centres into ever greater metropoli might be rapidly reversed.

Goldmark (1972b) has expounded his vision of the 'New Rural Society' in which selected growth of smaller rural towns, rather than the larger metropoli, would be encouraged by the provision of advanced telecommunications equipment so that the small town had all the same commercial, medical, educational and cultural opportunities available in larger centres. Another recent idea is the Neighbourhood Work Centre; a local suburban office would be in full telecommunications contact with other such centres or with central headquarters. Rather than the office worker travelling each day from the suburbs to a central office (a time-consuming, unpleasant and expensive process) to do no more than communicate with others face-to-face, via the telephone and via the written word, he would be able to travel to his neighbourhood work centre by foot, and carry out his work at a distance by telecommunications. Even more extreme is the conception that office work may well be done at home. Already authors and journalists do substantial portions of their work at home, but once new telecommunications devices are plentiful and cheap, will there be any substantial reason why computer programmers, accountants or lawyers cannot work from home? Again, the effectiveness and the acceptability of new telecommunications media for these potential applications have yet to be substantiated; however, if these telecommunication alternatives do prove feasible, the impact on the urban form could be massive.

Initially such impacts might take the form of businesses moving out of the larger metropoli into smaller cities and towns, perhaps leaving a *pied-à-terre* in their previous location, but in any case increasing their telecommunications use to compensate for their increased distance. The recent Hardman Report on *The Dispersal of Government Work from London* (Hardman, 1973), a massive attempt in this direction, recommends the removal of over 30,000 civil servants from central London. The report discusses the 'communications damage that might be thus caused and considers telecommunications as a means of repairing this damage'. Such exercises have, no doubt, taken place in many other large business and government organizations. If organizations have favourable experiences with their initial decentralizations, they might be more inclined to extend the process and break up their organization into smaller and smaller subunits. The concept of the Wired City (Coll *et al.*, 1974) may soon give way to one of the 'Wired Non-city', for telecommunications might remove a prime incentive for clustering together in such large agglomerations as present-day cities.

TELECOMMUNICATIONS AND SOCIAL ORGANIZATION

Cherry (1971) considers that the primary function of person-to-person telecommunication is organization. Marked alteration in our communication habits, such as could be produced by the widespread use of new telecommunications systems, may have an effect on the structure of social organizations.

Westrum (1972) is of the opinion that while the advent of advanced telecommunications tends to decrease geographic centralization, the reverse will occur with power and control: telecommunications will make it easier for the centre to control intimately the actions of the periphery. He states that 'with increased communication capabilities, control in the organisation tends to shift, if at all, from lower agents to the higher echelons of the organisation. Difficulties in communication, on the other hand, tend to decentralise control'.

A vivid, if somewhat exaggerated, example of such centralized control by telecommunications can be found in Orwell's *Nineteen Eighty-four* in which a primary method of the oligarchy for controlling the populace was intermittent video surveillance. A spy camera which could at any time be activated, together with two-way voice facilities, allowed constant invasion of privacy by government invigilators, going so far at one point as active behaviour control. Similar visions of centralized control by telesurveillance have occurred elsewhere (e.g. Chaplin's *Modern Times*), but even in lesser forms the increased ability for the centre to control the peripheral elements of an organization would be seen by many as anything but progress.

It is possible, however, that telecommunications could have the reverse effect, increasing rather than removing freedoms, and allowing the periphery greater control over the centre. It is a common complaint amongst disillusioned electors that politicians no longer take any notice of those who elected them. Would it not be possible for the very necessary feedback from the electors to the politicians to take place using new technologies? We can see the start of such procedures in the Gallup polls released on television or in the newspapers; the broadcast 'phone-in' is an even more recent development, but Etzioni (1972) and his coworkers on the MINERVA (Multiple Input Network for Evaluating Reaction, Votes and Attitudes) project foresee much more. They point out that using systems such as the conference call, small groups of people who would not normally go out to participate in political meetings could discuss local or national issues from their homes. If such small groups chose representatives for higher-level groups, and those higher groups chose representatives for even higher ones, one could achieve a form of government nearer the ideal of the Greek city states, in which everyone would, or at least could, be actively involved. A hierarchy of about seven levels could encompass a whole country (say 12^7 people). One can only speculate as to the desirability of this structure; one might anticipate overwhelming opposition to such potentially revolutionary proposals.

McLuhan has consistently made the point that media have their own effects and will alter the world in their own ways dependent on their own intrinsic natures:

'. . . a few years ago, General David Sarnoff made this statement: "we are too prone to make technological instruments the scapegoats for the sins of those who wield them. The products of modern science are not in themselves good or bad; it is the way they are used that determines their value". That is the voice of the current somnambulism. Suppose we were to say, "the smallpox virus is in itself neither good nor bad; it is the way it is used that determines its value".' (McLuhan, 1967.)

In the context of such apparent uncertainty about the feasibility and value of the applications of the new telecommunications, others might be tempted to side with General Sarnoff, but, whether one agrees or disagrees, the fundamental need for evaluation is inescapable.

TELECOMMUNICATIONS AND HUMAN RELATIONS

If contact via new media such as the videophone is essentially identical to face-to-face contact, one would expect that the major effect on interpersonal human relationships would be to weaken the ties of proximity. Festinger *et al.* (1950) and others have found that there is a strong relationship between physical closeness and the formation of friendships; the cost of maintaining a friendship when the separating distance is high could be more than the psychic rewards that the relationship would bring. However, telecommunications could be a great destroyer of distance, allowing people to maintain their contacts with others no matter what the intervening distances (unless telecommunications charges were strongly distance-related). This could happen particularly with the professional and managerial classes who move to or with their jobs but are then faced with serious problems if they wish to remain in contact with friends and relations. New friends can be made, but new relations cannot, and one of the consequences of greater mobility has been the decline of the extended family (Wilmott and Young, 1957). One could argue that telecommunications might allow the reinstatement of the extended family, enabling, for example, young mothers to rely upon *their* mothers for advice and comfort even if they were at opposite ends of the country. If, however, video and audio telecommunications are significantly different from face-to-face in this crucial area of interpersonal relations, the consequences may be very different. Any substitution of mediated for face-to-face communication in this case could lead to further breakdown in communication and friendly relationships, perhaps increasing the impersonality and mechanical aura which so many already abhor in our present society. Clearly, in this area, whether one should consider telecommunications boon or bane depends crucially on the empirical findings.

THE IMPACT OF TELECOMMUNICATIONS ON THE INDIVIDUAL

In the context of commercial information the telephone is already familiar as an information source (viz., the Yellow Pages advertisement 'Let your fingers do the walking'). Recent field experiments have expanded on the role of the telephone as an information source using more advanced hardware. For example, in Reston Virginia, the TICCIT project modelled the use of a cable television system to interact with a computer to allow the users to carry on activities such as learning languages, shopping and discovering the timetable of local events from the comfort of their own homes. Of particular interest in this context is the potentially liberating effect of telecommunications for the housebound (including not only the disabled but also such groups as the mothers of young children) who might thus be enabled to carry out a range of activities previously only available after travel.

The impacts of improved communications upon the individual may not all be favourable. One of the most unfavourable trends may be towards information overload. Toffler (1970) has pointed out that our society is becoming ever more rapid in its rate of change: goods last less long, friendships are quickly made and broken, the flow of news and information is ever increasing, the rate of technological change catches many unprepared. In such a situation, some people may suffer 'future shock' in which their information processing and learning capacities have been overcome by the rapid rate of change; they can no longer adapt fast enough. Meier (1962) has been particularly interested in the stresses produced by communications overload, and the reactions of individuals and organizations to such stress. Thus he says 'Observation of human interaction suggests that a prime cause of stress in human behaviour is the appearance of signals or cues calling for the initiation of a new operation before the current one is completed. A choice must be made as to which is more important. At the present time the telephone and "intercom" systems almost always win, and a flurry of calls leaves behind a debris of incompleted sequences of behaviour upon which effort has been expended but for which personal rewards have not yet been realised. Increasing interruptions seem to be associated with increasing stress. (. . . . . .) too much stress is destructive and even deadly. Each system has its outer limits of endurance'.

Will new telecommunications merely add to the overload already apparent in some people and organizations? Perhaps time spent travelling is not wasted, but is a necessary rest period between interactions. Are some of the new media more arousing or stress producing than others? It has been suggested that the advent of the videophone as a replacement for the telephone will increase stress; in telephone conversation one need control the impression given much less than would be the case over a videophone. On video, one could no longer sit in very relaxed pose, scratch, fidget, make faces or carry out any of the other activities which may act as tension releasers. Users may find themselves faced, at literally zero notice, with important 'face-to-face' interactions, and will inevitably feel flustered and inadequately prepared.

Meier (1962, 1973) discusses at length the adjustments which individuals and groups make to information overload. Two are particularly interesting; 'privacy shields' and 'dropping out'. A 'privacy shield' is a system, such as a secretary, which intercepts all communications and decides whether they should be routed to the person for whom they were intended. As the rate of communications input increases, perhaps even the secretaries will soon need privacy shields. 'Dropping-out' is a phenomenon which can be already observed, in which 'burnt-out cases', as Meier (1973) calls them, leave the 'rat race' and move to supposedly gentler pursuits such as farming, in which the communications load is not so great.

One of the most critcal aspects of the advent of new telecommunications systems will be this question of human adjustment, or lack of adjustment, to them. The number of little customs, and indeed subcultures, which have grown up around other technological innovations such as television, suggest a fascinating sociological study of the development of reactions to telecommunications.

THE ROLE OF SOCIAL PSYCHOLOGY IN THE ASSESSMENT OF NEW TELECOMMUNICATIONS SYSTEMS

In the last few pages, we have discussed potential impacts of telecommunications at every level in society. Some of these seem probable, others the reader may reject as unlikely. In either case, however, most of the ideas are founded mainly in speculation, with little empirical evidence which would allow one to decide whether a particular impact was highly probable, or so improbable that it could be forgotten.

It is the intention of this book to provide some of the answers to this problem. Clearly the task of collecting empirical data on all the factors that could affect all these possible impacts would be quite beyond even a lifetime's work. However, it is the authors' contention that there are some aspects which are more basic than others, and thus a directed research effort can provide useful preliminary information.

In Chapter 2, a framework for such a directed effort will be advanced; subsequent chapters will discuss the ways in which surveys and laboratory experiments have been used to give substance to this framework. It is important to note here that research work has not yet advanced to the stage at which definitive answers can be given to many of the problems and questions that have been advanced earlier in this chapter. Indeed, it could be argued that we are still at the 'guestimate' stage for most of the questions. However, the importance of these problems, offering, as they do, both hopes and threats for the future, makes the winning of even preliminary answers worthwhile.

2

The Telecommunications Impact Model

Discovering the impact of telecommunications on society may seem rather like trying to eat an elephant; it is difficult to know where to start. However, it is our contention that there are some places in which it is more profitable to start. The first and most fundamental of the questions to be answered is 'Will the new systems be used at all?'

It is by no means self-evident that all of these telecommunications systems will be used. History is replete with unsuccessful inventions, some of which reached an advanced level of production and use before eventually being abandoned (e.g. airships). It is quite possible that some of the new telecommunications devices and applications described earlier will prove, like the Zeppelins, to be but seven-day wonders. Certainly, initial American experience with the Picturephone has proved disappointing; optimistic predictions that there would be one million Picturephones in use in the USA by 1980 seem very unlikely to be fulfilled; indeed, it now seems almost as probably that there will be none at all in use at that date. If Picturephone never comes into extensive use, then we can forget about all its beneficial or harmful impacts as discussed in Chapter 1.

How, then, can we investigate whether these various devices will be used on any scale? The simplest approach is simply to ask people whether they would use telecommunications for particular meetings. A number of surveys of this type have been carried out, and these will be briefly described.

OPINIONS OF THE USEFULNESS
OF TELECOMMUNICATIONS SYSTEMS

Two recent surveys of potential users have had essentially a common format, with the following major aspects:

(a) Potential users were asked to describe a recent meeting.
(b) A series of telecommunications alternatives were described to them.
(c) They were asked to say which, if any, of the facilities would have been suitable for the meeting.

Klemmer (1974) reports on a survey of over 3000 Bell Laboratory personnel carried out by Snyder (1970) which found the results shown in Table 2.1.

Table 2.1.   Percent for whom the teleconference system would meet
stated needs for their meeting (from Klemmer, 1974)

System	Percentage satisfied
Conference room *audio* only	2
Audio plus *facsimile* (hard copy documents)	3
Audio plus *video for faces* of others	6
Audio plus *video for faces* plus *video for graphics* (blackboard, slides, etc.)	50
Audio plus *video for faces* plus *video for graphics*	85

85% of people were felt to need some form of telecommunications system as a substitute for their face-to-face meeting. Of these, the vast majority had their needs met only by a complex video system for faces and graphics. For 15% none of the above telecommunications systems could meet their stated needs.

These results suggest a rosy future for video conferencing facilities but poor prospects for audio. A similar, much larger survey carried out by Kollen and Garwood (1974) of Bell Canada found a rather different result. They gave survey questionnaires to approximately 30,000 business travellers using airplane, car, train or bus to travel between four major Canadian cities: Montreal, Ottawa, Toronto and Quebec City. As in the Klemmer and Snyder study, respondents were asked to describe the meeting they had just had, or were about to have. The questionnaire then gave verbal descriptions of various audio, graphics and video telecommunications devices, and asked whether they would have used such devices, had they been available, rather than make the trip. Of the 9688 who returned the questionnaires, only about 20% indicated that they would have telecommunicated instead of travelling, even if they could have had their choice of the telecommunications devices.

The discrepancy between these two sets of results needs some explaining. The difference between 85% substitution in the former and 20% in the latter is clearly more than can be dismissed as experimental error, or even as due to the differences between Canadians and Americans. One possible explanation is that there is a substantial difference between what can be provided to meet stated needs and what people would choose to use. To take a crude example, a private helicopter might meet one's transportation needs, but one would choose not to use it as it would be too expensive or too dangerous. Thus of the 85% in the Klemmer and Snyder study for whom the teleconference systems were supposed to be satisfactory for their meeting, a large proportion might nevertheless choose not to use them because they feel that they would be too expensive, or because they like making trips to get out of the office, or because they are making money on their business expenses. Clearly a large number of factors could be affecting the choice.

Even ignoring the discrepancy, however, one could with good reason reject both sets of results. The basic methodology which both have in common has a serious flaw: the respondents are being asked to *imagine* using various types of teleconference systems, and this leap of imagination may be too great. Few people have seen, let alone used, most of the novel teleconference systems which were described: indeed, some of the teleconference systems described have yet to be built. A brief verbal description of such a facility is really no substitute for actual use. Anyone who has worked with advanced telecommunications systems will have frequently had the experience of people coming up after using the system and saying 'It really was nothing like I expected'. After only a single use of some systems, hardened opponents of teleconferencing can become converts, and vice versa. A verbal description such as 'transmit and receive facsimile copies of documents quickly' may seem enticing to a potential user, until they actually use such a device and discover that 'quickly' can mean 4–6 minutes.

We, therefore, reject surveys which simply ask presumed potential users whether they might use novel types of telecommunications systems. An alternative method must be developed. Luckily, there is one, and although it is considerably more laborious, the eventual results can be expected to be considerably more reliable.

THE TELECOMMUNICATIONS IMPACT MODEL

This model, first described by Reid (1971), is likewise addressed to the problem of estimating the extent to which communications presently taking place face-to-face might be transferred to a range of existing or possible future telecommunications systems. The model has four stages as follows.

I. *The Amount Model*

'The purpose of this model is to discover what relationship exists between the amount of external communication generated (and attracted) by an organisation, and the characteristics of that organisation. The amount, mode and geographical spread of an organisation's communications may then be predicted within certain limits of confidence from a knowledge of the measureable characteristics of the organisation.' (Reid, 1971, p.3.) The basic input for this model is survey data, which measures the amount of face-to-face contact within organizations.

II. *The Type Allocation Model*

'The basis of this model is that some of the contacts which at present occur face-to-face will be transferred to other modes as more sophisticated telecommunications systems become available. They are being carried out face-to-face at present either because alternative, adequate systems are not yet commercially available, or because such systems are available, but it is cheaper to conduct these contacts face-to-face . . . The problem of type allocation is therefore one of deciding how many of the face-to-face contacts generated by an individual or firm may be assigned to each type category.' (Reid, 1971, pp.4–5.) There are three substages:

(a) The identification of types of face-to-face meetings: the DACOM study (Pye *et al.*, 1973) is such a typological exercise, and will be described in more detail in the next chapter.
(b) The measurement of the frequency of the various types identified. This will be a survey exercise, like those in the amount model, but will utilize the typology of meetings that has been developed. Such an exercise is the *1973 Office Communications Survey* (Connell, 1974) which will be described in the next chapter.
(c) The determination of the adequacy, or effectiveness of the various media for the various types of meetings identified. It is the achievement of this goal to which the controlled experiments described in Chapters 6, 7 and 8 are devoted.

III. *The Mode Allocation Model*

'Given that an individual, or an organisation, generates certain amounts of communication of various types (the outputs from Stages I and II of the model), how can one predict by which mode these contacts will be carried out? The purpose of Stage III is to predict this allocation, on the basis of the geographical (or other) separation between the participants, and the value of their time. This stage of the model will indicate the extent to which telecommunications is likely to substitute for business travel.' (Reid, 1971, p.6.) Mode here means medium of communication, particularly face-to-face contact, video conferencing and audio conferencing. In its initial conception, this stage only involved the measurement of the relative costs of travel and telecommunications, and assumed that, like the rational man of traditional economics, potential users would use the cheapest mode that allowed effective communication. This is in practice unlikely, and a series of other factors have had to be incorporated into this stage of the model. A number of these are discussed in subsequent chapters (particularly Chapter 9), but they will be briefly summarized here.

(a) *Attitudes.* Even though a medium of communication might be quite effective, this is not in itself sufficient to indicate that users will like using it. If there is a discrepancy between attitudes of the potential users, and the actual effectiveness of the medium, this discrepancy may not necessarily decrease in time, since initial attitudes may be so negative that the meetings during which the users could have discovered that the telecommunications system was not actually so unpleasant, may never occur. Some discussion of methods and results regarding attitudes to communications media can be found in Chapters 5 and 9.

(b) *Perceived effectiveness.* As well as the sheer aesthetic appeal of the communications medium, users may have attitudes towards its effectiveness for various types of activities (i.e. 'Can I make use of it?' as opposed to 'Do I like it?'). Again, this may be discrepant from actual effectiveness of the medium, though the two may with suitable experience, training and publicity come to correspond. Some data on the perceived effectiveness of various telecommunications media are presented in Chapter 9.

(c) *Inertia.* Any new system is likely to suffer a period of delayed acceptance, if only because we are all creatures of habit. The study of the diffusion of innovations is an active field (Warner, 1974). Clearly a delay in the adoption of an innovation can be very reasonable, in that it gives a chance for the potential users to assess the system more adequately; however, such delay may be much more extensive with interactive telecommunications systems simply because they are interactive. Thus if a person has a videophone, but all the people whom he might wish to call have only audio telephones, his videophone is completely useless. A videophone to the first person in the world to obtain one is worthless, but to the millionth person or the 100 millionth person it may be extremely valuable. The same applies to facsimile, conference television or any of the other systems; utility is directly related to market penetration. Thus inertia is more important for the adoption of telecommunications systems than for the adoption of non-interactive systems such as the car (indeed, for cars, the more people have one, the less useful they can become).

(d) *Spatial accessibility.* The convenience of telecommunication is mainly due to its time-saving capabilities. In many cases where the telephone is used rather than written or face-to-face communication, a major influence on the decision to use the telephone is its ability to allow immediate contact. Although some of the new telecommunications devices would allow similar immediate contact (e.g. telex or the videophone), others have centralized studios to which the potential user has to travel. In some cases this travel to the studio may act as a disincentive, particularly when, as discussed further in Chapter 9, *both* parties may have to travel to teleconference studios as an alternative to only *one* party travelling to a face-to-face meeting.

In the early days of teleconference systems, when the low rates of usage may not justify a very comprehensive network of studios, accessibility can be a substantial disincentive for potential users.

(e) *Other aspects of accessibility.* Apart from purely spatial aspects, other accessibility disincentives are often attached to new teleconference systems. Some teleconference studios have to be booked several days in advance, unlike either existing telecommunications facilities or most travel facilities. Computer-mediated conferencing has particular access problems on account of the codes and passwords necessary to gain entry to the computer and the program before one can 'attend' the conference.

(f) *Fringe benefits.* Associated with travel to face-to-face meetings are a number of fringe benefits, some of which may be greatly appreciated by those who receive them. Travel allows a person to escape from his office, with its interruptions or overclose supervision. Sometimes the travel is to new, exciting places, and a business trip can be almost as good as a holiday. Travelling expenses are often at a level which allow the recipient to enjoy more comfortable surroundings, better food and sometimes better entertainment than he could at home. In comparison, telecommunications usually offers no fringe benefits, except, perhaps, a cup of coffee and a vicarious feeling of importance in being allowed to use such an advanced piece of technology.

Mode allocation has thus been expanded to include all these factors, although few are as quantifiable as cost, and some have yet to be studied in detail. The final stage of the model is:

IV. *The Locational Change Model*

'The purpose of this model is to attempt . . . to predict the nature and extent of locational changes consequent upon telecommunications innovation. The . . . model takes, as its starting point, a population of firms, of defined sizes and characteristics, clustered together in a single city. The communications requirements of these organisations are derived from Stages I, II and III of the overall model (i.e. the Amount, Type Allocation and Mode Allocation Stages).' Reid, (1971, pp.7-8.) This final stage could also be considered overly narrow, in that the only impact of telecommunications on which it concentrates is locational change of business premises. The same information derived from the earlier stages of the model could also be used to predict the impact of new forms of telecommunications on the location of residences, on family life, on the structure of business or other organizations, on the psychological well-being of office workers, or any of the other possible impacts discussed in detail in Chapter 1.

One must stress, however, that the Stage IV activities mentioned in the previous paragraph depend on the outputs of Stages I to III; that is, the estimates of the extent to which telecommunications systems will be used. Until the methodological problems in these earlier stages have been resolved and some form of reliable estimates have been generated, it is premature to embark on detailed analysis of the impacts. For this reason, this last stage has not in general received a great deal of attention, though some pioneering work on office location (for example, Pye, 1972) has been carried out.

A STRATEGY FOR APPROACHING THE TELECOMMUNICATIONS IMPACT MODEL

Although the Telecommunications Impact Model is more satisfactory than the earlier, cruder approaches, if only because it allows for a much wider range of information and types of studies to bear upon the eventual output, there are still problems as to where to start. The studies described in detail later in the book are by no means all that which is necessary as input to achieve a perfect output from the Stage III (Mode Allocation) section of the model, telling us how much the various new telecommunications media will be used. Why, then, did we start where we did?

In fact, most of the research described later is most relevant to the Stage II (Type Allocation) step. Concentration on this stage can be justified in terms of the temporal stability of the various types of information. Social interaction between individuals does seem to be relatively invariant, with many aspects being constant across cultures, over time and between sexes and age-groups. In Chapter 4, we will review the evidence on the importance of visual, non-verbal cues in social interaction in detail, but to anticipate that discussion, it is clear that at least some forms of non-verbal behaviour have evolved before mankind became distinct from the apes, and are at least to some extent both hereditary and not under conscious control (Argyle, 1969). In view of this, it seems likely that the basics of social interaction are going to be relatively non-adaptive to the introduction of new telecommunications media, or to other future changes in the environment. If we discover that the use of audio-only communications leads to an impersonal atmosphere in a discussion, with a greater likelihood of disagreement resulting in a complete breakdown of the interaction, rather than to some constructive compromise, this finding is likely to be as useful and appropriate in fifty years time as it is now.

The situation is very different with many of the variables that we included in the Amount and Mode Allocation headings. For example, the price of a telecommunications system can be changed, virtually at a stroke of a pen, by the providers of the system. A futuristic study which concentrated too heavily on the prices of telecommunications systems would thus be in danger of being rapidly overtaken by events. The total amount of communication and its distribution between the various communications modes could be radically altered by price changes. Thus although useful work can be done on developing a basic methodology for discovering the influence of price on modal choice between travel and a variety of telecommunications media (see, for example, Cook, 1975), such calculations have to be continually reworked as prices change, and only the methodology is a permanent addition to the store of knowledge. While the costs of telecommunications systems may change more gradually than the prices, they may still change dramatically over the course of a few years with the advent of new technical developments, particularly in long-distance, wideband transmission (e.g. microwaves, satellites, waveguides and fibre optics, see Martin, 1971).

Even the more human-oriented variables under the Mode Allocation heading may be open to quite radical change over a few short years. For example, one could carry out careful studies of the way in which the use of telecommunications innovations spread through the population of potential users, so as to understand the inertial factors described earlier. However, it is more than probable that skilful publicity campaigns, or decisions by the management of organizations that funds for travel were to be reduced, could markedly alter the rate at which the new communications systems were adopted. Attitudes towards telecommunications may be more resistant, but one must still accept that with greater experience of telecommunications, and with detailed training programmes or saturation publicity campaigns, attitudes towards the systems might radically change. Studies of attitudes today seem likely to be of limited use in predicting the attitudes of the users of telecommunications systems even a decade or so hence.

We must thus reject detailed predictions of the future use of telecommunications systems which are too heavily based on the measurement of the present state of the various Mode Allocation factors, just as we rejected the simplistic studies discussed earlier, which merely asked potential users whether they would use a verbally described telecommunications system. The results from such methods are too readily influenced by short-term factors such as knowledge of the system, the attitudes of those around, company policy or what is read in the newspaper that morning. Thus while advance in methodology in any area is always welcome, we can conveniently leave detailed studies of the state of the Mode Allocation factors until we have solved more basic problems. We must concentrate first on that which is both more fundamental and more stable.

For this reason, most of the studies to be discussed later have been concerned primarily with Type Allocation questions, especially the following:

(1) What are the different functions and activities which take place in meetings presently occurring face-to-face?
(2) How are these functions and activities presently clustered or combined in face-to-face meetings (i.e. what are the types of meetings)?
(3) What are the approximate proportions of these types of meeting in present-day face-to-face meetings in business or government organizations?
(4) How are the outcomes of these types of meeting affected (either quantitatively or qualitatively) by the use of various person-to-person telecommunications media, as compared to each other and to face-to-face interaction?

The next chapter will deal with the first three questions, while Chapters 6 to 9 will discuss the last question.

By answering these questions one arrives not at a demand forecast for new telecommunications media (that is, how much they will be used at various times in the future), but rather at an indication of the upper bound of the extent to which these media could effectively replace existing face-to-face meetings. Clearly, if one then added data on the short-term trends in the Mode Allocation factors, one would begin to approach the situation where one could make demand forecasts. However, the Telecommunications Impact Model does have limitations, which make it unable to give perfect output in terms of either demand forecasts or measured extent of impacts. These limitations may well be unavoidable, since discussion in the next section will show that the problems which led to the limitations are relatively intractable.

LIMITATIONS OF THE MODEL

Although one can accept the Telecommunications Impact Model as a considerable advance over earlier ways of thinking of the same problems, it does nevertheless have two serious faults.

(a) *Substitution versus generation.* One can see that the Telecommunications Impact Model should allow for the possibility that new telecommunications devices may not merely be used for meetings transferred from face-to-face, but that meetings may be transferred from other media (e.g. from telephone to teleconferencing, so that more than two people can be in on a conversation) or may represent generated traffic (meetings that would not have occurred at all had the telecommunications system not been available). One can see this latter possibility being very real for a system such as computer-mediated conferencing, which does not attempt to approximate the face-to-face situation, but rather has novel characteristics of its own.

(b) *Effectiveness as an absolute*. The nature of the model is such that only types of meetings which have been determined as capable of transfer to telecommunications without any loss of effectiveness in the Type Allocation stage are considered in the Mode Allocation stage. This is equivalent to hypothesizing that 'No matter how overwhelming the favourability of other aspects such as cost, convenience, etc., any loss of effectiveness consequent on the use of a telecommunications system will not be tolerated by the users'. In cost-benefit terms, we are putting an infinite cost on the loss of effectiveness, which hardly seems reasonable. In some cases it may be true that effectiveness is the only, or overwhelming consideration; however, in other cases (e.g. where urgency is important) then effectiveness will be balanced against the other criteria for choice, and may prove not to be the most important.

Although it is easy to critizise by pointing out these omissions, it is less easy to see how they could be rectified. The prediction of generation effects would be the most tentative of futurology, in that one would be trying to discover what will happen under conditions that cannot be observed.

At a later stage it may become possible to do 'before and after' studies of organizations which are acquiring a new telecommunications system, with detailed audits of the use of all communications media including face-to-face meetings. In this way one could discover the extent to which the introduction of the new communications link increases or decreases the use of the existing links, and whether there is an overall increase in the amount of communication by all the links combined, stimulated by the new facility. However, as yet, the scope for such studies is limited and, what is worse, some generation effects may only come about as the penetration of connections becomes very high: as pointed out previously, for a telephone renter the telephone is daily becoming more useful as more people acquire telephones, and his usage may correspondingly increase. Furthermore, all sorts of other innovations may generate additional traffic: for example, the introduction of the Yellow Pages service, which lists businesses of various types, may generate additional traffic. To try to predict such effects, from our present situation when the systems are at their introductory stage, may seem more like an exercise in astrology than science.

Most of the potential users of the telecommunications media do not have the sort of detailed knowledge of the effectiveness of the various media in various situations and for various tasks which would allow them to put some cost on effectiveness losses: they may indeed be unaware of the existence of the media. Only having discovered the effectiveness of the various media, in terms of the ways that the outcome of the interaction could be changed, and having informed the potential users of these differences, could one hope for some measurement of the 'cost' of losses in effectiveness. However, as will become apparent from Chapters 6 to 8, even the goal of the accurate measurement of changes in effectiveness according to the communications medium has still only been partially accomplished.

Although neither of these flaws should be ignored, one can point out that omitting information on these aspects will affect the output of the Telecommunications Impact Model in the direction of making it more conservative. If one can expect a certain level of substituted traffic, then generated traffic is an extra, and will increase, not reduce, levels of use. Similarly, if one assumes that telecommunications will not be used in cases where such use would lead to a loss in effectiveness, then if such loss is sometimes acceptable, the actual level of telecommunications usage will be correspondingly higher. Thus the Telecommunications Impact Model, in omitting these factors, is likely to be underestimating the potential level of use, and thus size of impacts, that may occur.

METHODOLOGICAL CONSEQUENCES OF APPLIED RESEARCH

In order to satisfactorily answer the Type Allocation questions posed earlier, two basic approaches have been taken: field surveys of meetings, and controlled laboratory experiments (some additional interview studies will be mentioned later; however, they cannot be considered so central as they are concerned primarily with Mode Allocation factors). These methods are both familiar. However, the approach of the Telecommunications Impact Model does necessitate that the two be integrated to a greater extent than is usual. Thus, for example, the same types of situations, and indeed often the very same questionnaire scales, have been used in both methodologies. Other consequences of the integration of these two types of work into one stream will be discussed briefly.

(a) *Representativeness*. It is commonplace within survey research that the sample of respondents used should be representative of the population to which the results are to be generalized—and it is hoped that the subsequent description of some of the surveys which contributed to the Telecommunications Impact Model will show that they have met this criterion. The application of criteria of representativeness or realism to laboratory experiments is less well established: there has been a long tradition of social psychological research on college sophomores which is then generalized to the populace at large. Similarly, the experimental setting has usually been apparent as a laboratory, the experimenter may even wear a white coat, and the tasks have often been considerably divorced from those experienced in everyday life, even to the extent that they appear to be amusing games of trivial importance. Such unrealism has been recently challenged by several authors (Tajfel, 1972, Neufeld, 1970, Schultz, 1969) as an unnecessary threat to the external validity of the experiments (that is, a threat to the extent to which the results of the experiments can be generalized to the world at large). This may not be an important criticism if the intention of the experiment is to clarify some point of theory, but would be fatal within an area such as this, where the controlled experiments are but one segment of the input to a larger model, and thus must be compared with other information that has been collected under more realistic conditions (particularly the survey data). There has thus been a greater than usual emphasis on realism in much of the experimental work which is discussed in Chapters 6 to 8. Methods of obtaining realism have been several. Experimental participants have been selected to be typical office workers, largely civil servants. The laboratories have been designed to appear more as studios, and were generally referred to by the latter name. The experimental tasks have normally been specially designed so as to avoid the 'game-playing' mentality which can so easily appear if the tasks are trivial, childish or overcompetitive; in most cases they have been discussion of human interest problems, though usually with some partially disguised purpose (e.g. measurement of attitude change, or of coalition formation). Lastly, the communications media have been chosen so as to be as similar as possible to those which are likely to become available in the future (see Chapter 1)—possible manipulations such as having the participants talk through holes in the wall, or opaque screens, or having them wear masks to hide part of their faces have been rigorously avoided, even if they were of potential theoretical interest. As far as possible, realism has been the master of experimental design, though not to the extent of losing internal validity (through control groups, objective measurements, etc.).

One limitation to this emphasis on realism should be noted: experiments have not gone as far as to try to simulate the types of meetings which have been identified in the surveys, but have instead concentrated on the basic functions and activities which cluster to constitute these types. Thus although the surveys have identified meetings which involve both 'problem solving' and 'discussion of ideas', the controlled experiments have studied these two aspects separately. The reason for this deviation from realism is that one of the earliest effects of the introduction of new telecommunications media might be the development of new, generated meetings, which could have different combinations of the basic functions. Just such an effect was noted in one of our early field studies, that of the University of Quebec audio system (Short, 1973a). If the controlled experiments have studied only existing combinations of the basic processes, generalization to new combinations might be difficult. It is thus safer to study the processes at a more disaggregated level, and at a later stage to combine the results to predict the effects on meetings involving combinations of processes.

(b) *The Black Box Approach.* From the point of view of the

Telecommunications Impact Model, the important outcome from the
Type Allocation stage is the identification of the types of meetings
which can be transferred to telecommunications media without loss of
effectiveness (i.e. where the outcome is not affected by the medium of
communication used), and those which cannot be so transferred
without loss of effectiveness (i.e. those where the outcome is affected
by the medium of communication used). One consequence of this is
that negative results, with no effect of medium of communications
being found, are just as interesting (and indeed from the point of view
of the telecommunciations enthusiast, hopeful) as those where an
effect of medium is found. A more important consequence is that it
leads the experimental research to concentrate very heavily on the task
outcome, and much less on the communication processes. This neglect
of processes can mean that theories about the effects of medium on
interpersonal communication are difficult to develop.

Although this 'black box' concentration on interaction outcome
rather than interaction process has been consistent throughout most of
the experimental work in Chapters 6, 7 and 8, we have tried to balance
this with an extended discussion of the processes of communication,
and the way in which they might be affected by medium of
communication (Chapter 4), and of various theories of media
differences that have been developed, if not yet adequately tested
(Chapter 5). However, the heavy emphasis on outcome is, we feel,
appropriate. To those who wonder as they read further, 'How do the
media bring about these effects on the communication outcome?', we
can only reply, 'Does it *really* matter?'. Although we, like many others,
particularly in social psychology, might welcome further study of
processes and further developments of theory, from the point of view
of the Telecommunications Impact Model, and thus for the city or
transportation planners who might use its output, processes are very
clearly secondary to outcomes.

CONCLUSION

We have stated the approach we have adopted. To judge its
usefulness, it will be necessary to read on. Chapter 3 will present the
results of the surveys which identified and measured the frequency of
the types of face-to-face meetings. Chapters 4 and 5 will set the scene
for the controlled experimental work by discussing the importance of
visual non-verbal cues, and by setting forward alternative theories of
the effect of medium of communication upon social interaction.
Chapters 6, 7 and 8 will present the results of the experiments which
have attempted to measure the effects of medium of communication
on the outcomes of various types of task. Chapter 9 will broaden the
picture by discussing some of the Mode Allocation factors thereto
neglected, and the final chapter will try to derive some preliminary

conclusions as to the likely usefulness of new person-to-person telecommunications devices, and to discuss briefly the impacts that the likely levels of use might have upon our everyday life.

3

The Classification of Communication Episodes

INTRODUCTION

A widely accepted general taxonomy of meetings does not exist. In its stead are a multitude of distinctions on which individual theorists have from time to time focused. There is not even a generally accepted definition of communication. Barnlund (1968, p.5) states that, 'communication has been conceived structurally (sender-message-receiver), functionally (encoding-decoding), and in terms of intent (expressive-instrumental). It has been defined with reference to source (production of messages), channel (signal transmission), receiver (attribution of meaning), code (symbolizing), effect (evoking of response), and in ways that combine several of these criteria. To some, communication is "the process of transmitting stimuli" (Schramm), "the establishment of a commonage" (Morris), "conveying meaning" (Newcomb), or "all the procedures by which one mind affects another" (Weaver). To others, it is "interaction by means of signs and symbols" (Lundberg), "the sharing of activity, excitement, information" (Hefferline), or "the signals that individuals make to each other or which they detect in each other and which may be conscious or unconscious" (Cameron). Nearly every communicative element, function, or effect has been made the focus of some definition at some time.'

One classification of types of communication which is helpful primarily in that it sets the limits of our inquiry, is that of Applbaum *et al.* (1973). They describe seven levels of communication as follows:

(1) Intrapersonal communication.
(2) Dyadic communication.
(3) Small-group communication.
(4) Intercultural communication.
(5) Public speaking.
(6) Mass-media communication.
(7) Non-verbal communication.

The prime focus of the present discussion is dyadic and small-group discussion. Non-verbal communication is important in communication within dyads and small groups, and is affected by the medium of communication used, so it is central to the present area of research. It will be discussed in more detail later. The other levels of communication are less directly of interest, as they are not equally good targets for the introduction of new telecommunications devices. Our focus, then, is small-group (and dyadic) meetings.

Schein's (1965) definition of a group will serve to define what is meant in the present discussion: 'A psychological group is any number of people who (1) interact with one another, (2) are psychologically aware of one another, and (3) perceive themselves to be a group.' (Schein, 1965, p.67).

Schein's definition is particularly useful because it includes the concept of psychological awareness and identity with the group, not simply that of interaction. This is important because it provides a conceptual link with the concepts of person-orientation and social presence developed in later chapters which are believed to be important in understanding the psychology of teleconferencing.

Even within small-group communication there are many varieties. It would hardly be possible and certainly not helpful to list all the distinctions which have been made, but it is useful to review those which seem to be relevant to business communication.

FORMAL AND INFORMAL COMMUNICATION

The distinction between formal and informal communication is made by several theorists. Smith *et al.* (1972, p.272) define formal communication channels as 'those emanating from official sources and carrying official sanctions . . . Formal messages usually flow through these channels, thus acquiring legitimacy and authenticity.' Schein (1965, p.68) suggests that formal groups 'are created in order to fulfil specific goals and carry on specific tasks which are clearly related to the total organizational mission.' Schein suggests that such groups can be either permanent or temporary. Permanent groups include the top management team, work units in the various departments, staff groups and permanent committees. Temporary groups are committees or task forces created to carry out a particular job; for example, to review salary policies or to study the relationship between the organization and the community. Temporary groups can evolve into permanent groups. Both kinds of groups can engage in upward, downward, or horizontal communication (*cf.* Smith *et al.*, 1972). Communication is said to be upward when it is to a higher authority, downward when it is to a lower authority and horizontal when it is to an equal authority.

Informal communication channels, Smith *et al.* (1972, p.273) suggest, 'are not specified rationally. They develop through accidents of spacial arrangement, through friendships, and through the varying levels of ability in the organization's "boxes".' Schein (1965) suggests informal groups develop because man has needs beyond the minimum ones of doing his job and seeks fulfilment of some of these by developing a variety of relationships with other members of the organization. Informal groups can include individuals of differing authority in the organization (vertical groups), or be restricted to individuals of equal authority (horizontal groups) or be mixed. Their nature depends upon a variety of factors including past acquaintances, communities of interest and the ecology of the work area.

The experimental research and case studies described in succeeding chapters are concerned primarily with formal groups and horizontal communication.

PROGRAMMED, PLANNING AND ORIENTATION ACTIVITIES

Thorngren (e.g. Thorngren, 1972) distinguishes between three kinds of communication in business. 'Programmed' communication activities are routine, repetitive and standardized. They involve regular contacts between individuals who are well acquainted with one another. The subject matter discussed is specific rather than general; for example, giving or receiving orders, or making sales or purchases. In contrast, 'orientation' communication activities are novel, unstructured and complex. They frequently involve individuals who have not met before. The material discussed is general in nature. The orientation process allows the organization to adjust to changes in the environment, e.g. the availability of new markets, new products and changes in the legislation governing credit facilities. Orientation activities often suggest new alternatives. Between these two extremes are 'planning' activities. The planning activities result in the development and realization of alternatives suggested by the orientation activities.

These distinctions are conceptual rather than empirical. Thorngren himself and also Goddard (1971) have attempted to demonstrate the three types of communication empirically using self-completion contact diaries. Pye (1972) points to a major weakness in both attempts: most of the variables measured in the studies were not obviously related to the conceptual framework. Pye reanalysed the Thorngren and Goddard data using factor analysis and demonstrated that the variables used in Thorngren's and Goddard's latent profile analyses could be described more economically by a single factor: size. The more individuals involved in a meeting, the longer they talk, the more difficult it is to arrange the meeting at short notice and the greater the necessity for holding it face-to-face.

Despite the weakness in the empirical demonstrations, the conceptual distinctions between programmed, planning and orientation meetings are useful and bear a close resemblance to similar distinctions made by other theorists. For example, Ansoff (1965) distinguishes between strategic, administrative and operating activities, which are conceptually similar to orientation, planning and programmed activities, respectively. Simon's (1960) concepts of intelligence (searching the environment for conditions calling for decisions), design (inventing, developing and analysing possible alternatives) and choice (selecting a particular alternative), seem to overlap considerably with the concepts of orientation and planning.

THE BALES CATEGORIES

In a series of experiments in which subjects held simulated business meetings, Bales and his colleagues analysed the nature of the interactions that took place. The subjects in these experiments were tape-recorded and observed through a one-way vision screen. The observers recorded the nature of each interaction as it occurred. Bales (1955) has demonstrated that the following twelve categories can be coded reliably: shows solidarity; shows tension release; shows agreement; gives suggestion; gives opinion; gives information; asks for information; asks for opinion; asks for suggestion; shows disagreement; shows tension; shows antagonism.

Bales (1955) suggests that the 'types of acts in social interaction may be classed in four main categories: positive reactions, problem-solving attempts, questions, and negative reactions.' A further classification could also be of use. Bales's 'positive reactions' and 'negative reactions' could be classed together as person-oriented communications, implying that they reflect an attitude of one member of the group towards another. The other two categories, 'problem-solving attempts' and 'questions', could be regarded as non-person-oriented since they are concerned more directly with the task in hand and do not reflect the attitudes of the group members toward one another.

The distinction between person-oriented and non-person-oriented communication can be ambiguous because human behaviour is ambiguous. The ambiguity is recognized in the English language by terms such as 'sarcasm' and 'wit'. The style of doing something is often as important as what is done. For example, one can ask for information simply in order to receive specific information, or else, perhaps, to make the other person look a fool, or as a means of expressing an opinion or showing disagreement in an oblique way. Nevertheless, the conceptual distinction between person-oriented and non-person-oriented communication seems to be important in understanding the acceptability of teleconferencing and is developed further in later chapters.

THE DACOM CLASSIFICATION OF BUSINESS MEETINGS

The conceptual distinctions described above are limited in their usefulness for developing a taxonomy of meetings. The molar distinctions have theoretical rather than empirical bases, and deal with the whole range of communication activities, not just meetings. The molecular distinctions can provide profiles of particular meetings but have been developed in the laboratory under controlled experimental conditions and it is not clear whether they would provide a sufficiently comprehensive system of classification for meetings in the real world.

The Communications Studies Group (Pye *et al.*, 1973) undertook to develop its own, empirically based taxonomy of face-to-face meetings in a project called DACOM (Description and Classification of Meetings). The aim of this project was to develop a classification scheme based on the verbal descriptors which management personnel actually use in describing the meetings they hold. The scheme was to be based on a three-dimensional framework, namely the purposes (functions) of the meetings, the types of interactions which take place during the meetings and the atmosphere of the meetings. This three-dimensional framework was based on the belief that when a meeting is held it is always held for a purpose or set of purposes, that interactions occur between the individuals present, and the nature and style of these interactions determine the social atmosphere of the meeting; the atmosphere of the meeting may in turn constrain the kinds of interactions which are observed and may modify the purpose of the meeting.

First, a series of 65 open-ended interviews was conducted to elicit the words and phrases used to describe meetings. The interviewer asked the informants to describe the types of meetings they attended, and probed all three aspects of the meetings, i.e. their purpose, what went on and the atmosphere created. The informants were drawn from a range of different offices in Greater London, including general management, personnel, marketing and planning departments, amongst others. A random sampling of a comprehensive range of offices was not attempted since DACOM was conceived of as a pilot study.

Secondly, a questionnaire was constructed which asked informants to describe a single recent meeting. Questions concerning the length, arrangement and participants in the meeting were followed by questions derived from the preliminary interviews. One hundred and four descriptors were used in the form of rating scales. Informants were asked to give each descriptor a score from 0 to 6 to indicate its relevance to the meeting being considered. These questions were grouped into three sections: 'functions of the meeting', 'what went on at the meeting' and 'atmosphere of the meeting'. Three hundred and eleven questionnaires were completed by personnel in various business organizations.

Thirdly, several factor analyses were conducted, starting with different numbers of factors and performing different rotations.

(a) *Functions* A 9-factor varimax analysis accounting for 45% of the variance was most appropriate for the 'functions' scales. The highest loading items on the factors were as follows:

38

I. *Task allocation* (0.66), coordination of tasks (0.65), coordination of different stages of a project (0.64).
II. *Information giving* (0.71), information exchange (0.70), information seeking (0.61).
III. *Dismissal of an employee* (0.82), disciplinary interview (0.81).
IV. *Presentation of a report* (0.79), presentation of a draft report (0.58), discussion of implementation of a report (0.57).
V. *Problem discussion* (0.70), problem solving (0.62), problem review (0.61).
VI. *Appraisal* of another department's or organization's services (0.55), appraisal of another department's or organization's products (0.55).
VII. *Review of subordinate's work* (0.64), checking of subordinate's work (0.63).
VIII. *Tactical decision making* (0.60), policy decision making (0.56), policy discussion (0.53).
IX. *Advice-giving* (0.44), query answering (0.41).

(b) *Activities* A 6-factor varimax solution accounting for 47% of the variance was the most appropriate for the 'activities' scales. The highest loading items on the factors in this solution were as follows:

I. *Conflict* (0.80), disagreeing (0.74), arguing (0.72).
II. *Gathering background information* (0.70), asking questions (0.63), giving or receiving information (0.59).
III. *Problem solving* (0.66), decision making (0.65), giving or receiving orders (0.46).
IV. *Bargaining* (0.57), persuasion (0.57), compromising (0.57).
V. *Work-related gossip* (0.54), social chat (0.51), forming impressions of others (0.41).
VI. *Generating ideas* (0.51), exchanging opinions (0.50), expressing feelings (0.47).

(c)*Atmosphere* A 4-factor varimax solution accounting for 50% of the variance was the most appropriate for the 'atmosphere' scales. The highest loading items on the factors were as follows:
I. *Angry* (0.80), hostile (0.77), antagonistic (0.73), emotional (0.72), unpleasant (0.69).
II. *Constructive* (0.67), helpful (0.65), businesslike (0.64), cooperative (0.59).
III. *Cautious* (0.72), wary (0.68), defensive (0.61), competitive (0.51).
IV. *Informal* (0.77), friendly (0.54), easy going (0.44).

(d) *Combined analysis* A factor analysis which included all the 'functions', 'activities' and 'atmosphere' items together was also conducted. Items from different areas, e.g. 'functions' and 'activities', sometimes loaded on the same factors in this analysis. This does not invalidate the conceptual distinctions between these three areas but it does indicate that certain activities and certain kinds of atmosphere may tend to be associated with certain functions. It is to be expected that a meeting held for the purpose of negotiation is likely to involve bargaining and persuasion; the conceptual distinction between negotiation as a purpose of the meeting and bargaining and persuasion (or even negotiation) as activities which occurred during the meeting is still valid.

(e) *Cluster analysis* Whereas factor analysis describes the similarities between variables in terms of a set of hypothetical dimensions (factors) and their relationships to the original variables, cluster analysis describes the similarities between referents (in this case, meetings) by assigning them to groups (clusters) such that the referents within groups are more similar to each other in their characteristics than they are to referents in other groups. Two cluster analyses of the DACOM meetings were conducted.

The first cluster analysis was based on the similarities between the meetings in terms of their scores on six 'activity' scales (selected to represent the six factors described above). Pye *et al.* selected a 7-cluster solution as being optimal. The clusters in this solution were characterized as follows:

  (i) (32 cases) conflict and persuasion;
  (ii) (58 cases) persuasion;
 (iii) (50 cases) problem solving;
 (iv) (5 cases) a residual cluster;
  (v) (29 cases) social chat and gathering background information;
 (vi) (65 cases) gathering background information and problem solving;
(vii) (22 cases) meetings loading high on all six variables.

The second cluster analysis was based on the similarities between the meetings in terms of their scores on eleven scales drawn from the 11-factor solution of the 'functions' and 'activities' scales pooled together. Pye *et al.* selected a 12-cluster solution as being optimal in this analysis. The clusters were characterized as follows:

  (i) (14 cases) all variables except presentation of report, disciplinary interview and conflict;
 (ii) (32 cases) giving information to keep people in the picture;
 (iii) (46 cases) a residual cluster;
 (iv) (33 cases) policy decision making, not forming impressions of others, not information seeking, not giving information to keep people in the picture;
  (v) (13 cases) conflict, forming impressions of others, not negotiation, not problem solving;

(vi) (50 cases) giving information to keep people in the picture, information seeking, discussion of ideas, problem-solving;

(vii) (16 cases) negotiation, not conflict;

(viii) (19 cases) negotiation, conflict, policy decision-making;

(ix) (5 cases) disciplinary interview, conflict, presentation of report, delegation of work;

(x) (26 cases) forming impressions of others;

(xi) (25 cases) delegation of work, problem-solving, not forming impressions of others;

(xii) (32 cases) presentation of report, delegation of work, giving information to keep people in the picture, discussion of ideas, policy decision-making, problem-solving.

THE OFFICE COMMUNICATIONS SURVEY

The DACOM project was conceived of as a pilot study. A full-scale business communication survey leading on from the DACOM project was conducted by Connell (1974). The intention of this was to:

(a) confirm the clusters of meetings identified in DACOM;

(b) measure the frequency of these types in the 'office' environment;

(c) relate these types of meetings to other characteristics such as the use of documents, the location of the meeting, the pre-arrangement of the meeting, the number of participants and the length of the meeting (all of which have some implications for the suitability of various types of telecommunications devices).

In order to do this, a larger and more representative sample of face-to-face meetings was necessary. Connell (1974) achieved this by approaching 263 business customers of the British Post Office, each of which had at least two telephone lines, with probability of selection proportional to the number of telephone lines rented. 115 of these establishments agreed for their employees to participate in the survey, which provided in all 504 respondents who between them described 1791 face-to-face meetings. Various checks that could be made suggested that this was a representative sample of offices and of office personnel, and we can be reasonably confident that this is also a representative sample of business meetings.

Questions related first to the overall characteristics of the meeting (length, number of participants, etc.) and then asked respondents to describe the meeting by marking 'function' and 'activity' scales as in DACOM. Only the eleven scales which loaded most heavily in the 'functions and activities' factor analysis described earlier were used, with the addition of 'inspection of fixed object' (which has clear implications for telecommunication).

Cluster analysis allowed a very similar cluster of meetings as in DACOM to emerge. Actually, separate cluster analyses of two subsamples of 358 meetings were carried out. In each case 13 clusters was the optimal solution, and eleven of these, listed below, appeared from both samples. These eleven clusters, with the frequency of meetings in each, are shown below:

Cluster	Frequency
A. policy decision making; giving information to keep people in the picture; information seeking; delegation of work	6.9%
B. inspection of fixed object; information seeking	10.1%
C. giving information to keep people in the picture; problem solving	9.1%
D. giving information to keep people in the picture; discussion of ideas	8.7%
E. giving information to keep people in the picture; problem solving; information seeking; discussion of ideas	10.6%
F. presentation of report; information seeking; problem solving	4.6%
G. negotiation; problem solving; information seeking	6.3%
H. discussion of ideas; problem solving; information seeking	9.0%
I. delegation of work; giving information to keep people in the picture	8.3%
J. problem solving; information seeking	15.5%

The remaining 10.9% of the meetings in these two analyses fell in clusters which were unique to one subsample.

Other findings from Connell's survey were that 51% of the meetings lasted more than ten minutes, 49% involved people from another location and 34% involved travel for the respondent. With regard to documents, Connell found that for 53% of the meetings no documents were used, while for another 10% neither the postal service nor facsimile would have been feasible.

CONCLUSION

Here, then, we have a detailed classification of meetings, specially developed for the study of the substitution of face-to-face meetings by telecommunications. What remains is to decide which of these clusters could satisfactorily be carried out via telecommunications. This in turn requires an in-depth knowledge of social interaction via telecommunication media, with systematic variation of the meeting task. It is in search of this knowledge that we direct discussion first to the functions of visual cues in social interaction (Chapter 4), then to the several theories about the effects of telecommunications media on interaction (Chapter 5) and finally to the empirical studies of media effects (Chapters 6 to 8).

4

Visual Communication and Social Interaction

THE ROLE OF 'MEDIUM' IN THE COMMUNICATION PROCESS

As we saw at the beginning of Chapter 3 the word 'communication' has been used at different times with a wide variety of meanings; however, for our immediate purposes we shall use one of the more familiar social psychological definitions, that proposed by Cherry (1957): 'the physical signals whereby one individual can influence the behaviour of another'. It is readily apparent that constraints on these physical signals could affect the influence each individual has on the other. We use the term 'medium of communication' to describe the system of constraints on the physical signals available in any particular situation. Psychologists and others have long given extensive consideration to the ways in which one individual can influence the behaviour of another and the expression 'the medium is the message' has virtually achieved the status of a cliché. Surprisingly, however, in relation to the total effort expended on the investigation of social interaction, 'medium'—this apparently fundamental complex of variables—has received remarkably little attention.

Investigators have probed such points as whether or not one should counter the arguments available to the other side or simply give a partisan one-sided message. But scarcely anyone has looked into the question of whether or not one is more persuasive if physically present. The conditions conducive to effective problem solving have been extensively investigated but although the question of whether problems are solved more effectively when people are brought together in groups than when they merely act as individuals is a familiar issue, little effort has been expended on the means by which they are brought together. Do they need to be physically present to produce any sort of 'group cohesion'? Is audio contact sufficient to produce synergistic effects, or is visual feedback as to the reactions of others essential to effective group interaction? Again medium of communication is an almost forgotten variable.

The new media discussed in Chapter 1 are primarily directed at remedying what is the most obvious defect of the simple telephone—the fact that one cannot see the other person or group. Thus in discussing the effectiveness of these visual media, the fundamental question is—what is lacking in telephone communication that is present in face-to-face communication? If it is simply the lack of the visual channel, what sort of visual channel need be provided? In short, what is the function of the visual channel?

GENERAL FUNCTIONS OF NON-VERBAL SIGNALS AND THE EFFECTS OF MEDIUM

In normal face-to-face interaction, the participants exchange in addition to the verbal material, a range of non-verbal cues such as facial expression, direction of gaze, posture, dress and physical distance. Birdwhistell (1970) distinguishes two types of function for these cues. The first is directly concerned with the passage of information from one individual to another, the second is concerned with the 'integrational aspects' of the communication process. Integrational activity includes all behaviour that 'keeps the system in operation, regulates the interaction process, cross-references particular messages to comprehensibility in a particular context and relates the particular context to the larger contexts of which the interaction is but a special situation' (Birdwhistell, 1970).

Of the six functions for non-verbal cues during face-to-face interaction listed by Argyle (1969) three could be classified as integrational and three as informational. Starting with the three integrational functions, Argyle's six functions are as follows.

(1) *Mutual attention and responsiveness.* During the conversation there must be continuous evidence that the other is attending and responding. This is done chiefly by eye-gaze, head nods and gestures. However, mutual attention can also be signalled by brief utterances such as 'yes', 'ah ha', 'ummm' and so on. These are used in ordinary conversation and should function perfectly to take over the load borne by non-verbal signals. The fact that most people are practised in telephone conversation makes this replacement still more likely.

(2) *Channel control.* Head nods and eye movements are used in determining who shall speak and for how long. Interactors do not appear to be aware of making or receiving these signals. This function is likely to be more seriously affected by the removal of the visual cues. Argyle, Lalljee and Cook (1968) found that during two-person conversations there were more pauses and interruptions when the visual cues were reduced. Cook and Lalljee (1972) compared the conversation of subjects communicating face-to-face and those communicating over a microphone–loudspeaker system. They found that there were fewer interruptions, utterances differed in length and there were more requests for repeats in the no-vision condition. The explanation suggested for the unexpected result of more interruptions in the visible condition was that the subjects were more confident in their placing of interruptions. Jaffe and Feldstein (1970) found less

simultaneous speech in the no-vision condition together with shorter pauses both between and within speeches. Kasl and Mahl (1965) found more filled pauses in a no-vision condition. There is thus abundant, although sometimes conflicting, evidence of changes in conversational behaviour with the removal of the visual channel.

There is some evidence that such disturbances in conversational behaviour can be reflected in changes in more directly outcome-related measures. For instance, Miller and Hewgill (1964) found that when non-fluencies such as pauses were varied, ratings of the speaker on competence and power (although not trustworthiness) were lowered (similarly Sharp and McClung, 1966).

(3) *Feedback.* In order to plan his utterances, the speaker needs to know how the other is reacting to what has gone before. Non-verbal signals may sensitively track agreement or disagreement and other moment-to-moment changes in affect. In this respect, it is an important property of non-verbal signalling that it can go on simultaneously with verbal communication without interrupting it. If the visual channel is removed, the speaker must wait for a verbal reply from the listener before he has any feedback on his remarks. This could be sufficiently serious to lead to changes in the conversational topic: people might avoid topics (e.g. personal matters) where, lacking feedback, embarrassment or misunderstanding seems too probable. Speakers normally adapt the on-going message to the responses of the recipient (whether he is happy, comprehending, surprised, annoyed, etc.). The removal of this feedback could impair the efficiency of the adaptation of the message to the listener, and thus lower the speaker's persuasive impact. Consequently, one would expect that tasks on which the present behaviour of one individual is maximally contingent on the moment-to-moment affective reactions of the other, would be maximally sensitive to variation in the medium.

(4) *Illustrations.* Speech is accompanied by gestures of the hands which may be used to illustrate an object or action, to point to objects or directions, or for emphasis. The informational redundancy introduced by gesture will improve the clarity of the message (confirmed experimentally by Popelka and Berger, 1971). For articulate subjects this illustrative function is likely to be readily replaceable by words if the video channel is removed. But to the extent that this replacement does not occur, some of the impact of the message may be dissipated. 'The heart is stirred more slowly by the ear than by the eye', wrote Horace in his *Art of Poetry.*

(5) *Emblems.* This term is used to refer to gestures being used instead of a word, for instance a head-shake for 'No'. Except in special circumstances (such as the deaf) this category can be considered as less important than the others. It is in any case, by definition, replaceable by words in the absence of the visual channel.

(6) *Interpersonal attitudes.* Non-verbal cues may be used by the

listener as a vital source of information about the speaker's attitude to him and the speaker's intentions of, say, threat. Proximity, gesture, facial expression and eye-gaze—all the cues discussed earlier—may be used as sources of this affective information. Non-verbal cues can indicate changes in a relationship, for example the change from a relaxed to a more formal posture. Information is also conveyed about the speaker's affective reaction (pride, uncertainty, embarrassment or whatever) to what may be verbally a completely emotion-free statement. Thus, Argyle also includes under this heading the information about how the communicator sees himself and would like to be treated. For instance, Rosenfeld (1966) showed that subjects seeking approval smiled more and used more head nods.

Function (3) ('feedback') is to a large extent just a particularly important special instance of the interpersonal attitudes function. The former is primarily concerned with moment-to-moment changes (the perception of which is particularly liable to be affected by medium) and the latter with more long-term changes in affect. These two functions are together by far the most important functions of the visual signalling lacking in audio-only communciation.

While there has been very little discussion of the functions of the visual channel as a whole, there has been a considerable amount of research into the functions of the individual cues. Wiener and Mehrabian (1968) point out that each channel is likely to be differentially used according to its effectiveness for sending different types of information. Thus although certain common functions may be discerned, it would be wrong to expect each channel to carry the same kind of messages. Space does not permit a comprehensive review of the literature for each individual channel, but the following sections summarize some of the key literature to illustrate the principal role of the visual chanel—the provision of feedback on interpersonal attitudes.

PROXIMITY AND ORIENTATION

Physical separation is perhaps the factor which is most obviously varied when communication is by a telecommunications link rather than face-to-face. There is now a considerable volume of work on the importance of the distance at which people choose to converse, Hall (1963) suggests a four-point classification of degrees of proximity: up to 1½ ft 'intimate', 1½ to 4 ft 'personal', 4 to 12 ft 'social' and more than 12 ft 'public'. Each distance is thought appropriate for the activity after which it is named. Different non-verbal cues are thought to be relevant at different ranges; for example, pupil size may be relevant at the intimate distance (Hess, 1965) but at the public distance even eye-contact (mutual gaze) can no longer be discriminated sufficiently accurately to be useful. The distinction between these four degrees of proximity has never been demonstrated other than theoretically.

A variety of independent variables have been shown to affect the preferred distance for conversation. The simplest of these is culture: Arabs tend to sit closer than Americans (Watson and Graves, 1966) and British subjects in Cook's (1971) experiments showed positional preferences different from those of Sommer's (1965) American subjects. Personality factors are also relevant: extroverts tend to approach the experimenter more closely than do introverts (Patterson and Holmes, 1966). Argyle and Dean (1965) asked subjects to stand at a comfortable distance from (a) a life-size photograph, (b) the first author with his eyes shut and (c) the first author with his eyes open. Subjects stood closer when the author had his eyes shut than when open, and closer to the photograph than to the real person.

Although the material in the previous paragraph adds up to fairly convincing evidence that the distance people select for their conversation is not random, and a particular distance is preferred, precisely what is signalled by proximity is not clear. There have been attempts to demonstrate that distance can directly determine people's perceptions of one another: Porter, Argyle and Salter (1970) varied the distance between a confederate and the subject (3, 4 or 8 ft). However, proximity did not account for a significant proportion of the variance on any of the 21 rating scales. It could be argued that the variations in distance used in this study were not substantial. On the other hand, Scherer and Schiff (1973) found that perceived 'intimacy' increased as distance decreased (6, 4½ or 3 ft). Patterson and Sechrest (1970), using an interview situation with a stooge seated at different distances, found a significant negative relationship between distance (2, 4, 6 or 8 ft) and ratings of 'friendly', 'aggressive', 'dominant' and 'extroverted'. At the closer distance, this relationship was reversed, perhaps because of compensatory behaviour. Such compensation also appeared in an experiment by Argyle and Dean (1965) who found that visual interaction was reduced at close distances. To summarize: although there is substantial evidence that distance may be an indicative cue (relevant information for an outside observer), the evidence that it is of communicative worth (relevant for the participants) is uncertain.

Nevertheless, despite this uncertain evidence of communicative use, and doubts about what is signalled by proximity, proximity is important because there is evidence that it can affect the outcome of quite complex tasks. Albert and Dabbs (1970) investigated the variation of attitude change with distance of the communicator (1½, 4½ or 14 ft). Attitude change on the topic of the message was found to decrease linearly as distance decreased, being in fact contrary to the advocated direction at the closest distance. Selective attention to the message was found to be greatest at the middle distance (the conventionally appropriate distance) while, at either the excessively close or the excessively far distance, attention was apparently shifted to the physical appearance of the speaker. Ratings of the speaker on scales such as 'warm', 'sensitive', 'friendly', were not affected by distance. These results suggest that there may be an optimal distance (which probably varies with task) and that departures in either direction can impair performance. Sensenig, Reed and Miller (1972) had pairs of subjects play the Prisoner's Dilemma game (a simple game requiring a succession of choices between a cooperative and competitive strategy) seated either physically close or separated by a substantial distance (3 ft and 20 ft respectively). With greater distance, there were significantly fewer cooperative choices, smaller earnings and greater differences in outcome between the two players. In the 'far' condition, cooperative choices were practically non-existent in the later trials.

People select a particular orientation for their conversation just as they select a particular distance. For a competitive task people tend to sit opposite one another, while for a cooperative task the side-by-side position is preferred (Sommer 1965). McBride, King and James (1965) found that physiological arousal as measured by the galvanic skin response increases as a person gets closer to another and that this increase is greater for an approach from the front than for an approach from the side. Orientation may be important to the design of video systems: video systems impose an orientation (opposite one another) on the participants in a way in which neither an audio system nor face-to-face do (a very unnatural picture would result if the camera were not mounted in the vicinity of the monitor, i.e. opposite the subject). Evidence as to the effects of orientation is as yet too scant to make any hard predictions.

The influence of physical proximity on a telecommunicated interaction will be somewhat different from the influence on a face-to-face interaction. Behaviour concerned with approach and avoidance is simply not possible in a telephone interaction. One reason why proximity is important in face-to-face interaction is the effect it has on the salience of other non-verbal signals. In telephone conversation this ceases to be relevant and in conversation over a video link the analogous factor of image size is unlikely to be under the conscious control of the participants, being principally determined by the design of the camera and studio.

There is still, however, the possibility of effects of medium determined by the apparent (or psychological) proximity. The psychological proximity of a telephone contact is open to conjecture. It is probably affected by knowledge of actual physical location; system quality, task content, acquaintance with the other and many other factors. It does seem most probable that a telephone contact is apparently further away than any face-to-face contact, if only by analogy with the usual physical distance of a telephone contact (though McLuhan, 1964, argues the reverse). There is thus the important possibility that proximity, although unreal as a cue in any physical sense, may distort the interaction by imposing a constant distant level of apparent proximity on the interaction.

Some evidence to support such a hypothesis was produced in an experiment by Stapley (1972) in which subjects were asked to match the apparent sizes of a live face and a television picture. It was consistently found that the television picture had to produce a much larger retinal image to have the same apparent proximity.

It seems likely, then, that differences in apparent physical proximity produced by different media relate not only to the size of the retinal image of the other given by the system, but also to the 'social presence' engendered by the medium. The concept of 'social presence' will be more thoroughly discussed in Chapter 5, and we shall thus leave this line of thought until that chapter.

PHYSICAL APPEARANCE

In everyday life, physical appearance constitutes a very important source of information for individuals who do not know one another. In fact, initial judgements (apart from what is known in advance) must be made entirely on the basis of physical appearance. Thus, Thornton (1944) found that confederates wearing glasses were rated as more intelligent and industrious than those not wearing glasses. The effects, however, are only short-lived, for Argyle and McHenry (1971) demonstrated that they wore off rapidly with further acquaintance. There is evidence too that the outcome of interactions may be affected by variations in physical attractiveness (Singer, 1964) or by style of dress.

Thus, at least in interactions with strangers, physical appearance is one important cue which is not available in the absence of the visual channel. The effects of medium can be expected to vary with the level of acquaintance; that is to say, the video channel would be expected to be more useful for interactions with strangers than for interactions with familiar persons.

DYNAMIC NON-VERBAL SIGNALS FROM THE TRUNK AND ARMS

The dynamic non-verbal signals used in conversation can usefully be subdivided into those emitted from the regions of the body below the neck and those from above the neck (Ekman, 1965). We will consider first the information that can be derived from the lower region—the arms and trunk.

The simplest dynamic source of information is posture: standing, sitting, slouching, etc. Everyday experience, for instance in the interview situation, confirms that posture can be used as a source of information about personality and mood: is the other confident or relaxed, respectful or aggressive?

There is some laboratory work on the nature of the inferences made from posture. For example, James (1932), unfortunately only using still photographs of a masked male model, found four dimensions of posture on which subjects were able to agree on an interpretation; position of the head and trunk were found to be the most important indicators, with hand and arm position allowing for discrimination within the categories. Mehrabian (1968) also teased out some specific cues: forward lean of the trunk was found to convey a positive attitude towards the other, higher rates of gesticulation, smaller reclining angles, more head nodding and lower rate of self-manipulation were associated with greater perceived and intended persuasiveness. It could be argued that experiments such as this only demonstrate the existence of cultural stereotypes as to the meaning of various postures, but the existence of such stereotypes is difficult to explain if they do not, at least under some circumstances, form a basis of judgement.

As well as the everyday experience and laboratory evidence mentioned so far, there is also some observational evidence that subjects do respond to the cues emitted by the other. Scheflen (1965), for instance, showed that the posture of one person in a therapy group is related to that of the others with implications for his relationship to the others: for example, a posture consonant with others in the group may indicate sympathetic agreement.

Posture can only be changed at a relatively slow rate. The information capacity of this channel is therefore relatively low compared to that of the verbal channel. It is most appropriate for information relevant to long-term aspects of the conversation, acting as a background for the interpretation of other channels; mood changes only slowly through the interaction, and personality, also signalled by posture, does not change. Posture is, of course, a cue that is not available in the absence of the visual channel. If a picture of the other person is provided (perhaps by a television system) posture may or may not be available as a cue depending on the type of picture: if the picture is just of the head, as with many videophone devices, almost all the information from posture will be lost. If a more complete picture is provided, the postural cues will be retained, but at some trade-off against the smaller signals (such as eye movements) which are less visible with a more remote picture.

FACIAL SIGNALS

It is everyday experience that information is derived from people's facial expressions: are they surprised, interested, happy, sad, angry and so on? Indeed there are few nameable emotions which the very large literature has not investigated in relation to facial expression. Such work assumes that there are discrete emotional states such as 'joy', 'fear', 'anger' and indeed even more complex emotions such as 'pity', and that there are standard facial expressions for each. A review by Vine (1970) summarizes several serious inadequacies of these studies: for example, most have relied on still photographs of actors working without any context, to give very exaggerated poses.

However, more recent work by Ekman (1971), using still photographs and unobtrusive filming of facial expressions has shown that there is pan-cultural consistency in both the encoding (i.e. production) and decoding (i.e. interpretation) of facial expressions of emotion. This suggests that the earlier work cannot be easily dismissed as demonstrating merely cultural stereotypes as to the interpretation of posed facial expressions. Rather, it seems that facial expressions are consistent across many cultures, and may even be innately determined, as implied by Darwin (1872).

Another body of work on facial expressions (e.g. Osgood, 1966, Frijda, 1968) has attempted to factor analyse the responses to facial emotions. This is somewhat superior to the other approach, in that it does not rely so heavily on the arbitrary selection by the experimenter of the emotions investigated. However, such work has shed more light on the classification of emotions than on the part played by various non-verbal signals in the recognition of emotions.

There have been attempts to describe all the possible facial and bodily movements after the manner of structural linguistics (Birdwhistell, 1952). Birdwhistell introduced the term 'kinesics' for the description of such visible movements. Speech is typically accompanied by kinesic stress markers in synchrony with the vocal emphasis. For instance, an upward and lateral movement of the head together with elevation of the eyebrows typically appears in conjunction with a rise in pitch at the end of a sentence to indicate an interrogative. This is an example of the way in which non-verbal signals can interact with signals in both verbal and non-verbal channels to elaborate or modify the total message. However, this structuralist approach is concerned with the description of the cues rather than their function and is thus not itself directly productive in attempts to assess the effects of the removal of the cues.

An important limitation of most studies of facial expression is that they have ignored context effects. Contextual effects are known to be important even in the identification of one's own emotion (Schacter and Singer, 1962). They must be much more important in the identification of the emotion of others, for when internal cues are not available identification must depend on the external cues available. Context effects might be expected to be particularly important in situations where there are rapid moment-to-moment changes in the mood of the participants. This could be expected to interact with the other difficulties caused by the absence of the visual channel, thus rendering such tasks particularly sensitive to the absence of the non-verbal cues.

The variety of possible facial movements (Birdwhistell, 1968, lists 33 discrete movements or 'kinemes' associated with the face) taken with the rapidity of transition between these kinemes, probably accounts for the fact that, at least in our culture, the face is the most expressive part of the body. It is also the part of the body that is most visible and most attended to during interaction and thus usually the area that is most consciously controlled.

In line with Wiener and Mehrabian's (1968) remark that different channels can be expected to carry different types of information according to their suitability, there has been some theorizing about the different types of information communicated by facial and bodily cues. Ekman (1965) found the head to be more informative about the nature of the emotion (whether the person is angry, sad, etc.) while the body is more informative about the intensity of the emotion. If correct, this hypothesis would explain why research on the interpretation of non-verbal cues, has concentrated largely on the facial cues rather than the bodily cues. From arguments based on the relative sending capacities of the different channels, the extent to which they are under conscious control and the sender's awareness of the channel attended to, Ekman and Friesen (1969) suggest that the body and feet would be the most useful cues in the identification of lying. They may provide information at variance with the carefully controlled verbal and facial signals. Experiments provided partial support for this hypothesis. Deception situations may thus be a special case in which the body cues are particularly important. In such a situation, a video picture showing the whole person (as opposed to just the head) would be particularly useful. In other situations, the head is the most crucial region and accordingly a larger picture of the head would be more useful.

There is a limited amount of experimental material to support Ekman's (1965) hypothesis that the face is used in the recognition of emotion and the body in the judgement of intensity. Shapiro, Foster and Powell (1968) found that in judging genuineness, empathy and warmth in therapists, subjects responded more to facial than body cues; with body cues alone performance was negligible. Dittman (1962) found that high degrees of emotional arousal were accompanied by body movements which could not, however, be interpreted as meaning anything specific.

Whatever the relative importance of facial and bodily cues, there can be no doubt that both can constitute an important source of information about the mood and personality of the other—a source of information removed with the absence of a visual channel.

DIRECTION OF EYE-GAZE

Poets and novelists from Shakespeare to Sartre have long been aware of the importance of gaze in human relationships (Champness, 1970). In the last ten years, psychologists have also turned their attention to this channel. The comparative ease of obtaining objective measures of gaze may account for the great increase and considerable success of this type of work.

An extensive review by Kendon (1967) describes three functions of gaze. Firstly, 'monitoring' looks at the other can serve to provide feedback at points where this is required: for example, in deciding whether to continue speaking to clarify a point, whether to change the subject, or whether to yield the floor to the other. Gaze also fulfils a 'regulatory' function being related to floor apportionment (when each person speaks in a conversation). A speaker looks away as he starts to speak and terminates his speech with a sustained gaze. A speaker wishing to hold the floor at a pause point, looks away. Inappropriate eye movements are related to non-fluencies and interruptions: if a speaker fails to look up on completion of an utterance, reply is delayed in 71% instead of the ordinary 29% of instances. Finally, there is the 'expressive' function. Kendon's data were collected from recordings of two-person conversations during the course of which it was noted that subjects tended to look away at points of high emotion. Another example of the expressive function is the sustained gaze associated with interruptions and short questions when the speaker 'bears down' on the other.

Eye-gaze can also be a stable measure of individual differences (Exline and Winter, 1965, Exline, 1971). Strongman and Champness (1968) used frequency of looking away from eye contact as a measure of dominance. Consistent dominance hierarchies were found in groups of subjects who met one another in all possible pairs. Absence of this visual channel, apart from disturbing the regulation of the interaction and the integration of one person's behaviour with the other's, removes what is both an important expressive tool and a vital source of information about the other.

MUTUAL GAZE AND ARGYLE'S INTIMACY EQUILIBRIUM

Argyle (1969) suggests that one function of looking is to establish a relationship: for example, a person will look more if he wants to establish a closer relationship. Eye-contact (mutual gaze) is thought to be particularly significant. Argyle and Dean (1965) postulate an optimum level of 'intimacy'. 'Intimacy' is a function of eye-contact, proximity, conversation topic and so on; changes in one will produce compensating changes in the others. The hypothesis was produced in response to the observation that eye-contact is generally sought after, but too much creates discomfort; for instance, eye-contact is reduced when people are placed very close together (Argyle and Dean, 1965, Goldberg et al. 1969).

A number of observations were linked by Argyle with the equilibrium of intimacy hypothesis. Exline and Winter (1965) found that a person looks more at someone he likes. Exline (1963) found that people high on affiliative motivation look more in non-competitive than in competitive situations. When the conversation topic is more intimate there is less looking (Exline, Gray and Schuette, 1965). Indications of the predicted compensatory changes in non-verbal expressions of intimacy have also been found (Patterson, 1973). However, the ambiguity as to the direction of causality reduces the predictive power of the theory.

Consider an example to illustrate this. If an audio medium increases the apparent distance and reduces eye-contact, would one predict an increase in the friendliness of the conversation (to restore the optimum level of 'intimacy') or a decrease in the friendliness of the conversation (to be consistent with the level of 'intimacy' suggested by the non-verbal signals)?

Eye-contact has been shown to have communicative as well as indicative worth. Ellsworth and Carlsmith (1968) found that with positive verbal content, frequent eye-contact produces more positive evaluations of a confederate, while, with negative verbal content, frequent eye-contact produces more negative evaluations. The converse result (negative verbal content, frequent eye-contact, more positive evaluations) has also appeared (Scheritz and Helmreich, 1973). Results appear to be dependent on the sex of the dyads and the level of personal involvement in the interaction. Kleck and Nuessle (1968), using silent films of a confederate in conversation with a subject, in which the confederate had either high or low amounts of eye-contact (80% or 15% of the time), found that subjects rated the high eye-contact confederate as friendlier, warmer and so on. Stass and Willis (1967) showed that subjects were more likely to choose as partners for an experiment those with high eye-contact during an introduction than those with low eye-contact. Finally, Nichols and Champness (1971) showed that the galvanic skin responses (palmar sweating) of subjects were greater during periods of eye-contact with another than in periods of unreciprocated gaze; heart rates, too, give indication of greater emotional arousal under condition of eye-contact (Kleinke and Pohlen, 1971).

Many of the above experiments used confederates with a very artificial pattern of looking. One experiment relevant to the intimacy equilibrium theory that did not, was conducted by Champness (unpublished). In any interaction, a chance eye-contact (based on the assumption that subjects do not interact and eye-contact arises by chance) can be obtained:

$$\text{Expected eye-contact} = \frac{\text{A's looking time x B's looking time}}{\text{Total time}}$$

Subjects discussed issues on which they were known either to agree or disagree. The discrepancies between the actual eye-contact and the 'expected eye-contact' were examined. There was an interesting effect such that when subjects disagreed there was less eye-contact than expected by chance, while when they agreed there was more than expected by chance.

Eye-contact is thus an important cue that is not available in telephone conversation. The visual channel available in most video systems does not restore eye-contact as a cue; it makes things even worse. The camera cannot be placed exactly in line with the picture of the eyes, so if person A thinks he is looking person B in the eye, he will appear to B to be looking elsewhere (shiftily sideways if the camera is mounted on the side, modestly downwards if the camera is mounted above the monitor). The regulatory function of eye-contact may thus be worse than removed, its operation may be reversed. For example, when thinking he is looking away during an utterance, A may look at the camera; on such occasions B may experience eye-contact and take it as his turn to speak. This effect could be sufficient to account for the disturbances in interrupting behaviour found by Champness (1971) when a video condition was compared with an audio and a face-to-face condition. Some experience and training in the use of video systems may be required before such problems are overcome.

Removal of the visual channel prevents the integrative functions of eye-gaze cues. Replacement of the ordinary visual channel by a picture of the other might distort these functions. The same holds for the expressive functions: reducing apparent eye-contact might affect evaluations of the other, vary the intimacy of the conversation and alter the apparent level of conflict. Thus, as was the case with proximity, altering a non-verbal cue (in the video condition) may have very definite negative implications which may be qualitatively and not just quantitatively different from the effects obtained by removing the cue altogether (as in telephone conversation).

COMPARISONS OF VERBAL AND VISUAL COMMUNICATION

Much of the information available in the visual channels is also available in the audio channel from such cues as tone of voice, choice of words, pausing behaviour, and so on. If there is complete duplication of the information (redundancy in the information theory sense of the word) no effects of removing the visual channel would be expected. At the other extreme, if there is no duplication of information between channels, the effects of removing the visual channel would depend on the relative importance of the visual and auditory cues. Reality is likely to lie between the two extremes. The relative importance of the two sources of information is thus a matter of some interest. There have been a few investigations of relevance.

In an experiment by Shapiro (1968) trained raters were asked to rate segments of therapy presented via one of three modes (audio only, video only, or audio + video channels). In general, the two partial modes were equal in their agreement with the combined mode, suggesting that the visual cues were as powerful as the auditory cues. Further, as the judges were trained on audio-only material, the procedure was probably biassed against the video mode.

Rowley and Keller (1962) using a procedure involving the operant conditioning of a class of verbal behaviour and employing as reinforcers either the verbalization 'good' or a head nod, found that the verbal reinforcer was significantly more effective. One wonders what would have been the result had the head nod been more vigorous and accompanied by a smile. Another experiment was conducted by Argyle et al. (1970). Subjects rated a video recording of a confederate who read three passages in various tones of voice with corresponding facial expression such that the non-verbal information sometimes conflicted with the verbal content of the messages. The results showed that, in this context, the non-verbal cues had more impact than the verbal cues.

Such experiments tackling the relative importance of verbal and non-verbal behaviour are up against an almost insuperable problem in having to choose what non-verbal behaviour and what verbal behaviour are to be compared in efficacy. Furthermore, designs in which the isolated channels are compared are unsatisfactory because it is not clear to what extent the information normally conveyed in one channel can, if necessary, be conveyed by the other; the two types of information can interact. Finally, there is the point that even a source manyfold less important than another source can still have some importance. The only safe conclusion is that the relative importance of the various channels varies according to the particular people, situation and subject matter involved, and attempts to compare them in this way are of dubious value.

Thus, although at first sight relevant, these comparative studies provide only more evidence for the already well-substantiated conclusion that non-verbal behaviours are important sources of information in some circumstances.

Are qualitative comparisons of verbal and non-verbal behaviour any more fruitful in the attempt to assess the implications of the removal of the visual channel? Ruesch (1966) gives a full list of the similarities and differences. The most significant of the differences is the relative sophistication of the verbal system. Most individuals would find it difficult to transmit non-verbally high-level cognitive information such as the possible effects of alteration in the bank rate on inflation. Verbal communication is manifestly coded (language) but non-verbal communication is coded to a much smaller extent. Some meanings are culturally determined and there are special sign languages for the deaf, but most non-verbal signalling is more universal (laughter, shoulder-shrugs and startle reactions for instance, see Ekman, 1971). The information in the non-verbal signals is more of an affective than a cognitive nature.

This is not to deny that affective information is also transmitted via verbal channels, but it does mean that where the affective information is of critical importance, the absence of the visual signals may be particularly damaging to effective communication. Tasks in which two people combine to solve arithmetic problems would, from this point of view, not be expected to be affected by the removal of the visual channel.

What sorts of information are carried specifically by the visual non-verbal channels? One obvious category is that which the communicator does not want to express verbally. For example, in an ordinary business context there is something of a taboo on direct expression of attitudes towards others; boredom, similarly, is more likely to be expressed non-verbally than verbally.

A second category of information carried particularly by the visual non-verbal channels is 'unconscious communication'. A series of studies on experimenter bias have shown that non-verbal cues may have considerable effect, even unintentionally. Rosenthal (1967) lists smiles, head-nods and other facial movements among the cues with which the experimenter may unwittingly influence the subject. In mixed-sex interactions, sex-related differences were found in the relative reliance on the visual and auditory channels for such signals, suggesting the possibility of sex differences in reaction to the removal of the visual channel.

MULTICHANNEL COMMUNICATION

A key issue in the interpretation of the literature on the functions of the individual non-verbal signals is the relationship between the various individual channels.

Birdwhistell (1970) pointed out that while communication is 'a continuous process made up of isolable discrete units, these units are multifunctional, they have distinguishable contrast meaning at one level, and cross referencing function at another. *None of these units has meaning in and of itself.*' In attempting to assess the functions of the visual channel, it is therefore dangerous to confine attention at any one time to individual cues such as posture, eye-gaze, proximity and the like. The channels do interact (see for example Argyle and Dean, 1965). In particular one must beware of moving from the observation that a particular channel is 'redundant' (in the strict information theory sense of 'conveying no new information') to the position that it is without function and could be removed without distorting the communication process and outcome. Studies of media must look at relevant combinations of channels. Important overall properties of communication may be missed if attention is restricted to individual channels.

The addition of the visual channel to the audio-only system represented by the telephone, permits the use of a variety of new signs transmitted in the visual channel. This information must be combined with that from the audio channel. Understanding the communication is thus a bisensory perception task. It is not appropriate to go deeply into the literature on bisensory perception because the experiments and the theory (which draws heavily on signal detection theory) have largely been concerned with the detection of simple physical stimuli (Loveless *et al.*, 1970, for review). Any extrapolation of the results to complex stimuli extended in time such as occur in freely interactive conversations would probably be unwarranted. However, there is one distinction that is relevant in the present context; this is the distinction between the case in which the two channels are both relevant and that in which only one channel is relevant.

The latter case is usually referred to as 'accessory stimulation'. An important practical example of this is noise. There is no simple relationship between noise level and performance; it seems that noise can function either to distract or to alert the subject, depending on the task (Hockey, 1969). The tasks relevant in the present context are not vigilance tasks; the distraction function is therefore more likely. Irrelevant information (perhaps provided by the video channel) could under some circumstances be a positive hindrance.

When the information in both channels is relevant, the addition of the second channel will have the effect of improving the chances of detection of difficult stimuli (provided that the human system is not already loaded to its maximum channel capacity). For example, insincerity might be more easily detected by observation of tone of voice coupled with gaze aversion, than by either separately. Similarly there is experimental evidence to support the widely held view that audio-visual channels are better than either separately for educational instruction purposes (Hsia, 1968).

Referring strictly to the informational aspects of communication, the addition of the visual channel to the 'audio-only' system will improve performance on signals for which it is relevant and, in so far as it is a distraction, impair performance on activities for which it is not relevant. The possible distraction effect may depend on task complexity. The impairment associated with the addition of irrelevant information (Shaw, 1958) is more likely to be serious if the task is complex and the participants therefore susceptible to 'stimulus overload' (Milgram, 1970).

Another important issue concerning the interaction between channels is the possibility of substitution between signals. The foregoing overview has noted a number of examples of apparent compensatory behaviours between channels such as eye-gaze and physical proximity. Shulman and Stone (1970) noted that people used voice volume to adapt to difference in proximity. Much of the information conveyed by the visual non-verbal signals can also be conveyed verbally. Indeed there are a number of auditory non-verbal signals (such as tone of voice pausing behaviour, and paralinguistic material such as 'um', 'ah', 'er' and so on) conveying information very similar to that conveyed by the visual non-verbal signals, whose operation is not likely to be significantly affected by the variations in medium of communication with which we are concerned. The extent of the likely substitution between signals is very uncertain. This being the case, one can not even say with certainty that communication outcomes will be affected by the removal of the visual channel; one can only point to the type of tasks most likely to be affected and the effects to be expected.

VISUAL COMMUNICATION—OVERVIEW

Cherry (1957) defined communication as an exchange of 'signs' (physical signals by which one organism affects the state of the other in a two-organism system). This definition is conveniently operational and in some senses general, for it allows that the signal be emitted either intentionally or unintentionally and be received either consciously or unconsciously. The constant problem is to know whether the signals emitted by one party are used by the other. A distinction is thus commonly made between cues which signal a certain state in the sender ('indicative cues') and cues to which the other responds in some way or another ('communicative' cues). The foregoing summary provides abundant evidence for the indicative worth of visual signals, but the evidence is in many cases somewhat incomplete when it comes to the communicative worth. Lack of evidence of use is, of course, not to be interpreted as evidence of non-use. Whilst for some types of visual information it may be an assumption to say that they are used, it is every bit as much an assumption to say that the information is derived from the auditory channel only. We must recognize that the communication stream is a total stream and it is dangerous to isolate items of information in individual channels from the total message. Information that may be duplicated, set in context or amplified, in another channel may still be important.

In most cases, the functions of the non-verbal cues have been in some way related to forming, building or maintaining the relationship between the interactants. The absence of the visual channel reduces the possibilities for expression of socio-emotional material and decreases the information available about the other's self-image, attitudes, moods and reactions. So, regarding the medium as an information transmission system, the removal of the visual channel is likely to produce a serious disturbance of the affective interaction; one would expect the transmission of cognitive information to be relatively unaffected.

Thus, the tasks which would be expected to be most sensitive to variation in the medium of communication are tasks in which the expression of emotion (and perception of this emotion) is an important part of the interaction, tasks with a great need for timing and coordination of the speaker's activity with the responses of the other, and finally, tasks on which there is the greatest need to manipulate others. On tasks on which there is no need to manipulate others, the performance of the pair will approximate more nearly the sum of the performances of the individuals, and as such is less likely to be disturbed by variations in the link between them.

5

Theoretical Approaches to Differences Between Media

INTRODUCTION

Although the initial motivation for the study of the differences between communications media was an interest in the practical implications of a wide-scale switch from face-to-face towards mediated communication, the area does also have implications for the study of social interaction. In order to draw out these implications, three alternative theories of the effects of varying medium of communication are presented in this chapter. The theories can be considered hierarchical, in that while the later ones take into account all the factors allowed for in the earlier ones, they also extend their scope to include other processes and new phenomena. The earlier two theories, the 'efficiency' and the 'non-verbal' theories have been implicit in the previously published literature; the third, the 'Social Presence' account, is relatively novel.

SIMPLE THEORIES IN TERMS OF EFFICIENCY

Most previous studies relevant to the effect of removing the visual channel have only incidentally manipulated medium of communication, the main interest has been elsewhere. It is probably for this reason that no well-articulated body of theory relating to medium has grown up, and that a very common interpretation of differences is a naive view that focuses on the 'efficiency' of the interaction.

It is widely assumed that the reduction in cues in a telephone conversation will reduce the efficiency of the interaction. Hence the expectation of greater cooperation in face-to-face bargaining than in telephone bargaining, or of more rapid problem solving face-to-face, or the reports of greater persuasive impact for live speeches as compared to speeches heard over a loudspeaker (see Chapter 6). So far as it goes, and in the situations to which it refers, this view may be reasonable, but, although efficiency can be unambiguously defined in, for example, a problem-solving situation (by the quality of the solution or length of time to solution) this is not always the case. The predictive usefulness of the theory is then much diminished. For example, in many conflict situations such as a negotiation in which it is possible to cooperate to mutual advantage, individual and collective interests conflict. What outcome will be favoured by the most 'efficient' communication? No clear answer emerges.

The logic of the theories in terms of efficiency can also be somewhat loose, for there is no compelling reason why removal of cues at the level of the mechanics of the interaction should always lead to a reduction in the overall efficiency. The cues removed might have been distracting and their removal might serve to concentrate attention on the important aspects of the interaction, thus making the overall outcome more efficient. This is important, for there is evidence that on some tasks, certain media may allow too much personal contact; one might expect that in tasks involving a high degree of confrontation or interpersonal tension, such would be the case. Interviews confirm this: asked about the sort of tasks for which they would prefer to use the telephone rather than see the other person face-to-face, people cite high conflict or embarrassing situations (particularly, it seems, when the outcome is not in doubt, as when reprimanding a subordinate or refusing someone for a job.) Participants in Sinaiko's (1963) Summit II game were also reported to have preferred to negotiate via telephone because of its 'depersonalized' nature and the absence of distraction by non-verbal cues. Christie (1972) asked a sample of businessmen to list the advantages of the telephone as compared to face-to-face. One of his factors (labelled 'impersonality') loaded highly on 'conceal identity if required' and 'allows for less stress in unpleasant tasks'. Thus under some circumstances, impersonality may be preferred. On other tasks—perhaps, for example, the interview situation examined by Reid (1970) (see Chapter 8), media such as the telephone may be too impersonal.

Perhaps most important of all, simple theories in terms of efficiency provide no grounds for distinguishing those situations in which the outcome is affected by medium from those in which it is not. As we shall see in the chapters discussing the experimental work, some tasks do appear to be sensitive to medium and others do not. Broadly speaking, those tasks in which interpersonal relationships are important are sensitive to medium while those involving simply cognitive material (e.g. problem solving, information exchange) are not. On the naive efficiency interpretation this result is hard to predict for it appears that it is amongst those tasks whose efficiency can be most clearly defined that the effects of medium are least frequently found. Some more sophisticated explanation is required.

THEORIES EMPHASIZING NON-VERBAL COMMUNICATION

A more sophisticated approach would be to attempt to predict the effects of media by extrapolation from the known qualities of the medium and the known functions of non-verbal cues. Chapter 4 discussed a number of non-verbal cues, some of which are transmitted by all media (e.g. tone of voice) some of which are only transmitted face-to-face (e.g. touch) and some of which are distorted in transmission (e.g. proximity and eye-contact in video systems). In many cases the functions of these cues are at least suspected, if not conclusively demonstrated.

A reasonable, but still naive, hypothesis, would thus be: we can predict the effects upon interaction of varying medium of communication by listing the cues that are not transmitted via the different media, by discovering the functions of these cues by reference to research on face-to-face communication, and then deducing the way in which the outcome or processes of the conversation would be altered by the absence of these cues. An example of the working of this hypothesis would be as follows:

Audio-only media do not transmit facial expressions;
Facial expressions are important in face-to-face conversation for communicating emotional mood;
Therefore, it will be difficult to transmit or receive indications of emotional mood in telephone conversations.

This hypothesis is naive and illogical for various reasons, four of which we will describe here.

(a) Firstly, non-verbal cues are not transmitted or received in isolation; they are always combined with other non-verbal cues and usually with a verbal message. A good example of a constellation of cues has been provided by Duncan (1972) for cues to termination of speech. According to Duncan, a speaker who is preparing to yield the 'floor' to the listener will engage in some combination of the following behaviours: (1) a shift in pitch at the end of the phonemic clause, (2) a drawl on the final syllable, (3) the termination of a hand gesture or relaxation of a tense position, (4) a 'sociocentric' expression such as 'you know', (5) a drop in loudness and (6) the completion of a grammatical clause. To this list one could add (7) the resumption of eye-gaze, following the work of Kendon (1967).

It is therefore necessary to extend the argument to the point where one knows the *combination* of cues which transmit a particular type of message and to examine the combination for its reliance on the visual channel. Thus, in the above example, five of the cues are transmitted by the audio channel while two are transmitted visually. In so far as the visual cues are not simply redundant, turn-taking will be less well synchronized in telephone conversation. However empirical results generally fail to support this hypothesis (Cook and Lalljee, 1972, Williams, 1975b, and Rutter and Stephenson, 1974), finding on average *less* interruptions, though more pauses in telephone conversations than in face-to-face conversations.

(b) One reason for such failure to confirm empirical predictions is the likelihood that, aware of the reduced-cue situation, the actor will modify his behaviour; thus head-nods indicating agreement may be replaced by verbal phrases such as 'I quite agree'. There is experimental evidence to support this hypothesis: analysing the Watergate transcripts, Wilson and Williams (1975) found that the telephone conversation transcripts contained more verbal expressions of agreement or disagreement with the other's opinion than did the face-to-face transcripts. This constitutes a clear case of interchange-ability between non-verbal cues (in this case head-nods and facial expressions) and verbal messages (in this case explicit expressions of agreement or disagreement). With such possibilities for substitution and even overcompensation always present, it is impossible to make predictions with any degree of confidence.

(c) The situation is further complicated by the possibility that particular cues or combinations of cues are not invariant in their meaning across situations. To take an exaggerated example, consider how in the face-to-face situation failure to smile and shake hands would be interpreted as a sign of unfriendliness. If contact were by telephone, clearly no such interpretation of the same behaviour would be made! Thus the absence of non-verbal cues in telecommunicated interactions is not necessarily equivalent to their absence in face-to-face conversation. We need therefore to take into account the actors' feelings about the total situation.

(d) Finally prediction is hampered by the lack of knowledge about the (probably tenuous) relationship between the use of the visual cues and the outcome of the interaction. If one is interested principally in simple behaviours such as interruption, non-verbal theories may be productive. However, the level of analysis is inappropriate when considering more complex behaviours.

Simplistic extrapolations based on the normal functions of the visual non-verbal cues share too many of the faults of the 'efficiency' theories discussed above. Although they represent an improvement over the simple 'efficiency' theories in so far as they can be used to predict differential sensitivities to medium of communication, such theories are still too simplistic.

A THEORY BASED ON FEELINGS OF 'SOCIAL PRESENCE'

Douglas (1957) proposed that in any interaction Person and Other are concerned both with acting out certain roles and with developing or maintaining some personal relationship. These two aspects can be distinguished as 'interparty' and 'interpersonal' exchange. Morley and Stephenson (1969) applied this distinction in their analysis of media effects. They proposed that there existed a balance between these two, which could be affected by medium of communication such that in telephone conversations there would be a greater emphasis on the interparty exchange at the expense of the interpersonal exchange. Thus, 'negotiators are likely to be less concerned with the presentation of the self, pay more attention to what is being said and to be more task-oriented' (Morley and Stephenson, 1969, p.543).

Although, at least in their published material, Morley and Stephenson did not explicitly tie in the proposed effects of medium on the interperson/interparty balance, with the functions of the visual cues that are eliminated, their view is certainly consistent with the functions of these cues. The key roles of the visual cues are in the communication of interpersonal attitudes (see Chapter 4). If the availability of this type of information is reduced attention must focus instead on the cues which are available—the verbal channel containing the interparty, task-oriented, cognitive material.

Morley and Stephenson devised this conceptualization of the effects of varying the medium of communication in the context of negotiations. We believe, however, that the degree of salience of the other person in the interaction and the consequent salience of the interpersonal relationships is an important hypothetical construct that can usefully be applied more generally. We shall term this quality 'Social Presence'. This critical concept needs further clarification. We regard Social Presence as being a quality of the communications medium. Although we would expect it to affect the way individuals perceive their discussions, and their relationships to the persons with whom they are communicating, it is important to emphasize that we are defining Social Presence as a quality of the medium itself. We hypothesize that communications media vary in their degree of Social Presence, and that these variations are important in determining the way individuals interact. We also hypothesize that the users of any given communications medium are in some sense aware of the degree of Social Presence of the medium and tend to avoid using the medium for certain types of interactions; specifically, interactions requiring a higher degree of Social Presence than they perceive the medium to have. Thus we believe that social presence is an important key to understanding person-to-person telecommunications. It varies between different media, it affects the nature of the interaction and it interacts with the purpose of the interaction to influence the medium chosen by the individual who wishes to communicate.

We conceive of Social Presence as a single dimension representing a cognitive synthesis of all the factors discussed in Chapter 4 as they are perceived by the individual to be present in the medium. Thus, the capacity to transmit information about facial expression, direction of looking, posture, dress and non-verbal vocal cues, all contribute to the Social Presence of a communications medium. How they contribute, the weights given to all these factors, is determined by the individual, because we conceive of the Social Presence of a medium as a perceptual or attitudinal dimension of the user, a 'mental set' towards the medium. Thus, when we said earlier that Social Presence is a quality of the medium we were not being strictly accurate. We wished then to distinguish between the medium itself and the communications for which the medium is used. Now we need to make a finer distinction. We conceive of Social Presence not as an objective quality of the medium, though it must surely be dependent upon the medium's objective qualities, but as a subjective quality of the medium. We believe that this is a more useful way of looking at Social Presence than trying to define it objectively. In Dashiell's (1935) experiment (to be discussed in Chapter 6) it was not the objective fact that there were others in a nearby room working on the same problem as the subject which was important, but the subjective fact that the subject was *aware* of this which was important in influencing behaviour. Similarly, in understanding the effects of telecommunications media, we believe that it is important to know how the user perceives the medium, what his feelings are and what his 'mental set' is.

MEASURING SOCIAL PRESENCE

The chief method for measuring Social Presence in the laboratory is the semantic differential technique (Osgood, Suci and Tannenbaum, 1957), the experimental subjects being asked to rate the communication media on a series of seven-point, bipolar scales such as

impersonal _ _ _ _ _ _ _ personal.

In the classic semantic differential technique, it is usually found that the ratings on the individual scales reflect only about three major factors. These have been labelled Evaluation, Potency and Activity, and have been referred to collectively as the E-P-A factor structure. However, this factor structure is most commonly found when both the rating scales and the items judged are heterogeneous (Miron, 1969) and it is perfectly possible to find that the ratings are determined by other factors when the range of items judged is limited, as it is limited, in our research, to communications media.

We have found that the Social Presence factor is typically marked by scales such as unsociable-sociable, insensitive-sensitive, cold-warm and impersonal-personal. Media having a high degree of Social Presence are judged as being warm, personal, sensitive and sociable. Sometimes, however, depending upon the range of media examined and the number of rating scales used, the Social Presence factor merges with another factor, which is usually separate, to form a combined factor. This process, 'factor fusion', is not uncommon. Even in the very early days of this research it was noted that the Potency and Activity factors of the classical E-P-A factor structure would sometimes combine to form a compound 'Dynamism' factor (Osgood, Suci and Tannenbaum, 1957). In our experiments, we have found that the Social Presence factor tends to fuse with a factor we call Aesthetic Appeal when the range of communications media is limited.

The fusion of the Social Presence factor with the Aesthetic Appeal factor occurred in the first experiment (Champness, 1972a) to examine users' attitudes towards different media using the semantic differential technique. In this experiment, the reason for the fusion was not only the limited range of media but also the fact that only two scales which we now know measure the Social Presence factor were included in the set of rating scales.

The subjects in this experiment (72 managerial civil servants) used one of three media (face-to-face, closed-circuit television or an audio system) to discuss items taken from the Kogan and Wallach choice-dilemmas (decision-making problems, in which the acceptable degree of risk is chosen by subjects). Each pair of subjects had three conversations, one over each medium. After each conversation the subjects were asked to rate the medium they had just experienced on twenty-four semantic differential scales, selected to be representative of the factors from Snyder and Wiggins' (1970) study.

The ratings of the media were factor analysed, treating each subject–medium combination as a single case. The first factor was a combination of the Social Presence factor and the Aesthetic Appeal factor. The highest loading scales all had connotations of aesthetic appeal: colourless–colourful (0.76), small–large (0.74), constricted–spacious (0.68), boring–interesting (0.63), and ugly–beautiful (0.62). The two scales measuring Social Presence: unsociable–sociable (0.60) and insensitive–sensitive (0.57), had lower loadings.

Because the fusion of these two factors makes interpretation based on the factor structure of the ratings difficult, it is probably more instructive to examine the individual scales which, in the light of our later research, we know measure Social Presence. Twenty of the 24 scales distinguished between the audio medium and the two visual media to a statistically reliable degree, so we can attach little significance to the fact that both of the Social Presence scales distinguished between these media. However, only four scales distinguished between the video medium and face-to-face, and the scale unsociable–sociable was one of these. (The other three were: meaningless–meaningful, public–private and true–false.) There is therefore some indication in the results of this experiment that Social Presence is a good discriminator between communications media. As would be expected from our theory, the ratings were such that face-to-face was rated the most sociable medium, video was rated the next most sociable and the audio medium was rated the least sociable.

The results of this initial study of users' judgements of communications media supported the hypothesis that Social Presence varies significantly between different communications media. However, only three media were examined, and these three differed from one another markedly. One was an audio telecommunications medium, one was a telecommunications medium having a visual channel and one (face-to-face) was not a telecommunications medium at all. A more stringent test of the importance of the Social Presence dimension was made in a second study by Champness (1972c). In this study, he tested the hypothesis that the Social Presence dimension would discriminate even between two variations of the same telecommunications system.

Three media were compared in this experiment: audio, video and face-to-face media as used in the first experiment. However, in this experiment, subjects participated in groups of three, not in pairs. In each of the telecommunications conditions, two subjects were seated in the same room, with the third subject in a different room. In the video condition, the lone subject viewed a picture showing the other two participants, their chairs and the small table at which they sat. The two subjects who shared a room viewed a head-and-shoulders picture of their colleague. It was hypothesized that the video system as perceived by the lone subject viewing two small images of his colleagues would have lower Social Presence than the system as perceived by the two subjects viewing a close-up picture of their colleague. The task and procedure were the same as in the first experiment. The set of rating scales was modified to include a total of four scales measuring Social Presence: unsociable–sociable, insensitive–sensitive, impersonal–personal and cold–warm. Ninety civil servants participated.

The factor analysis of the ratings resulted in four factors in this experiment, of which the first was again a fusion of Social Presence and Aesthetic Appeal. The highest loading scales reflected Aesthetic Appeal: constricted–spacious (0.74), small–large (0.73), closed–open (0.68), colourless–colourful (0.67) and ugly–beautiful (0.62). However, the next highest loading scale below these was cold–warm (0.60), and the remaining Social Presence scales also had fairly high loadings: unsociable–sociable (0.58), impersonal–personal (0.52) and insensitive–sensitive (0.47). Differences between the media were tested by an analysis of variance on the factor scores. This confirmed that the three media differed in their scores on the factor and also that higher scores were given to the video medium by the two subjects who saw a close-up picture than by the lone subject viewing the picture with two small images of his colleagues.

The hypothesis that Social Presence would vary even between two versions of the same communications medium was thus supported. The results of the two experiments considered together are therefore encouraging. However, in neither experiment was a truly separate Social Presence factor isolated. Furthermore, the experiments succeeded in demonstrating differences between the visual and the non-visual media, and even between media within the 'visual' class, but what about differences between different audio media? If social presence is as important as we believe it is, we should expect to find differences between different audio media as well.

Both of these points were answered in an experiment by Christie (1973a). Thirty-six businessmen in groups of six used in turn each of five media to discuss 'the major problems facing modern business in New York and Connecticut'. The five media were: face-to-face, closed-circuit television, speakerphone (a commercial loudspeaking telephone), a high-fidelity improved speakerphone and a multispeaker audio system in which each person was represented by a different loudspeaker. After experiencing all five media, subjects completed a thirty-scale semantic differential questionnaire.

The factor analysis of these ratings produced six orthogonal factors. The first factor was clearly identified as Social Presence. The three highest loading variables were: passive–active (0.74), insensitive–sensitive (0.72) and unsociable–sociable (0.58). The high loading for passive–active indicates that the media having high Social Presence were also seen as being more 'active' in this experiment. The Aesthetic Appeal factor appeared as a separate factor, and was marked by hard–soft (0.79), erratic–periodic (0.71) and ugly–beautiful (0.69). (The scale ugly–beautiful had a loading of only 0.03 on the Social Presence factor, confirming that the conceptual distinction between Social Presence and Aesthetic Appeal is a real one.)

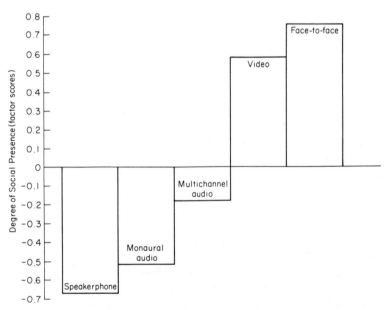

Figure 5.1   The relative Social Presence of five communications media.

Mean factor scores for the five media are presented graphically in Figure 5.1. The difference between the video and face-to-face conditions is not statistically significant, and neither is the difference between the speakerphone and the monaural audio. However, the multispeaker audio system is significantly higher on Social Presence than the other two audio media and is significantly lower on this factor than the two visual media.

The results of this experiment demonstrate that Social Presence is relevant to group conferencing situations as well as meetings between two or three people. The experiment confirms the usefulness of distinguishing between Social Presence and Aesthetic Appeal, since these appear as separate factors. It supports the hypothesis that Social Presence varies even between different audio systems. Finally, although not all the differences between the media reached statistical significance, the media are ranked in Figure 5.1 exactly as would be predicted from our theory.

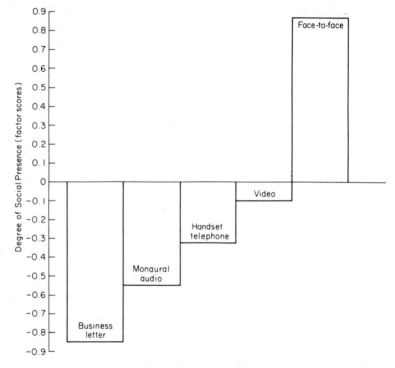

Figure 5.2 The relative Social Presence of five communications media.

A further experiment by Christie (1974) lends some generality to these results. This experiment differed from the original in three ways, (a) the subjects were British Civil Servants rather than American businessmen, (b) the scales used in the semantic differentials were chosen as representative of those elicited from businessmen in free descriptions of media and (c) the range of media used was slightly expanded to include also the written medium. The results clearly supported the pattern obtained in previous results (see Figure 5.2). A clear Social Presence factor emerged marked by the scales:

impersonal–personal, cold–hot, dehumanizing–humanizing, insensitive–sensitive. Although as in Figure 5.1 not all the differences
between media reach statistical significance, the ordering of the media
is as one would expect and there are a sufficient number of significant
differences between media not adjacent to one another in the ordering
(e.g. face-to-face versus letter) that we can have some confidence that
the rank order shown in Figure 5.2 is not simply due to chance.

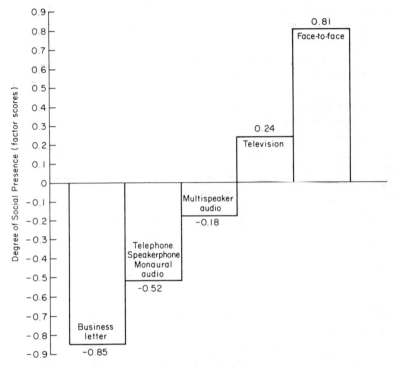

Figure 5.3   Social Presence of several communications media.

The results of Christie's two experiments can be combined in a single
bar chart (Figure 5.3). Here we have averaged over all the audio media
except the multispeaker audio system which was the only system that
differed significantly from the others. The values displayed for the
video and face-to-face media are the averages of their values in the two
experiments. The value for the video medium is therefore very
approximate and is likely to vary markedly depending upon the
conditions of testing (e.g. the size of the image on the screen).

The differences between the media shown in Figure 5.3 should not
be regarded as conclusive. It would be premature to say *this* is the way
the media are ordered. We would rather say that our results so far
suggest that Figure 5.3 might show the approximate pattern of
relationships to be demonstrated more conclusively by future research.
It is, however, a useful heuristic device. It suggests that, if Social

Presence is an important determinant of media effects in experiments in which we measure objective performance, then most of the effects we observe are likely to discriminate between the visual and the non-visual media. We would also expect to observe differences between audio systems in which each individual is represented by a different loudspeaker and systems in which this is not the case. We might also expect differences between the audio media and the written media. Whether or not we would expect differences between the video medium and face-to-face would seem to depend upon the details of the experimental conditions, including, for example, the size of the subject's image in the television picture. We would not expect to find substantial differences between different types of monaural audio media.

These experiments support our hypothesis that communications media can be distinguished by their degree of Social Presence. Since the concept seems, therefore, to have some value we should ask: how does Social Presence relate to other concepts in social psychology? Two such concepts would seem to be particularly relevant: Argyle and Dean's (1965) concept of intimacy; and Wiener and Mehrabian's (1968) concept of immediacy.

Argyle and Dean (1965) proposed that when two people enter into a conversation each is both attracted to and repelled by the other. This approach–avoidance theory predicts that the two people, if they are seated face-to-face, will try to adjust their seating positions until an equilibrium is reached. But an equilibrium of what? The answer to this, Argyle and Dean suggest, is an equilibrium of the factors affecting the overall level of intimacy. These factors include, apart from physical distance: eye-contact, smiling and personal topics of conversation. This theory leads to many predictions. For example, it suggests people will tend to avoid eye-contact and will increase their physical separation if personal topics are to be discussed. In this way, they can maintain an optimum level of intimacy.

We would like to suggest that the Social Presence of the communications medium should be included in the list of factors contributing to intimacy. Thus, the use of television rather than audio-only communication makes for greater intimacy, other things being equal.

Immediacy is related to Social Presence in a different way. Immediacy, as conceptualized by Wiener and Mehrabian (1968), is a measure of the psychological distance which a communicator puts between himself and the object of his communication, his addressee or his communication. According to Wiener and Mehrabian, negative affect, low evaluation and non-preference for any of these things are associated with non-immediacy in communications.

Wiener and Mehrabian originally applied the concept of immediacy to an understanding of speech. They showed that immediacy in speech can be manifested in many different ways. For instance, the choice of 'Let us . . .' or 'We . . .' as opposed to 'I . . .' or 'You . . .' may be significant. The former connote a feeling of closeness and association, the latter separation.

The concept of immediacy can be extended to include a consideration of other aspects of communication apart from speech itself. Thus, a person can convey immediacy or non-immediacy non-verbally as well as verbally (e.g. by physical proximity, formality of dress, and facial expression). Some (e.g. Heilbronn and Libby, 1973) have gone further and suggested that immediacy or non-immediacy can also be conveyed by which medium of communication is used. They suggest that, in general, the more information a medium can transmit, the greater its immediacy. Thus, the use of face-to-face communication implies greater immediacy than the use of the telephone or even interactive television. This kind of immediacy has been termed 'technological immediacy' as opposed to 'social immediacy' which is conveyed through speech and associated non-verbal cues.

Technological immediacy may seem very similar to our own concept of Social Presence, but there are important differences. This is evident from the fact that the immediacy implied by the use of a particular medium of communication may vary even when Social Presence does not. For example, if a person uses his telephone to speak to someone in an adjacent office when it would be just as convenient to go and see him, an impression of 'distance' and non-immediacy is likely to be created, especially if the person making the call is the other's superior. However, the non-immediacy associated with the use of the telephone in this instance is less likely to be replicated when the two parties are separated by considerable physical distances. In these cases, where face-to-face communication is not practicable, the use of the telephone does not carry the same connotation. Although immediacy varies in these two kinds of situation, the Social Presence afforded by the telephone will be the same (unless, of course, the quality of the sound is affected by the distances involved; if so, Social Presence will be *greater*, not less, when the two parties are in adjacent offices).

In some cases, immediacy and Social Presence may vary together. For example, if a person has both a voice telephone and a picture telephone available, both immediacy and Social Presence will be greater if he chooses to use the latter.

A final point to make is that, for any given medium of communication (e.g. telephone) and situation (e.g. long-distance call), immediacy may vary even when Social Presence does not. Thus, the person making the call may choose to speak in such a manner as to give an impression of aloofness and 'distance' (non-immediacy) or he may choose to adopt an attitude of informality and comradeship. In either case, the degree to which he is perceived as a 'real person'—the Social Presence afforded by the telephone—will be the same.

To clarify the concept of Social Presence further and to derive suggestions as to how this may affect behaviour in using the media, one further study will be described. Users' comments about new media frequently relate to what we conceptualize as Social Presence: 'more realistic', 'three-dimensional, gives feeling of group', 'vividness of expression' and 'maintains one's sense of individuality'. Champness (1973) in an evaluation of a commercial video system systematized this type of material. Users of the system were asked to rate their agreement or disagreement with a number of such statements collected from interviews with users of other systems. A factor analysis of the responses yielded four orthogonal factors. The first factor was clearly a Social Presence factor, the highest loading items being:

One does not get a good enough idea of how people at the other end are reacting (−0.76)

One gets no real impression of personal contact with the people at the other end of the link (−0.65).

One can easily assess the other people's reactions to what has been said (0.64).

It provides a great sense of realism (0.60).

One gets a good 'feel' for people at the other end (0.60).

It isn't at all like holding a face-to-face meeting (−0.59).

It was just as though we were all in the same room (0.54).

People at the other end do not seem 'real' (−0.50).

I would be happy to use the system for a meeting in which I intended to persuade other people (0.46).

I couldn't get to know people very well if I only met them over this system (−0.44).

Champness reports that each of the eight highest-loading items on this factor of the questionnaire correlated significantly with the semantic differential scale personal−impersonal.

Even the crude measures of Social Presence used in the laboratory so far suggest that reliable differences between media can be observed. The greatest differences seem to occur between the visual and the non-visual media. This is not surprising in terms of our theory because a large class of the non-verbal signals which form a part of normal face-to-face interaction are visual. We would expect that blocking the transmission of these cues would result in much lower Social Presence. However, Christie's experiment confirms that even within the range of audio-only media there are observable differences in Social Presence. This is important for our theory since we hypothesize that Social Presence depends upon not only the visual non-verbal cues transmitted, but also more subtle aspects such as the apparent distance of the other (influenced, perhaps, by voice volume) and the 'realness' of the other (influenced, perhaps, by the fidelity of speech reproduction). Our prediction regarding differences in the Social Presence of various media is *not* simply that some media will be 'better' or more 'effective' than others. On the contrary, we hypothesize that the suitability of any given communications medium for a specified type of interaction will depend upon two things: the degre of Social Presence of the medium, and the degree of Social Presence required by the task. In particular, we would expect to observe the greatest distortions compared with face-to-face communication when a medium having a low degree of Social Presence is used for a type of person-to-person interaction requiring a high degree of Social Presence. We would expect, for example, that whenever the nature of the communication requires the individuals concerned to attend to one another's idiosyncrasies, to constantly assess each other's reactions, to assess accurately the 'atmosphere' of the meeting, to be on guard against allowing personal conflicts to break up the meeting, to be sensitive to the personal feelings of the group members—then, under these circumstances, the outcome of the meeting would be seriously affected by the communications medium used. We would expect to observe greater and greater differences from the face-to-face outcome as the communications medium was further and further impoverished with respect to its degree of Social Presence. On the other hand, where the task does not require a high degree of Social Presence, we would not expect the Social Presence of the communications medium to be important. Thus, we would predict that in tasks where the emphasis is not on the people involved, and where the outcome does not reflect on the personal qualities of the individuals communicating, the outcome will be unaffected by the degree of Social Presence of the medium. Such tasks would include, for example, information transmission and simple problem-solving tasks.

We will see in Chapter 6 how the limited experimental evidence supports these general notions about the areas of sensitivity to variation in the medium of communication derived originally from the literature on the functions of the visual cues. We have seen in this chapter how the theoretical notions thus derived receive empirical support also from the literature on laboratory subjects' attitudes to media. Two interview studies confirm that these hypotheses agree with everyday opinions on the sort of task for which particular media are appropriate.

Westrum (1972) conducted a series of semi-structured interviews to evaluate the necessity of letter, telephone and face-to-face contact for a variety of tasks. On the basis of these, he concluded that face-to-face contact was especially necessary in those communication situations which involve a high degree of emotional contact (such as conflict resolution, authority relations and the development of trust).

Champness (1972b) asked a sample of 112 civil servants how suitable they thought various media (face-to-face, loudspeaking audio and two types of video system) were for various activities. Four factors were obtained in the analysis:

(1) 'Interpersonal relations' which loaded highly on scales such as 'maintaining group morale', 'getting to know others' and 'staff relations'.
(2) 'Factual information' which loaded highly on 'exchange factual information', 'giving orders'.
(3) 'Interpersonal conflict' which loaded highly on 'resolving conflicts', 'settling differences of opinion' and 'persuading people'.
(4) 'Chatting'; an uninterpretable residual factor.

No effects of medium were found on factor (2), factual information. Both factors (1) and (3) showed substantial effects of medium. The face-to-face medium was, for these activities, considered much superior to the audio system; the video systems were considered rather similar to the audio system on factor (1) and intermediate on factor (3). Further results by Champness and others using similar techniques in the field will be presented in Chapter 9. These results in general confirm the earlier laboratory results.

Intuition, laboratory studies of attitudes and theoretical notions derived from the literature on non-verbal communication thus all converge on the same areas of likely sensitivity to medium. It is to experiments in these two areas—interpersonal relations and conflict situations—that we must look if we are to test and refine these theories about medium. Chapters 7 and 8 will discuss detailed experimental work in each of these two critical areas, but first it seems appropriate to review in detail other work relevant to the comparison of communication media.

6

Communication Modes and Task Performance

There have been many studies which have explored the effects on performance of various types of task of varying the link between the participants. To what extent do these experiments bear out our general hypotheses about the functions of the visual channel? What sort of tasks have been found experimentally to be sensitive to the medium of communication and what is the nature of the sensitivity?

A large percentage of the literature of social psychology could be construed as relevant but we can discuss only those in which medium has in some sense been manipulated. Unfortunately, medium of communication has seldom previously been the variable of central concern and most of these studies therefore have, for our present purpose, one or more serious limitations. Variations in the medium have frequently been very crude (e.g. communication versus no communication); interaction is often constrained by extraordinary means (e.g. no partner to communicate with); the tasks have usually been very artificial and clearly distinct from normal work tasks, and finally investigators have often been more concerned with the process than the outcome, so that outcome measures have not been obtained. Nonetheless much of the material is instructive.

THE EFFECTS OF THE PRESENCE OF OTHERS

Before considering the more subtle effects of medium on complex interactions, it is appropriate to consider the simplest way in which an individual can impact on another: the mere presence of others has been shown to affect performance on a variety of tasks. Two isolated individuals unaware of one another's existence and with no communication can naturally have no influence on one another, but as soon as contact occurs, performance is affected. The effects of the presence of others can be either facilitative (for example, on signal detection, Bergum and Lehr, 1963, and chain association, Allport, 1920) or detrimental (on tasks such as nonsense syllable learning, Pessin, 1933). These seemingly conflicting results can be reconciled by assuming that the presence of others increases the individual's arousal (Zajonc, 1965). It is reasonably well accepted that experiments on learning have shown that high drive (or arousal) enhances the emission of dominant (well-learned) responses. If, for a given task, the dominant responses arc largely correct this will improve performance, but if, as is more likely to be the case in a learning task, the dominant response is incorrect, the presence of other people will impair performance. In a similar vein, Allport (1920) concluded that complex intellectual processes were impaired in the presence of others, while response production was facilitated. Thus he found that subjects writing refutations of arguments produced longer but worse passages in the presence of an audience. In support of the hypothesis of an increase in motivation, it was found that it was the slower individuals who were most affected by the audience.

There is now a variety of evidence taken to support Zajonc's hypothesis. Although much of this is based on experiments using animals, experiments using human subjects have given similar results. For example, Zajonc and Sales (1966) demonstrated that on a task in which the subjects tried to identify what were, in reality, meaningless sets of lines, the likelihood of practised responses was increased relative to that of the less practised ones in the presence of an audience. Increased arousal may not be the whole story, for there is some evidence that the presence of others can arouse social motives which inhibit task performance. For example, on word-association tasks, the presence of an audience can make subjects more cautious and lead to longer response latencies (Wapner and Alper, 1952). This would also explain the more usual and less individual associations found by Allport (1920) with a similar task.

The word 'presence' need not be taken too literally. The effects of audience are also obtainable with the knowledge that others are working on the same problem in another room (Dashiell, 1935). Wapner and Alper (1952) found that an invisible audience known to be watching through a one-way mirror was even more inhibiting of response than a visible audience. The latter result is potentially important, because the telephone likewise represents a system in which one's performance is being monitored while one has relatively little feedback as to the reactions of the other party.

Medium of communication could be said to vary the presence of the other, as in our Social Presence hypothesis. What effect then would be expected on task performance? The evidence for Zajonc's hypothesis is as yet sufficiently limited that one hesitates to draw any firm conclusions. The chief obstacle to inference is the definition of the response; which responses are relevant and which are dominant? In animal experiments with a single performance measure, this poses relatively little problem, but consider a concrete example to illustrate the difficulties of applying the theory—a debate between two individuals who initially disagree and must come to some agreement. What is the dominant response? Perhaps it is each person expressing his own point of view; in this case conflict would be exacerbated face-to-face. Perhaps it is each compromising to reach agreement (that is the object of the interaction); in this case agreement would be easier in the face-to-face condition. Perhaps the dominant response is something else altogether, such as the community consensus view on the issue under dispute. Finally, there is the added complication that the dominant response might differ for the two individuals. In the absence of any simple behavioural measure directly related to individual motivation, the value of any prediction is dubious.

This work suggests that just the physical absence of the other (as in telecommunication) would be expected to affect task performance, but, owing to ambiguities of response definition, specific effects on performance in complex interactive tasks are not easy to deduce from the previous work on mere presence.

CONFORMITY AND ANONYMITY

There is another body of work in which the effects of the presence of others has been examined: the literature on conformity. The paradigmatic experiment in the conformity literature involves the subject in giving judgements of simple stimuli while confronted with judgements, purporting to come from other members of a group, which are at variance with his own initial position. In such a situation, subjects tend to shift their stated views towards the view suggested by the others. The conformity effect is particularly marked with difficult problems where there is no objectively correct, clearly defined, answer (Blake and Mouton, 1961). The problems used in the attitude-change literature and the sort of problems encountered in everyday business both usually answer this description.

The relevance of this work stems largely from an independent variable which has been examined in relation to this phenomenon: anonymity. It is a well-substantiated finding that anonymity decreases the magnitude of the conforming response. 'Anonymity' should not be taken too literally, for although sometimes meaning 'not having to give one's name' before responding (e.g. Mouton, Blake and Olmstead, 1956) it can also mean physical separation (e.g. Deutsch and Gerard, 1955). In this more general sense, 'anonymity' could be varied by medium of communication. Although the two experiments just mentioned used simple physical stimuli (metronome clicks and line lengths respectively), the same effect of anonymity is found with judgements of more complex stimuli such as the artistic merit of a painting (Argyle, 1957) or the action that should be taken to deal with a juvenile delinquent (Raven, 1959).

On the assumption that removing the visual channel increases the anonymity of the situation, one would therefore expect less conforming when communication was over an audio link. It is perhaps unwise to put too much weight on this conclusion, for the following reasons:

(a) There are situations in which anonymity can increase conformity. For example, Gerard (1964) reanalysing the Deutsch and Gerard (1955) data found that among those individuals who were initially unconforming, those tested subsequently in the anonymous condition showed more yielding. The presence of the visual channel, while decreasing anonymity, might be felt to increase commitment to one's initial discrepant position. Thus, removing the visual channel, while making it easier to remain independent when independence was felt to be appropriate, might make it easier to yield when yielding could be interpreted as loss of face or otherwise inappropriate.

(b) Deutsch and Gerard (1955) drew a distinction between informational and normative social influence: the former in which subjects conform as a result of the information provided by the group, and the latter in which they conform because of the sanctions conferred by the group for non-conformity. Normative influence is dependent on the degree of interdependence among group members and the attractiveness of the group to the individual. Anonymity manipulates the normative influence. However, informational influence might also be affected by medium; this latter effect could work in the opposite direction (more conforming in the audio condition). It is thus difficult to predict what effects, if any, should be expected.

(c) Finally, all the above studies were non-interactive in the sense that free verbal interaction was not permitted (Argyle allowed note-passing but the others permitted only knowledge of the judgement of others). Extrapolation to interactive situations may be unjustified.

STUDIES OF MEDIA DIFFERENCES IN THE MECHANICS OF INTERACTION

Some studies have been concerned with the mechanisms of interaction rather than the outcome of the task (for instance, Cook and Lalljee, 1972, found little effect on a number of simple measures such as number of questions and pauses, when the visual channel was not available).

Two such experiments, however, are relevant. In one, Argyle, Lalljee and Cook (1968) conducted a series of experiments in which the visibility of one member of a dyad was systematically varied with the use of masks and dark glasses. Interaction was found to be disturbed in various ways as the visual cues were removed (the person with visual feedback tended to dominate the encounter, there were more interruptions and greater reported difficulty of interaction). However, a later experiment in which visibility was reduced symmetrically, although finding some effects on pauses and interruptions found little reported difficulty of interaction. It appears that the asymmetry was the basis for the previous effects. The other relevant experiment, by Moscovici and Plon (1966), showed that compared to subjects who sat face-to-face (whether visible or screened from one another) subjects who sat back-to-back or side-by-side spoke in a style that was more formal, like the written form. Here again, the effects of medium seem to derive from the unfamiliarity (of the two latter orientations) rather than the physical constraints imposed by the removal of the visual channel.

These two studies are noteworthy because they suggest that some effects of medium may be due more to strangeness than to the objective constraints of the system. The usefulness of a strange system such as a closed-ciruit television might therefore be expected to increase with experience.

A more recent study (Wilson and Williams, 1975) compared telephone and face-to-face conversations from the 'Watergate' transcripts. There were three initial hypotheses:

(a) That there are verbal substitutes in telephone conversations for visual cues (following Cook and Lalljee, 1972).
(b) That the uncertainty engendered by lack of non-verbal feedback on the telephone influences verbal processes.
(c) That telephone conversations are, or are felt to be, less pleasant than face-to-face ones (following the Social Presence hypothesis, that suggests that telephone communication is intrinsically less sociable, more impersonal, and that, unless the task requires such psychological 'distance', the mismatch is felt to be unpleasant).

A number of measures were extracted from the transcripts (e.g. length of conversation, number of agreements and disagreements, number of questions, length of utterances), and the various significant differences found were felt by the authors to support the 'lack of feedback' and 'telephone unpleasant' hypotheses, though there was less evidence for the 'verbal substitutes for visual cues' hypothesis.

STUDIES OF INFORMATION TRANSMISSION

Let us consider now what could be viewed as the simplest true type of communication: information transmission. This is a necessary element of all meaningful interaction including problem solving. How is this fundamental type of communication affected by the medium used?

This question was first examined by Champness and Reid (1970), who explored the accuracy with which their subjects (students) were able to transmit the contents of a business letter over three media of communication (face-to-face, telephone and 'face-to-face' with a separating opaque screen). No effects of medium of communication were found on any of the experimental measures, which included time to complete the task and several measures of accuracy, nor did the subjects perceive any difference in accuracy.

This experiment represents an example of what appears to be a whole class of person-to-person interactions which for all practical purposes may be relatively insensitive to the effects of communications media. Tasks in which only one individual is active and where the feedback function is consequently of little importance have generally been found not to be affected by the medium used. This result is obtained over and over again in a variety of experimental contexts.

Davies (1971) conducted experiments to compare face-to-face and teletype as media for the communication of factual information. The only effect of medium was that the teletype was found to be the most effective mode (provided that time was adequate); a result consonant with the rest of the literature on the comparative effectiveness of the written and spoken word. Reanalysis of Davies' data shows that there was a tendency towards better recall of the arguments in the two audio-only conditions than in the two conditions where the visual channel was available. However, the effect was not statistically significant and there was no effect on confidence in accuracy of recall. Nor was there any effect on the response strategy selected on the basis of the material presented or on opinion change in response to the communication.

While these two experiments may seem insufficient for generalization, it seems that the initial hypothesis, that since information transmission does not require a close interpersonal relationship to be successful, then we will find no effect of medium of communication for such tasks, is likely to be confirmed.

EFFECTS OF COMMUNICATION IN BARGAINING GAMES

McClintock, Nuttin and McNeel (1970) examined the effect of visual presence on behaviour in a two-person bargaining game. The task involved both persons making simultaneous choices from two alternatives, so as to give one of four possible combined choices, each of which was associated with a particular payoff for each individual. Auditory communication was not permitted. The visual presence of the other did not affect choices in the game.

A number of experiments have investigated the effect of a variable referred to as 'communication' on cooperation in two-person games. There is general confidence that increasing communication increases cooperation (Swensson, 1967, Daniels, 1967, Voissem and Sistrunk, 1971). However, the evidence for this has not been altogether consistent (see Terhune, 1968, for a review). The reason for the inconsistency is probably the variation in the tasks used and the wide range of definitions of what constitutes communication: for example, Loomis (1959), Daniels (1967), and Voissem and Sistrunk (1971) allowed the passage of standardized notes, Terhune (1968) allowed subjects to compose their own messages, and Deutsch (1958) allowed free speech.

Although this work does at first sight suggest some very definite effects of medium, any general inference is unjustified. Firstly, investigations of communication have typically been confined to the presence or absence of communication (e.g. Deutsch and Krauss, 1962) rather than to variations in the type of communication. This, in turn, has meant that the tasks are of such a nature that they can be conducted without any verbal communication. Neither the variations in communication nor the type of tasks used have been appropriate to the present purpose. Secondly, increased communication will not necessarily increase cooperation; Krauss and Deutsch (1966) point out that subjects must use the opportunity to engage in communication relevant to cooperation (this was not found to be the case in their own 1962 experiment). The effect is therefore very task dependent. If it is mainly threats which comprise the communications, then bargaining efficiency and cooperation are more likely to be impaired than improved (Froman and Cohen, 1969).

Finally, the tasks used in these studies have always been simple games in which it has not been possible to interpret unambiguously what is meant by cooperation; for instance, cooperation is frequently confounded with efficient bargaining (as in the Prisoners' dilemma game). Whilst it may be true that this is reasonable because the two are usually confounded, it is nonetheless an obstacle to inference when either (or both) could be affected by medium.

COMMUNICATION MODALITY AND ATTITUDE CHANGE

There is some early work on the question of modality in the literature on attitude change. This is mainly directed at the relative impact of the written and the spoken word. The weight of this evidence is that the spoken word has more persuasive impact (Cantril and Allport, 1935, Elliot, 1937). There have been some contradictory observations (e.g. Wall and Boyd, 1971, found more attitude change in response to a written than in response to a live presentation).

Despite observations that the impact of the spoken word is as great or greater, comprehension is generally found to be greater with the written word (Toussaint, 1960). Two possible explanations suggest themselves. The first is that there is more yielding to the spoken message; McGuire (1969) summarizes: 'There must be some felt difference in the receiver's relation to the source depending on whether he is listening or reading the message. Perhaps he feels more anxiety or greater pressure from self interest or good taste to conform when the more personalised modality is used'. Another possibility would be that many people read by subvocal or internalized speech and in so doing impose their own intonation on the material. This would have implications for meaning in that the force of the material could be dissipated or misdirected. These two possibilities are not mutually exclusive and both would predict an increase in impact with the addition of the visual channel to the audio-only channel. The visual signals could either reduce the ambiguity of the message and so sharpen the argument, or increase the awareness of the other and so add force to the message.

A third possibility, however, is that the difference between the written and live presentations arises because the written mode allows the possibility of rereading or checking difficult or important passages. In view of this possible effect, it is probably unwise to argue from the comparison of these two media to other media comparisons.

Evidence on the relative effectiveness of live and taped speeches is slight. McGuire (1969) cites a study by Wilke (1934) as showing that a speech heard directly produced more opinion change and less hostility than one heard over a loudspeaker. Also cited are attempts to communicate hypnotic suggestion via a tape recorder (Estabrook, 1930); however, it is not known whether any attempts were made to evaluate the effectiveness of this procedure. Frandsen (1963) had subjects attend to high or low threat appeals presented live, by television or by tape. He hypothesized that the degree to which the speaker's threats were personalized would interact with his 'closeness' to the audience. There was no significant effect of medium on the dependent measures (shift in opinion and recall of argument). In both cases, there were trends such that in the face-to-face condition there tended to be more opinion change and more recalled than in the taped condition. The results must therefore be considered inconclusive.

However, Croft et al. (1969) in a similar experiment did find a significant difference between the media used. Students watched a live presentation or a videotape of the same person giving a short, antiathletics talk. Post-experimental measures showed significantly greater attitude change amongst those who had received the face-to-face presentation, although the 'videotape' group also changed their attitudes to a significant degree.

Finally, Wall and Boyd (1971) presented subjects with a live, a written and a videotaped message. It was found that the written message produced more attitude change than either of the other two (which did not differ). An audio-only condition was not included in this experiment.

In summary, this evidence, all from non-interactive situations where a source communicated with a recipient but not vice versa, suggests that there may be more opinion change in face-to-face situations than with audio-only communication, though written communication may be the most effective of all. However, it would be unwise to generalize from this data to conclude that the same result will occur in a more interactive attitude change situation, where each party is simultaneously (or nearly so) trying to persuade the other. Results from such situations will be described in Chapter 7.

PROBLEM SOLVING

More important for our present purposes than the foregoing are the experiments which did require genuine two-way interaction between the participants; a number of studies of cooperative problem solving meet this criterion.

First in this category is that of Champness and Davies (1971). Participants in this experiment were required to discuss a problem and agree on the best possible solution; the 'problem' was what to do about an old, loyal worker who is holding up a serial production process in a motor-component factory. Pairs of subjects discussed the problem either face-to-face or by telephone, having in both cases twelve minutes to reach agreement. None of the outcome measures (including nature of the solution, satisfaction with the solution or agreement between individuals) was affected by the medium used. However, an important result of the experiment was that despite the fact that the outcome was not affected, other measures indicated that medium did affect what went on before the final solution was agreed.

At the level of the mechanics of the interaction it was noted that whilst in the face-to-face condition there was a highly significant correlation ($p < 0.001$) between the speech lengths of the two members of each pair, there was no such correlation in the telephone condition. This indicates a more satisfactory matching of their behaviour in the presence of the visual channel. A more startling finding was obtained from the analysis of the content of the conversation when it was found that a significantly ($p < 0.02$) higher proportion of the solutions discussed in the face-to-face condition than in the telephone condition were concerned directly with the problem worker. In assessing the effects of medium of communication on problem solving it may thus be necessary to distinguish between different levels. At the level of the processes leading up to the final solution, effects can be observed. However, as we shall see, at the level of the outcome a whole series of experiments have failed to find effects of medium (at least within the range of media studied).

For example, later experiments by Davies (1971a and 1971b) used a task which was almost antithetical to the problem used above. Whereas the task in the Champness and Davies experiment was 'open-ended', the new task was a closed deductive type of task which permitted precise scoring of the quality of the final solutions. Neither experiment found any indications of any effect of medium (telephone or face-to-face) on the quality of the final solution. It seems improbable that this absence of effect was due simply to the crudity of the measuring instrument, for the scoring procedure did readily distinguish between individuals who had had varying times for individual thought about the problem prior to the discussion with their partner. Although there were thus no effects of medium on the outcome, effects were again observed in the processes leading up to the solution. The principal finding in this respect was that subjects took significantly longer in the face-to-face condition (this fact accounted too for subsidiary findings such as the observation that more suggestions were discussed in the face-to-face conversations than in the telephone conversations). Since the face-to-face discussions were longer but failed to produce better solutions, one is tempted to argue that the telephone conversations were more efficient. It is a recurring finding in interviews with users of new audio conference systems that the interactions are shorter than they would have been had the meeting been conducted face-to-face (there is further discussion of this finding in Chapter 9). In some cases (as for instance Davies' experiments) the time difference may arise from the discomfort of holding a telephone handset for long periods of time; but with systems where the audio quality is excellent and there are loudspeakers rather than handsets, this argument cannot apply and there may be real grounds for believing that the face-to-face interactions are in some way more enjoyable. Such effects may occur in problem-solving situations but it is obvious that unless they affect aspects of the interaction relevant to the final solution, no effect on the outcome will be observed.

Other researchers have manipulated medium of communication primarily out of an interest in man's abilities to interact with computers (Chapanis, 1971, Chapanis, Ochsman, Parrish and Weeks, 1972). The experiments arising from this source all follow the basic paradigm of one subject seeking information from another in order to solve a problem. Chapanis *et al.* (1972) describe two problems that have been used: in the 'equipment-assembly problem' the 'seeker' had to assemble a lightweight trash-can toter, having been given the parts and tools but not the instructions (which were with his partner). In a second problem, the 'seeker' had to find the nearest doctor to a designated address in Washington.

A wide range of communication media (from face-to-face to written communication) were investigated. The problems used had only one correct solution and all subjects eventually reach the solution; it is therefore not possible to examine the quality of the solutions. The most revealing measure is the time taken to reach the solutions. This did not differ significantly between the 'communication-rich' mode (full face-to-face) and audio-only communication. Predictably, the written media were considerably slower than the others, but a more striking finding was also obtained: the subjects in the audio-only mode exchanged ten times more messages than the subjects in the handwriting mode, and the subjects in the communication-rich mode exchanged more messages than the subjects in the voice-only mode. It seems that the face-to-face medium actually encourages conversation, with the result that the less-rich media are more efficient (per message though not per minute, in this case).

A similar experiment by Woodside, Cavers and Buck (1971) also used simple cooperative problems in which the information was split between two participants. One task was a crossword puzzle, the other a simple resource-allocation task (one side given the properties of the resources and the other side the specifications). No effects of medium (face-to-face, telephone or telephone with a graphics sending facility) were found.

The cooperative tasks we have been considering in this section would not seem to require a close personal relationship between the two subjects. We would therefore not expect the Social Presence of the medium to be important for the satisfactory completion of the task. A cold, impersonal medium should be as satisfactory as a warm, personal one. It is noteworthy that generally we do not find media effects at the level of task outcome, but only at the more subtle level of the person-to-person interaction that precedes task completion. How much of this interaction is directly related to the task, and how much is social, we do not know, but we would hypothesize that many of the media effects observed at this level reflect a greater emphasis on social, as opposed to directly task-oriented interaction over the warmer more sociable media such as face-to-face.

MISCELLANEOUS MEDIA COMPARISONS

Various other experiments have compared the effects of different media of communication on tasks that do not fit neatly into our previous categories. One of the most important is that of Milgram (1965). He used a similar paradigm to his earlier experiments, in which a naive subject, under the instructions of an 'experimenter', was persuaded to give seemingly very painful shocks to another person (in actuality, the other person was a confederate, and did not receive any shocks, but as far as the subject knew these shocks were getting through and, at the higher levels, were causing severe pain). In this experiment, both the immediacy (and the Social Presence) of the 'victim' and of the experimenter were varied, to see the effect on the willingness of the subject to give shocks. To compare with the base condition, where the 'victim' was invisible and inaudible (except for pounding on the intervening wall), Milgram used a 'voice-feedback' condition, where the 'victim' could be heard but not seen, a 'proximity' situation where the victim was face-to-face with the subject, and finally a 'touch proximity' situation where the subject actually had to hold the victim's hand down on the shock plate. Each of these increases in immediacy produced a corresponding decrease in obedience: in the 'remote' condition, 34% of subjects defied the experimenter; in the audio-only condition, 37% defied him; in the face-to-face condition, 60% defied him; and lastly, in the 'touch proximity' situation, 70% defied the experimenter.

The other variation was in the proximity of the experimenter. Here there were just two conditions: the experimenter was physically present (face-to-face), or he was at the other end of a telephone link. It was found that three times as many subjects were obedient in the face-to-face condition as in the telephone condition, a statistically significant difference. Clearly the experimenter was less able to obtain obedience when he was not physically present, and this was further emphasized by the observation that some of the 'obedient' subjects in the telephone condition in fact cheated by giving lower voltage shocks than required, and lying to the distant experimenter about their actions.

A later experiment (Penner and Hawkins, 1971) using a situation in which a fast reaction time allegedly delivered an electric shock to a victim, found that performance was not affected by whether the 'harmer' and 'harmed' were in visual contact. Identification of the victim by name however did reduce aggression. Anonymity again appears to be affecting task behaviour.

Two experiments have investigated the effects of the presence of the visual channel using the Kogan and Wallach choice-dilemma problems. The typical finding using this instrument is the so-called 'risky shift' (that after a group discussion, individuals make riskier decisions than they did before the discussion): Lamm (1967) had non-participating subjects listen to the group discussion, a second group could see as well as hear the discussion. The viewers showed more risky shift than the listeners but the difference was not statistically significant. Kogan and Wallach (1967) separated the members of the groups such that during the discussion they could not see one another. The results were similar to those from face-to-face groups run on previous occasions. There is some doubt that affective processes are involved at all in the production of the risky shift (Vinokur, 1971), as the crucial factor may be merely the exchange of information relevant to the task. It would then be consistent with the affective nature of non-verbal communication, that there was no effect of removing the visual channel.

A number of studies in an educational context have compared the effectiveness of instructional television with ordinary face-to-face teaching. Generally such studies fail to find any difference (Allen, 1971). Audio-only presentations also appear to have been satisfactory in the context of language laboratories. However, in view of the number of possible confounding factors and the difficulties of assessing effectiveness, any conclusion on the basis of these studies as to whether or not there is any difference between the face-to-face and televised presentations is probably unjustified.

OVERVIEW OF AREAS OF SENSITIVITY TO MEDIUM

The experimental evidence thus far bears out our general hypothesis derived from the literature on non-verbal communication as to the tasks which would be insensitive to medium of communication (tasks with little need for rapid feedback about the other person's reactions). While some of the experiments have found minor effects of medium, these scattered positive results do not critically test any coherent general theory either about which tasks will be sensitive or about how they will be affected. The next two chapters provide more stringent tests of the theories in the areas of greatest expected sensitivity.

7

Conflict

INTRODUCTION—THE LIKELY SENSITIVITY OF CONFLICT SITUATIONS

The negotiation situation is one which might be expected to be particularly sensitive to variation in the medium of communication. Each side's actions are highly contingent on his perceptions of the other's previous moves. Any changes in the communications link which might affect the information available about the other and thus distort interpretations of his actions could have strong implications for the eventual outcome. In view of this expected sensitivity to medium, the negotiation situation represents an important testing ground for theories about the origins of any effects of medium of communication.

In contrast to the studies in cooperative situations, studies of the effects of medium in conflict situations—at least, those which do not restrict verbal interaction—have usually found significant effects of medium.

EFFECTS OF MEDIUM ON BARGAINING GAMES

Unlike other studies of the effect of varying the amount of communication in bargaining games (see Chapter 6), Wichman (1970) did investigate variations in the medium of communication. His subjects played the Prisoners' Dilemma game (a simple two-person game in which cooperation or competition are both possible) under one of four levels of communication: no communication, video only (subjects forbidden to talk and white noise played over a speaker), audio only (subjects screened from one another) and normal face-to-face. The results showed an increasing degree of cooperation with an increasing number of communication channels. The most substantial change was with the addition of the auditory channel. Ability to see the other also increased the overall level of cooperation and allowed a stable level of cooperation to be achieved at an earlier stage.

In explanation, Wichman hypothesized that the availability of a greater number of cues gives subjects the feeling that the other can be influenced more, and therefore that there is some point in playing cooperatively (if the other is not influenced, playing cooperatively is to one's disadvantage). Dorris (personal communication) speculated along the same lines to explain similar results in his own study (unpublished). He found that subjects allowed visual contact in a two-person zero-sum bargaining game rated themselves after the game as more cooperative than did those not allowed visual contact (they were also in fact more cooperative).

Another study using the Prisoners' Dilemma game was conducted by Laplante (1971). Although in this study subjects did not in fact interact, they played against a series of programmed responses set by the experimenter which led them to believe that they were playing against a real person; the same result was obtained: cooperation increased as communication opportunities increased. Face-to-face subjects were the most cooperative, as compared to those who received messages from the other via closed-circuit television, telephone and written notes. Laplante's analysis of his results hinged on the notion that the opportunity to communicate should 'help subjects to arrive at a mutual understanding with respect to their proposed game behaviour'. As subjects are oriented towards gaining as much as possible and this end is, in the Prisoners' Dilemma game, confounded with cooperation, an increase in the number of cooperative responses would be expected.

Dorris, Gentry and Kelley (1972) investigated (among other things) the effects of opportunity for visual interaction on a two-person mixed-motive non-zero-sum game. In outline, the game consisted of a two-minute discussion on how to split a number of points between the two. Each person's payoff was related in a complex way to the manner in which the points were shared. Subjects stood facing one another, either with or without a screen intervening. Mode of interaction (presence or absence of visual contact) influenced the outcome only on the first of the four games that each pair played. In this game, the average joint payoff per pair was higher in the vision than the non-vision condition. The authors surmised that perhaps the removal of the visual channel increases the time necessary to develop a reliable estimate of their partner's approach. In all four games non-vision subjects took longer to reach agreement and had fewer settlements than the vision subjects. All these effects were more marked for the competitively oriented subjects.

Mode of interaction was not found to have any effect on the number of bids, the number of lies or number of cooperative statements. Subjects in the non-vision condition thought that their partner was striving for a greater share of the points than did the subjects in the vision condition. On the post-conversation questionnaire they rated their partners as being more active, stronger and less peaceful and sociable, than did partners in the vision condition.

The subjects who were cooperatively oriented expressed strong preferences for negotiating under visual conditions but those who were competitively oriented were ambivalent about this choice: on the one hand increased contact would provide more information to facilitate exploitation of the other, on the other hand increased contact would be more likely to expose their motivation (an event assumed to be detrimental to the public image of the competitively oriented subjects).

In discussion of their results, Dorris *et al.* suggested that the removal of the visual cues vital to the accurate perception of motivation interfered with the development of trust. This could have been the basis for the observed greater verbal exchange and lesser agreement in the early stages of bargaining. However this explanation was not substantiated in any other way.

There has only been one failure to find effects of medium in conflictful situations. Vitz and Kite (1970) investigated (among other things) the effect of medium of communication (face-to-face, written messages or intercom) on behaviour in a two-person bargaining game. Outcomes unfortunately were not measured and the evidence was largely of an observational nature. No differences were noted between face-to-face and intercom communication. Those negotiating by written messages took more time and used more formal language than those negotiating face-to-face.

SIMULATED NEGOTIATIONS

Smith (1969) compared the outcomes of negotiations carried out face-to-face and negotiations where communication was restricted to written messages. Subjects were cast in the roles of either the defence council or the plaintiff's attorney in a role-playing simulation of a suit by an individual against a drug company. The results showed that settlement was more likely and that there was a greater dispersion of the results of the settlements in face-to-face negotiations. Smith argued that the latter effect was due to the more successful negotiator being better able to push the settlement in his preferred direction when communication was face-to-face. Neither the time to reach settlement nor the satisfaction with the settlement was affected by medium.

Morley and Stephenson (1969 and 1970) used student participants in a simulation of an industrial wage dispute. Playing the role of either the management or the union representative, subjects communicated either by telephone or face-to-face to negotiate a settlement of the dispute. The background to the proposed dispute provided specimen arguments for each side, giving an initially stronger case either to the management representative (Morley and Stephenson, 1969) or the union representative (Morley and Stephenson, 1970). Combining the data from the two experiments, the side with the stronger case was found to be significantly more successful in telephone than in face-to-face negotiations (although the effect was in the same direction in both experiments, it in fact only reached significance in one experiment). This result seems incongruent with Smith's (1969) hypothesis that the successful side was able to manipulate the other more successfully in the face-to-face condition: for this would predict that the 'strong' case would be more successful face-to-face. Tortuous reasoning, to the effect that the successful side was the one that had the weak case, because the stronger case should have won more convincingly, would be needed to save Smith's hypothesis.

THEORETICAL ANALYSES OF EFFECTS OF MEDIUM ON CONFLICT

The four sets of studies which have found effects of medium (Wichman, 1970, Dorris, Gentry and Kelley, 1972, Smith, 1969, and Morley and Stephenson, 1969, 1970) have been those which have used the tasks which the literature on visual communication suggested would be sensitive, that is, tasks in which the personal relationships of the participants are relevant to the solution of a problem necessitating interaction.

Much of the theorizing by the investigators who have found effects has however centred on the *efficiency* of the interaction: thus, subjects are thought to perceive the other more accurately (Dorris, Gentry and Kelley, 1972) more quickly (Dorris, Gentry and Kelley) and are therefore motivated to act more cooperatively in competitive situations (Wichman, 1970, Laplante, 1971, Dorris, unpublished) and this in turn is translated into more effective action either from an individual point of view (Smith, 1969) or from the point of view of the joint payoff (Wichman, 1970, Dorris, Gentry and Kelley, 1972). So far as it goes, and in the situations to which it refers, this view may be reasonable; but, as pointed out in Chapter 5, it is not productive when there are several possible measures of efficiency. Is individual or collective interest favoured by the more efficient communication?

In Chapter 5 we discussed briefly Morley and Stephenson's theorizing as to the effect of medium. Distinguishing between interaction concerned with the personal relationships of those involved and interaction concerned with the object of negotiation they proposed that there existed a balance between these aspects (termed interperson and interparty exchange respectively) which could be affected by medium of communication. They argued that in a telephone negotiation there would be a relatively greater emphasis on the interparty exchange at the expense of the interperson exchange. This would have the consequence of a greater likelihood of a settlement in accordance with the objective merits of the case in telephone negotiations. Such a hypothesis could explain Smith's finding of greater variance in the results in the face-to-face condition.

Morley and Stephenson also introduced the concept of 'formality', which was defined in terms of the number of social cues available. They hypothesized that the more 'formal' the communication link the greater the emphasis on the interparty exchange at the expense of the interperson exchange and the less the 'norm of reciprocity' inherent in interpersonal exchange would impinge upon the interparty exchange to influence the outcome of the negotiation. In the context of media comparisons, we would identify a 'formal' medium as one high in Social Presence.

The concept of 'formality' was the rationale for another of Morley and Stephenson's experimental manipulations; the restriction of the freedom to interrupt the other. If freedom to interrupt is not present, the stronger case is again more successful than when the freedom to interrupt is present (independent of the medium). The mechanism through which 'formality' affects the balance between the interperson and the interparty exchange is not clear; further discussion will elaborate on this point. This theorizing seems implicitly to assume that more information must improve cooperation and efficiency, but as we shall see, this may not always be the case.

Morley and Stephenson's argument that use of the telephone shifts the emphasis from the interpersonal towards the interparty exchange, is more satisfactory. Such a theory lacks the evaluative overtones of the 'efficiency' interpretations and can conceive of situations for which the telephone would be more effective than face-to-face (an interaction in which personal considerations were an irrelevant distraction). Such an argument can also readily distinguish between the tasks which have, and those which have not, been found to be sensitive to the effects of medium. If personal considerations are irrelevant to the outcome, and medium affects primarily the personal considerations, the outcome would not be expected to show any effects of medium.

Although Morley and Stephenson did not explicitly connect the proposed effects of medium on the interperson/interparty balance with the functions of the visual cues, their hypothesis is quite consistent with the known functions of these cues. Equally, such a hypothesis is compatible with the 'efficiency' interpretations, for, in so far as 'interpersonal' is equivalent to 'friendly' predictions will coincide.

TESTING THEORIES IN ASYMMETRICAL NEGOTIATION SITUATIONS

Morley and Stephenson's experiments (1969, 1970) were particularly significant because they were the only experiments to have used relevant variations in the medium of communication for realistic tasks. Wichman (1970) and Dorris, Gentry and Kelley (1972) both used material comprising a simple conflict of interest; negotiations were brief, interaction limited and the participants' individual opinions were not relevant to the negotiation.

The effects reported by Morley and Stephenson are therefore of critical importance. Unfortunately, although the combination of the results from the two published studies (Morley and Stephenson, 1969 and 1970) showed a significant effect of medium of communication (the 'strong' case was found to be more successful in telephone than in face-to-face negotiations), there remained some reservations. Although in the first of the two published experiments the trend of the data was in the same direction as that of the later experiment, it was not sufficiently marked to reach statistical significance in that experiment taken on its own. Morley (1971) also conducted a third large experiment which failed to find any effect of medium of communication. This third study used a different, more complex set of material (although similar in that it outlined a situation in which one side had the stronger case). Subjects may have needed more than the time actually allowed to master the brief: it could be simply that the failure to replicate the result was due to subjects' failure to master the instructions.

With such uncertainties it was felt necessary to replicate this fundamental media effect. Accordingly an experiment (Short, 1971a) was designed in which thirty pairs of subjects playing the role of the union and management representatives trying to resolve an industrial dispute negotiated either face-to-face or by telephone. The material—a four-page background to a complex industrial dispute—was that used by Morley (1971). It had been designed such that one side (in fact the union side) had very much the stronger case.

The results of this experiment showed firstly that there were significantly more failures to reach agreement in telephone negotiations than in face-to-face negotiations ($p < 0.05$): six out of the seven such failures occurred in the telephone condition. More importantly, the results supported those obtained in Morley and Stephenson (1969, 1970). The outcomes in the telephone condition were significantly more favourable to the side with the stronger case than were the results in the face-to-face condition (Mann Whitney $U = 67$, $p < 0.05$). The result has since received further support in the work of Brown (unpublished) and can now be taken as reasonably well established.

Interpretation of the result hinges on the interpretation of the term 'stronger'. However it is not possible to do this unequivocally. In this context 'stronger' could refer to several variables all of which are relevant in some degree. Morley had defined 'strength' in terms of the number of arguments available to each side (ignoring the possibility that a single argument might prove overwhelming). A meaning nearer to most people's understanding of the word would define strength in terms of success in the final agreement (but overall both sides were almost equally successful). Then again there is the 'strength of one's convictions'. The side with the weak case may not have believed in the arguments he was presenting. Power can be defined in terms of scope for influencing the other's actions, the 'strong' case could therefore be thought of as the side that is the more important in determining the outcome. Theories discussing media in terms of efficiency would predict that this side should be more successful in the *face-to-face* condition (the reverse of the result actually obtained). Whatever the relevant meaning of the term 'strong' it is interesting to note that the subjects found no difficulty in agreeing which side was stronger.

To investigate the nature of the difference between the two sides which interacted with medium, a further experiment (Short, 1974) was devised which rendered the two individuals differentially dependent for good outcomes on interpersonal and interparty exchange. In Morley and Stephenson's experiment the intrusion of *interpersonal* considerations (in the face-to-face condition) was held to represent an advantage for the 'weak' case. The next experiment examined the complementary situation; one in which the intrusion of *interparty* considerations would be expected to represent an advantage for the 'weak' case, because the 'strength' was this time based in interpersonal considerations rather than in interparty considerations (as was the case in Morley and Stephenson's experiment).

The critical difference between this experiment and Morley and Stephenson's experiment was in whether or not the subjects' personal views were consonant with the case their role required them to argue. In the earlier experiment, subjects were randomly assigned to roles and their personal feelings were not systematically relevant to the conflict. In the second experiment, personal opinions were made relevant to the conflict which formed the centre of the negotiation. One side always believed in the case he was asked to argue; the other side's personal view was not consistent with his case, indeed in many cases his actual views may have been dissonant with the view he was required to advocate.

The experimental hypothesis was that in this situation the party who 'had the strength of his convictions' would be relatively more successful under face-to-face than under telephone conditions, i.e. when interpersonal considerations were more salient in the negotiation.

Forty-eight pairs of civil servants used one of three media (face-to-face, closed-circuit television or loudspeaking audio) to negotiate a settlement of a specially designed bargaining task. Briefly, the task involved agreement on three items from a list of nine, each of which had a separate payoff for each side. Each side was to persuade the other to agree a solution which maximized his individual payoff. However, although the payoff structure was symmetrical, the task was asymmetrical. One side had previously chosen his order of priorities among the nine alternatives (which were named and described in a background brief as options for management in a given industrial situation). The payoffs for this side (henceforth called 'A') were arranged so as to be in the same such order as his own opinions on the desirability of the alternatives. The payoffs for the other side 'B' were simply an inverse rank ordering to those of A, irrespective of B's opinions. A's instructions emphasized that personal conflict would be involved while B's instructions pointed out the conflict of interest with A and emphasized the need for bargaining skill to maximize his payoff. The experimental hypothesis was that A would be relatively more successful under face-to-face conditions than under telephone conditions.

An analysis of variance of the outcomes showed the results to be consistent with this hypothesis, there being a significant interaction ($p < 0.05$) between medium of communication and 'personal involvement', whereby the side whose interests were consonant with his convictions was relatively more successful face-to-face (see Table 7.1).

Table 7.1 Means and standard deviations of payoffs

	Face-to-face		Audio		Video	
	mean	s.d.	mean	s.d.	mean	s.d.
A (consonant)	135.6	35.2	112.3	24.7	134.4	33.3
B (not consonant)	110.00	30.2	129.8	29.2	108.3	30.6

A large payoff represents a good outcome.

To clarify the origins of the hypothesized effects of medium, a third condition (communication by closed-circuit television) was included in the experiment. If the *lack of the visual channel* was the basis for the effect, this condition would be expected to be similar to the face-to-face condition; if the physical *isolation* in the audio condition was the basis, the video condition might be more similar to the audio condition.

The outcomes in the video condition were very similar to those in the face-to-face condition. As in the face-to-face condition, A was more successful than B. A two-way analysis of variance with repeated measures including all three media conditions did not show a significant interaction of medium with 'personal involvement' ($0.1 < p < 0.05$). The non-significance of this interaction, primarily due to the close similarity of the video and face-to-face conditions, concealed a difference between the video and audio conditions. A two-way analysis of variance with repeated measures of the payoffs to each side in the video and audio conditions showed a significant ($p < 0.05$) interaction between medium and 'personal involvement'. It would therefore appear that the lack of the visual channel rather than the isolation in the audio condition was the basis for the effect of medium on the outcomes. Usage of the visual channel (in the video condition) varied almost from 0 to 100% of the time (mean 23%). If one person is not looking at the monitor—his partner may see only the top of the other's head as he bends studying papers—the usefulness of the visual channel will be much reduced. There is indeed a correlation ($r = +0.46$, $n = 16$, $p < 0.05$) between the amount that members of each pair look at the monitors. One might expect that these substantial differences in the use of the video channel might relate to outcomes; in those pairs where the video channel was heavily used the outcome would be more like that face-to-face. However, no significant, or even appreciable, correlation was found between outcomes and use of the video channel.

Although far from conclusive and much in need of replication with more sophisticated measures, this result does raise an interesting hypothesis: perhaps the video channel affects the outcomes not through its functional importance as a channel for the transmission of information, but more generally through its effects on the dispositions of the participants. It has been found in other circumstances not only that there is more cooperation when people have the opportunity to communicate, but also that there is more cooperation when the opportunity to communicate is present although not used (Management Science Centre, 1967). Perhaps the mere *presence* of the visual channel affects behaviour.

As one would expect, the A's rated their own case as much more reasonable than did the B's. The A's were also rated by their partners as 'stronger', more 'active' and more 'successful' than were the B's. Clearly, therefore, if one wishes to apply the term 'stronger' in the context of this experiment one must apply it to A (the side whose case was consonant with his own views). If this is done, there is an apparent contradiction with the results of Morley and Stephenson (1970), where the 'strong' case was more successful in telephone conditions. The concept of 'strength of case' can not cope with the experimental evidence. What then is the difference that interacted with medium?

It could perhaps be argued that it was the difference in the perceived justification that was the basis for the effects of medium. It is likely that with less information available, insincerity would be harder to detect. There is some experimental evidence that eye-contact is avoided when telling lies (Exline *et al.*, 1961). It could thus be that there is a positive advantage in the audio condition for the insincere side. However, this explanation cannot reconcile the result with that of Morley and Stephenson (1970) for those subjects were assigned at random and it must have been the 'weak' case that believed less in his own case, but the 'weak' case was more successful face-to-face.

In this experiment, there may have been an expectation on the part of both sides that the insincere side should give in. If so, the situation can be likened to that used by Morgan and Sawyer (1967): they found that a bargainer was more willing to accept a lower outcome (in a situation in which he thought that this was expected of him) when negotiating against a friend than when negotiating against a non-friend. Perhaps medium of communication affects the variable referred to by Morgan and Sawyer as 'friendship'. Morgan and Sawyer's experimental manipulation may have operated through the same intervening variable through which medium operates, i.e. may have affected the salience of the other individual as a person as opposed to an impersonal opponent in a bargaining game.

METHODOLOGICAL ISSUES FACING LABORATORY STUDIES OF CONFLICT

There is a potentially important implication for the methodology of laboratory studies of negotiation. Comparison of these results with Morley and Stephenson's experiment suggest that the processes and outcomes of laboratory negotiations can be affected by whether or not subjects' personal views are consonant with the case they are asked to argue. Laboratory studies of negotiation typically assign subjects at random to roles which may or may not be consonant with their personal opinions (e.g. Druckman, 1968, Bass, 1966). The consequences of this procedure merit some attention, for variations in laboratory procedure can completely change the nature of the conflict.

It is a familiar problem that realism in laboratory tasks is obtained at some loss in experimental control. We have already seen how the realism of the Morley and Stephenson simulations of industrial disputes is gained at some cost in control. In particular, realistic conflicts are complex. There is first an element of conflict of interest; what one side gained the other side lost. This is the conflict element captured in typical laboratory bargaining studies (see for example Morgan and Sawyer, 1967, Daniels, 1967). Secondly there is a conflict between the value systems of the two sides; to put it simply, ideological differences may exist between the two parties to a wage negotiation. This element is seldom captured in laboratory studies of negotiation for even if values are relevant to the two sides' cases, they often do not coincide with those of the subjects owing to the random assignment of subjects to roles (e.g. Druckman, 1968, Bass, 1966). Finally, there may be an element of personal conflict. In real life there is likely to be some existing relationship (be it friendly/hostile, trusting/suspicious) which may be further developed in the interaction. Naturally this third element is very difficult to bring into the laboratory, for real subjects and real tasks would be required.

The idea that conflict is not a unitary phenomenon, but needs to be analysed more carefully if we are to attempt to reproduce it in the laboratory, is supported by classifications of real-life meetings. For example, in Chapter 3 we described the DACOM study of Pye et al.

(1973). The factor analysis of the 'activities' scales showed six activity factors, two of which seemed to have elements of conflict. The first, which incidentally accounted for the most substantial single proportion of the variance, loaded heavily on 'conflict', 'disagreement' and 'arguing'. It seems reasonable to identify this with the conflict between value systems and personal conflict as described in the previous paragraph. The second loaded heavily on 'bargaining' and 'compromising', and thus seems more similar to the cool-headed conflict of interest described in the last paragraph.

While it is clear that these different types of conflict may all be involved in some situations, it would be useful from an analytical point of view if we could separate them in the laboratory situation, and study, for each separately, the effects that medium of communication might have. Experiments attempting to do that will now be described.

A LABORATORY STUDY OF THE EFFECT OF MEDIUM ON BARGAINING

The analysis of a two-person game poses certain problems. Consider an example to illustrate the difficulty: Deutsch (1960) distinguished three motivational orientations to bargaining: the individualistic, the cooperative and the competitive. It is not improbable that the individual's approach would vary with medium as he feels more or less distant from his partner and as he sees the opportunity for various types of influence on his partner. In a hypothetical situation in which a subject bargained against an individual whose behaviour was governed by the same motive regardless of the medium of communication or the other's strategy, any variation in the subject's approach would presumably be reflected directly in the outcome: thus individualistic subjects would maximize their own score, cooperative subjects would maximize the total score for themselves and their 'opponent', while competitive subjects would maximize the difference in score between themselves and their opponent. The hypothesized effects of medium would thus, if valid, inevitably be reflected in the outcome.

Unfortunately, the situation is not so simple. There are two parties to the negotiation and corresponding changes may occur in the other subject which nullify the changes in the first. Suppose, for example, that over one medium of communication there were a general increase in competitiveness; far from increasing the difference between the scores this might actually decrease the difference as the loser became unwilling to accept any sort of raw deal. In the literature on bargaining, attempts have been made to overcome problems such as these by having subjects play against a stooge who played a controlled strategy (such as making concessions at a fixed rate independently of the behaviour of the subject—e.g. Komorita and Brenner, 1968). In some circumstances where interaction is limited and subjects may be unaware of what is happening this may be a useful procedure, but if the experiment is to be realistic, the use of this approach in more complex situations is not feasible. Such a procedure loses the elements of contingency of one person's behaviour on that of the other. In communications studies, where the effects of one individual's behaviour on the other are the main item of interest, this contingency can on no account be neglected.

Thus despite the difficulties of interpretation it is imperative to study bargaining procedures in a genuine two-person game. A third experiment (Short, 1971b) was conducted using a specially constructed two-person mixed-motive bargaining game. Subjects were assigned at random to a partner and a media condition and the task material was such that their personal opinion was in no way relevant to the conflict. The payoff structure and the task were similar to that used in the above experiment (Short, 1974)—the intention being to compare and contrast the results of this experiment with those of the previous experiment with a view to isolating the critical factors which previously had interacted with medium of communication.

This third experiment, which had no pre-task manipulation of the individuals' belief in their own case, presented a symmetrical task situation (both sides were identical); in a symmetrical situation it is no longer meaningful to describe the outcome in terms of favourability to one side or the other. To describe the outcome of such a task four indices can be used: (1) A plus B, the combined payoff which represents the effectiveness with which the two sides coordinated to mutual advantage; (2) A minus B represents the extent to which the winner succeeded in imposing on the loser (c.f. Smith's hypothesis about the greater success of the winner); (3) the winner's payoff; (4) the loser's payoff. Sixteen pairs bargained over each of two media (face-to-face and telephone): two parallel versions of the task had been constructed and each pair performed one version over each medium of communication. No effect whatsoever of medium of communication was found for any of the four indices described above nor on the number of agreements reached (all pairs succeeded in reaching agreement). A detailed analysis of the pattern of offers in the transcripts of the tapes of the negotiations also showed no effect of medium of communication.

Although one can strictly speaking never confirm a null hypothesis, this failure to find any effect of medium on a task so similarly structured to that used in the second experiment (Short, 1974) does suggest that the effects of medium in that experiment may have resulted from factors not present in the later experiment: the most conspicuous of these being the relevance of personal beliefs and genuine disagreement over values, as opposed to the conflict of interest. This type of 'cognitive conflict' has been notably neglected by social psychological studies of conflict (Hammond, 1965).

THE EFFECTS OF MEDIUM ON THE RESOLUTION
OF A CONFLICT OF OPINION

A fourth experiment (Short, 1972a) was therefore designed to investigate this type of cognitive conflict—the other of the two types of conflictful meeting identified in the Pye *et al.* (1973) study. Although the 'attitude change' literature represents a vast body of work investigating the factors which determine how much an individual is affected by various types of influence attempt, this literature has almost totally neglected the simple interactive situation in which two individuals who disagree, discuss an issue with a view to reaching agreement; experiments have instead concentrated on the one-way situation in which the sender generates a message received by the subject who has no chance to act back on the sender. The reason for this is probably simply that the underlying interest behind the work on attitude change has been in the effectiveness of public propaganda campaigns conducted through the mass media which are essentially one-way. However, even within the context of public campaigns, the concentration on the one-way situation is surprising in view of the considerable support for the hypothesis that much of the impact of such communications—such as it is—is obtained not directly, but through the person-to-person interaction of opinion leaders with those around them (Katz and Lazarsfeld, 1955).

In this fourth experiment thirty pairs of subjects discussed controversial issues using one of three media of communication (face-to-face, closed-circuit television or loudspeaking audio). The experimental material consisted of a pool of 19 controversial statements about topical social issues (examples were 'students should be financed by loans rather than grants'. 'public transport in large towns should be heavily subsidized out of taxation to discourage the use of the private car' and 'foxhunting should be forbidden'). On entry into the laboratory, subjects recorded their agreement or disagreement with each statement on an eleven-point scale ranging from 'strongly agree' to 'strongly disagree'. Topic items were then selected for discussion according to responses to this initial questionnaire.

In the first experimental condition (the 'real' disagreement condition) two items were selected such that the subjects disagreed on the issue, i.e. one agreed with the statement and the other disagreed with the statement. The interpretation of previous experiments was complicated by possible effects of medium of communication on the ease with which a person could argue a case counter to his actual beliefs. To explore this situation a second experimental condition (the 'false' disagreement condition) was included in which the issues for discussion were selected such that the two individuals in each pair agreed in reality but one individual was asked to be a 'devil's advocate'. The stated objective of all discussions was to reach agreement on a point somewhere along the scale from 'strongly agree' to 'strongly disagree'. Each pair discussed two items in each of the two agreement conditions ('real' and 'false'), using the same medium of communication throughout, and fifteen minutes were allowed for each conversation. Medium of communication had no significant effect on the agrements reached in either of the two agreement conditions ('real' and 'false'). Since the situation in the 'real' condition is symmetrical, no effect would be expected on which side won. The 'false' condition resembles the situation used in the second experiment (Short, 1974)—an insincere individual is arguing against an individual who is sincere in his case. Although the differences obtained were in the same direction as those in the previous experiment, they did not approach statistical significance. The results thus fail to support any interpretation of the results of the previous experiment in terms of sincerity of argument. It will be recalled that such an interpretation was in any case incapable of reconciling the results of Short's (1974) experiment with the Morley and Stephenson results.

After each discussion subjects were again asked to record their private individual opinions on each of the issues which they had discussed. Opinion change was scored by subtracting the opinion recorded after the experiment from that recorded before the experiment (the sign being taken as plus if this change was away from the pole which they were initially nearer). Table 7.2 gives means and standard deviations for the opinion change in each condition. The analysis of variance shows that there is a significant main effect of medium on opinion change (F $(2,57)$ = 3.36, $p < 0.05$). There was

Tabl 7.2 Means and standard deviations of opinion change scores (Short, 1972a). Opinion change is scored by subtracting final opinion from initial opinion. The signs are plus if this change was away from the pole which was nearer the initial opinion

	Person	Real mean	s.d.	False mean	s.d.	Overall mean
Face-to-face	A	1.35	2.3	1.40	2.36	
	B	1.13	2.1	1.98	3.0	1.46
Video	A	2.25	2.67	1.73	2.61	
	B	1.50	2.86	2.08	2.67	1.91
Audio	A	2.20	2.65	2.23	2.85	
	B	1.78	2.36	2.80	2.89	2.25

Newman–Keuls procedure gives a critical ($p < 0.05$) value for the difference between the means separated by two steps of 0.73. The actual difference between audio and face-to-face exceeds this critical value. The same procedure gives a critical value of 0.61 for the means separated by one step. No other differences are therefore significant.

significantly more opinion change in the audio condition than in the face-to-face condition with the video condition intermediate and not significantly different from either. Inspection of Table 7.2 shows that the effect of great opinion change in the audio condition appeared to an approximately equal extent in all experimental conditions.

It could be suggested that this effect is conforming behaviour, in that an isolated individual brings his stated views into line with those of his partner. Indeed superficially the result bears some resemblance to that of Gerard (1964), discussed in Chapter 6. Reanalysing the data of Deutsch and Gerard (1955) he found that in a conformity situation, among those who are initially non-conforming, those tested subsequently in anonymous conditions showed more yielding than those tested publicly. Removing the visual channel (making the situation more anonymous) could be taken to decrease the loss of face associated with yielding; in this way there might be less 'opinion change' in the face-to-face condition where perceived commitment to one's initial position is higher. However, the conformity explanation is inadequate because such a hypothesis would predict that the change for the insincere individual in the 'false' condition would be a 'boomerang' effect (i.e. *towards* the pole nearer the initial opinion). In fact, however, the change for these individuals is in the same direction as with all the others (away from the initial opinion). Furthermore, it is well established in the conformity literature that conforming is less under anonymous conditions (Deutsch and Gerard, 1955, Mouton, Blake and Olmstead, 1956) and if this were conformity one would therefore expect that opinion change would be greater in the face-to-face condition, which is the reverse of the effect actually obtained.

THE EFFECTS OF MEDIUM ON ATTITUDE CHANGE

Considering that the finding that there is more attitude change after a telephone discussion than after a face-to-face discussion is, at least on first sight, counterintuitive, it was felt necessary to repeat the experiment. In fact, four repetitions have been reported, three by Short (1972b, 1972c, 1973b) and one by Young (1974b). In Short's (1972b) and (1973b) experiments and in Young's (1974b) the task was identical with that used by Short (1972a); various other manipulations were incorporated into the experiments, so that they were attempts to extend the finding by noting its limitations and relation to other processes and outcomes rather than simply replications. Short's (1972c) experiment, however, used a slightly different paradigm. Subjects were first asked to rank order the seriousness of eight problems in Britain today. They then discussed the issues to reach an agreed ranking, and again ranked them privately.

All four experiments showed the same effect; in all cases the opinion change, in terms of the differences between initial opinion and final individual opinion, was greater after audio conversations than after face-to-face conversations, with closed-circuit television conversations being intermediate. In two of the experiments (Short, 1972c, 1973b) the effect was sufficiently large to be statistically significant; in the other experiments, it was too small to reach significance. The mean amounts of opinion change for the five experiments are shown in table 7.3. With the mean amount of opinion change over all five experiments set at 100 in the face-to-face condition, the comparable figures are 145 for video and 157 for audio. Combining the results of the five experiments using the method outlined in Winer (1962 p.44) indicates that there is significantly more opinion change in both the audio and the video conditions than in the face-to-face condition, (audio v. face-to-face, $z = 3.43$, $p < 0.0005$, video v. face-to-face, $z = 2.06$, $p < 0.02$) but that there was no difference between the two telecommunications conditions (video v. audio, $z = 1.16$, n.s.), despite the fact that the amount of opinion change was slightly more in the audio than in the video condition in all four experiments. It would, however, be unsafe to conclude too glibly that the telecommunications conditions are always more like each other than they are like face-to-face; in the (1972c) experiments, video is much more similar to face-to-face than to the audio, which may be due to the different experimental task used.

The finding of greater opinion change after audio-only interactions than after face-to-face interactions is in apparent contradiction with Festinger and Maccoby (1964) and Shamo and Meador (1969) who suggest that irrelevant visual stimulation (a slide show) during message reception *increases* attitude change. In terms of the topic of conversation, the visual channel during face-to-face conversation could be considered irrelevant visual stimulation. The finding was only statistically significant in one of Festinger and Maccoby's three experiments but the result was substantiated by Shamo and Meador (1969). In accounting for their slightly paradoxical results, Shamo and Meador made reference to 'ability to raise counter arguments': with less distraction by irrelevant visual stimulation, better counter arguments would be raised and less opinion change would result. But here there is a critical difference between the interactive situation and the non-interactive situation, for in the interactive situation counter arguments are raised anyway (simply to sustain one's end of the conversation). If subjects are already doing their utmost in counter arguing, small changes would be expected to have less effect. The contradiction between the present results and those obtained in the non-interactive situation raises important questions about the generality of results of attitude change studies in non-interactive situations.

Distraction may still be relevant, for if attention to the argument

106

Table 7.3 Means (and standard deviations in brackets) of opinion change scores (adjusted so that the face-to-face mean = 100 in each experiment)

	Face-to-face		Video		Audio		Number of subjects per condition
	mean	s.d.	mean	s.d.	mean	s.d.	
Short (1972a)	100	(178)	152	(223)	160	(205)	40
Short (1972b)	100	(134)	123	(1126)	133	(166)	48
Short (1972c)	100	(54)	107	(73)	133	(57)	28
Short (1973b)	100	(159)	198	(238)	221	(227)	24
Young (1974b)	100	(157)	—		138	(158)	24

N.B. The results of the (1972c) experiment are not strictly comparable to the other results due to the different method used.

is better under audio conditions, one might expect a greater modification of the subjects' original (relatively extreme) positions. This hypothesis could account for the fact that the effect was in the same direction for the insincere individual in the 'false' condition. Despite the observation of an increase in attitude change, Shamo and Meador did in fact find that irrelevant visual stimulation *decreased* the 'recall of argument' score. There is thus some evidence of a distraction function though what is distracted may depend on the situation.

Such results indicate that there is more to attitude change than simply attention to and comprehension of the arguments presented. Another relevant factor is the 'credibility' of the sender (the extent to which he is perceived as a reliable source of information). Although credibility has been shown to affect attitude change (e.g. Aronson and Golden, 1962) such experiments finding effects on attitude change have frequently failed to find any effect on the learning and retention of the message content (Watts and McGuire, 1964, Hovland, Janis and Kelley, 1953). To explain such results it has even been suggested (Bauer, 1965) that the arguments used are only relevant if the standing of the communicator is unclear. Thus when the communicator's standing is clear, only his conclusion, and not his argument, is relevant to the receiver's attitude change. In the same way, when there is less information available about the communicator's opinion (as with the removal of the visual channel) it would be expected that the arguments used would be more critical in determining the amount of attitude change.

Thus a vital issue is the perception of one's partner and his opinion. One replication of the opinion-change experiment (Short, 1972b) explicitly tackled the question of perceptions of the other person. Twenty-two seven-point rating scales were used to assess subjects' perceptions of one another. The scales used drew heavily on those found by Williams (1972, 1975a) to be sensitive to medium of communication. In addition, a number of scales were included which were aimed at the social evaluative aspects of perception (friendly–unfriendly, pleasant–unpleasant, sociable–unsociable), and a few scales were included which were felt to be relevant to this type of task (persuasive–not persuasive, reasonable–unreasonable, etc.). After each conversation subjects rated their partner. There were several significant main effects of medium. People in the audio condition were generally rated more favourably than those in the other two conditions: they were rated more 'pleasant', 'reasonable' and 'trustworthy' (all $p < 0.05$) than those in other conditions and also tended to be rated more 'sincere', 'sensitive', 'sociable' and 'trusting' (all $p < 0.1$). To condense this mass of data, a factor analysis of all the rating scales was conducted. The analysis was based on the oblimin criterion and the factors restricted to being orthogonal, for an additional oblique rotation did not notably improve the simplicity of the factor loadings. The detailed structure can be found in Table 7.4. Factor scores were obtained for each subject and the mean factor scores in each media condition are to be found in Table 7.5. Separate analyses of variance were conducted for each of the five factors. These analyses showed that there is a significant main effect of medium on factor 1, 'trust'. One might have expected that with less information available one would be less willing to trust one's partner, but the results contradict this view: audio partners were rated more favourably on factor 1; that is to say, they were considered more 'trustworthy', 'trusting', 'sincere' and 'fair'. There were no significant effects of medium on the other factors, but the direction of the differences was also that audio partners tended to be evaluated more favourably. These results suggest that in tasks involving a high degree of confrontation or interpersonal tension, conversations over audio links (and the persons encountered over audio links) might be preferred to those encountered over the more intimate media (video or face-to-face).

Table 7.4 Results of factor analysis on scales for rating the interaction partner (from Short, 1972b)

Factor 1	Factor 2	Factor 3	Factor 4	Factor 5
Trustworthy	Persuasive	Emotional	Friendly	Tenacious
Trusting	Informed	Personal	Pleasant	Strong
Sincere	Successful		Sociable	Active
Fair	Informative		Informal	Aggressive
	Reasonable			Competitive
	Strong			
10%	16%	6%	11%	13%
				Total 58%

Table 7.5 The means of the factor scores from the factors in table 7.4 (Short, 1972b). The adjectives indicate which end of the scale is a + score

	Face-to-face	Video	Audio	
Factor 1	0.14	0.25	−0.39	Untrustworthy
Factor 2	−0.10	−0.06	0.16	Persuasive
Factor 3	0.23	−0.18	−0.04	Unemotional
Factor 4	0.10	−0.01	−0.09	Unfriendly
Factor 5	0.14	−0.04	−0.10	Tenacious

Observations made in the course of these experiments and elsewhere are also consistent with this hypothesis. Asked about the sort of tasks for which they would prefer to use the telephone rather than see the person face-to-face, many subjects cite embarrassing situations. Participants in Sinaiko's (1963) Summit II game were also reported to have preferred to negotiate via telephone because of its 'depersonalized' nature and lower distraction by non-verbal cues.

The question then arises as to whether the effect of medium on the rating of partner is related to the effect of medium on opinion change. The median score for each factor in each media condition was calculated. Subjects were divided into those rating their partner above and below the median on each factor. It was found that the 'trust' factor was the only factor which discriminated between those who change their mind a lot and those who change little. (Interestingly, the factor 'persuasive' did not discriminate.) Over the experiment as a whole, those rating their partner as more than normally trustworthy do change their minds more ($t = 2.47$, $p < 0.02$). This in itself was striking, for it will be recalled that the 'trust' factor was the only one which showed any effect of medium, but an even more striking result is obtained when the foregoing analysis is repeated for each medium separately. In both the face-to-face and video conditions, the relationship between trust and opinion change was as expected (more trust, more opinion change). However, in the audio condition this relationship was reversed (more trust, less opinion change, $t = 2.56$, $p < 0.02$ two-tailed). This latter relationship is paradoxical; it seems more reasonable to suppose that in fact in the audio condition there is no causal relationship between trust and opinion change. The reason for the negative relationship could be simply that those who have a friendly conversation, not about the official topic for conversation, both give their partner a favourable rating and are relatively uninfluenced in their opinions. In contrast, in the face-to-face conditions, the more normal relationship (high trust, high opinion change) is obtained. However, the reason for the observed effects remains open to speculation.

CONCLUSION—THE PROBLEMS OF INTERPRETATION

In contrast to problem-solving discussions, conflict is clearly a major area of sensitivity to medium of communication. Medium can affect the likelihood of reaching agreement, the side which is more successful, the nature of the settlement reached, the evaluation of the other side and the individual opinions after the discussion. Understanding these effects is therefore important. All the results can be reconciled with the underlying hypothesis that since the audio medium is low in Social Presence, discussions over that medium are more task-oriented, less person-oriented than face-to-face discussions.

The main competing line of explanation is in terms of efficiency of the interaction. This latter hypothesis is inadequate to explain many of the results of these experiments, notably Morley and Stephenson's result (the strong case is more successful after telephone negotiations), the difference between their experiment and Short's (1974) experiment, and the finding of greater opinion change under audio conditions. There have been repeated failures to find effects of medium on indices of the efficiency of the negotiation such as the sum of the individual payoffs (though there are some exceptions, such as Wichman, 1970, where efficiency may have been confounded with cooperation). A more versatile explanatory tool such as that afforded by the Social Presence hypothesis is required.

One hesitates, however, to put an evaluation on these effects and to say that the telephone is either better or worse for negotiation. It very much depends on one's criterion. There have been indications that agreement is less likely in telephone conversations, but victory rather than agreement may be the main objective, in which case a good medium for one side is a bad medium for the other. One might suggest that it is good that both sides should be influenced away from their initially divergent views and that the audio medium is consequently advantageous, but against this one could set the possibility that the audio medium, by decreasing the importance of self-presentational aspects, may increase the likelihood of socially disapproved behaviour such as obstinacy and exploitation, or perhaps result in a less permanent settlement.

It is also important to consider the total nature of the conflict. As already indicated, most real-life conflict has several components and the effects of medium may differ for the different components. Druckman and Zechmeister (1970) confirmed that a conflict of interest linked to a conflict of value is more difficult to resolve than a conflict not so linked. When the two types of conflict were linked, the resolutions were more characterized by unilaterial domination than by the compromise which characterizes the resolution of a pure conflict of interest. This is potentially important if medium is thought to affect the apparent nature of the conflict. If the face-to-face medium shifts the emphasis to personal considerations, there may be more emphasis on the conflict of values. Effects similar to those found by Druckman and Zechmeister (1970) would then be expected face-to-face: resolution might be more difficult.

A second problem stems from laboratory procedures. When the relationship between the participants is consonant with that given by the conflict of interest, antagonistic intrusion of the personal relationships would be expected to impair the prospects of resolving the conflict. However, in the laboratory (where subjects are often assigned at random to roles) the personal relationships will generally not coincide with those given by the task. Indeed quite the reverse of the real-life situation is likely to be the case: personal relationships will often be good, as most people will be motivated to present a positive image to their partner by being friendly. In that case intrusion of the personal relationships would be expected to facilitate resolution. One must be very careful in extrapolating from laboratory findings using simple conflict of interest situations to any more general 'real-life' conclusion.

8

Person Perception, Interpersonal Attraction and Group Cohesion

INTRODUCTION—THE SIGNIFICANCE OF 'GETTING TO KNOW SOMEONE'

The second critical testing ground for theories of media sensitivity is in the area of interpersonal relations. Within this area of sensitivity, one might anticipate that media effects would be particularly marked when the interactors are relatively unacquainted. While people are still getting to know one another, any small additional piece of information can markedly affect overall judgements; later on in the acquaintance process, small changes in the available information would be expected to have less effect.

Face-to-face contact seems to have special importance in the process of getting to know someone. Thus one user of a conference television system expressed his feelings:

'If you know people well, going out for dinner or a drink would not add anything, but if it is someone you are meeting for the first time there are benefits of the get-together. One tends to relax more after you have met the person and had a few jokes so as to develop some sort of friendship. This helps to make you more efficient as both parties tend to say what they really mean'.

The speaker here seems to have had in mind social aspects both inside and outside the meeting. There is reason to believe that this broad process of getting to know people is an important aspect of many meetings: Collins' (1972) survey of 6397 civil servants' face-to-face meetings showed that at least 20% involved the presence of strangers. This percentage may well be higher with the greater separating distance likely to be associated with the parties to a teleconference. Thus, Champness (1973) surveying 193 meetings over the Confravision system, reported that 70% had involved at least one complete stranger at the other terminal. 'Getting to know someone' is seldom the main purpose of the meeting or even 'on the agenda'; it is, nonetheless, an important subsidiary process in a substantial proportion of meetings. Collins (1972) reported that 34.8% of his respondents gave 'assessing other's reactions' or 'maintaining friendly relations' as the reason why the meetings had to be face-to-face. Another survey of 311 face-to-face meetings in business organizations (Pye *et al.*, 1973) found 13% of respondents gave 'forming impressions of others' as a major activity at the meeting. 'Getting to know someone' can be an explicit as well as an implicit purpose of the meeting, as for example in interview situations.

We have used the term 'getting to know someone' rather loosely since this is the broad term used by interviewees. The term however covers a number of processes which, although closely interrelated, are distinct. This chapter will consider all of these processes, but separately under the conventional social psychological terms: person perception, interpersonal attraction and group cohesion.

PERSON PERCEPTION

Tagiuri (1969) defines person perception as '. . . the processes by which man comes to know and to think about other persons, their characteristics, qualities and inner states' (p.395). This clearly covers a wide range of processes. The characteristics judged will vary in assumed temporal constancy from personality states (which are generally assumed to be lifelong) to interpersonal cues such as smiles (which vary from moment to moment). They will vary in the channel by which they are transmitted, with verbal, paralinguistic, facial, gestural and postural being only a selection of the variety. Furthermore, the dimensions of judgement will vary from judge to judge, and from situation to situation, though some major dimensions can be distinguished.

Individuals are not all identical in the dimensions by which they judge others; they have their own 'implicit personality theories' (Smith, 1967) or 'personal constructs about people' (Kelly, 1955). There is, however, some agreement as to the major dimensions for the judgement of others. Schlosberg (1952) has shown that judgements of facial expressions of emotion can be adequately described by two factors: pleasant–unpleasant and attraction–rejection. Judgements of interpersonal behaviour have also come up with two dimensions, which can be described as pleasant–unpleasant and dominant–submissive (Lorr and McNair, 1965). Kuusinen (1969) in factor analysing ratings of the personality of other people, identified five dimensions of which three were identified as evaluation, potency and activity, the other two being designated 'tolerance' and 'self-confidence'. A similar study by Warr and Haycock (1970) produced six factors: two evaluative factors, two potency factors and two activity factors. In general, then, the structures of judgements of other people are not very dissimilar from the classic EPA structure derived by Osgood, Suci and Tannenbaum (1957).

We have seen in Chapter 5 how the evaluative dimension, or that

114

segment of it identified as 'Social Presence', is particularly important in discriminating between media. One can hypothesize that evaluation of the medium of communication will be related to evaluation of people met via that medium, and thus that the medium of communication used will affect judgements by the users of the mood of others contacted via the medium. This effect would be particularly marked in the evaluative judgements, especially those relating to the Social Presence of the other: scales such as 'personal', 'sensitive' and 'sociable'.

The relationship between judgements of medium of communication and the person met via the medium could be due to either of two processes. It is possible that interactors, on realizing that they are using a medium that is low in Social Presence, change their behaviour in a congruent direction: because they feel the situation is formal, they feel obligated to act formally themselves, and the other parties in the interaction then perceive veridically that they are behaving in an impersonal and formal manner. Alternatively, it could be that the interactors are emitting the non-verbal cues of friendliness and warmth at their normal rate whatever the medium, although with a telecommunications medium many of these are not transmitted. In this latter case, the effect upon the perception of the other person would be due to a misattribution of the non-reception of the non-verbal cues of warmth. The telecommunications user concludes that the other is unfriendly because he interprets the observation that he is receiving no cues to social warmth as due to sending no such cues rather than due to the medium not transmitting the cues. In practice, both processes probably occur: the user changes his behaviour and his behaviour is misinterpreted. We thus have a vicious circle.

An aspect of person perception likely to be especially sensitive to this type of experiential impact of medium of communication is in the formation of 'metaperspectives' (Laing, Phillipson and Lee, 1966), that is, the situation where the 'judge' rates not how he sees the target person but how he thinks the target person sees him. It seems possible that people will doubt their ability to project their personality adequately over new media, and may feel less confident, and act in a less confident manner.

One of the most serious methodological problems in person perception research relates to the measurement of accuracy of perception. In our present research, we are interested in discovering whether the non-transmission of various non-verbal cues over some media means that the accuracy of perception of the other's personality or mood state is lowered. However, Cronbach (1955) has pointed out that a number of different components of accuracy need to be distinguished. For example, one can sometimes 'perceive' the other's personality fairly accurately merely by stereotyping him (e.g.

he is a student, therefore he is long-haired and left-wing). Stereotype accuracy may be possible without non-verbal cues (by just knowing the age, sex or occupation of the other); we are therefore in a stronger position to detect media differences if we can eliminate such 'spurious' accuracy, and Cronbach has described ways of doing so.

INTERPERSONAL ATTRACTION

The term 'interpersonal attraction' has been used to cover all the affiliative emotions such as liking, love, respect, admiration or wish to interact that one person might feel for another. There is a substantial area of overlap between person perception and interpersonal attraction. As was discussed previously, the perception of another person is usually primarily in terms of the three basic dimensions, Evaluation (E), Potency (P) and Activity (A). The perception by Ego of Alter as having a positively evaluated personality, or having other characteristics which are positively evaluated by Ego, is very similar to Ego liking Alter. Thus while there are certain areas of non-overlap (such as the perception of 'potency' or 'activity' traits, or the perception of passing mood states or behavioural indices of interpersonal attraction), the area of overlap is interesting to students of both.

This overlap is apparent in some of the measures of interpersonal attraction, which often bear a strong resemblance to person perception measures. For example, Fishbein (1965) used rating of others on seven-point scales, summing across the evaluative scales to obtain a measure of interpersonal attraction.

A number of factors have been found to affect interpersonal attraction. Some pertain to the judge (such as the 'need for affiliation' studies of Atkinson, 1958, and others). Others pertain to the person judged, who is liked better if he is of high social status (Hurwitz et al., 1960) or relatively intelligent (Bonney, 1944). A number of factors relating to the social situation have been found to affect attraction between people in that situation, examples being group success (Heber and Heber, 1957) and democratic leadership (White and Lippitt, 1960). A hypothesis which could explain all these effects of the situation is that any factor that makes the interaction with the other person or the group more pleasant, is likely to lead to the interpretation that the other people actually are more pleasant, so that they are better liked.

Non-verbally rich media are more favourably evaluated than non-verbally poor media (see Chapter 5) particularly on the Social Presence scales. Feelings about the medium might thus directly affect feelings about the pleasantness of one's conversation partner. We have seen in Chapters 6 and 7 how medium of communication can actually affect the success of the interaction, for example by making agreement more likely in a negotiation. It is known that the success or failure of the interaction can affect the participants' attitudes towards their discussion partners (Heber and Heber, 1957). Such effects may be a consequence of the participants' incorrectly attributing the success or failure to their partners rather than to the communications medium. If this were so, it seems possible that the effect could be abolished or even reversed by giving the participants information about the likely effects of medium (just as Schacter and Singer, 1962, found that the direction of perceptions of arousal could be influenced by attributions as to its causation).

One of the most important determinants of liking is the similarity between the individuals. Similarity in spatial location, i.e. proximity or propinquity, has frequently been found to be a determinant of friendship, whether the proximity is in living quarters (Festinger et al., 1950), the work place (Gullahorn, 1952) or seating position in a classroom (Kendall, 1960). Similarity in attitudes has also been found to be an important determinant of attraction (Newcomb, 1961, Byrne, 1969) and similarity in age, sex, race, religion and personality have all at various times been found to increase attraction between individuals.

Any systematic distortions in the perception of the other person's attitudes could thus affect attraction. Such effects could result directly from the non-transmission of cues to 'friendliness' or 'pleasantness'. One might then predict less liking for those encountered over media which transmit fewer cues. In interactions where non-verbal cues to dislike predominate, the reverse might hold. However, the former situation is probably more common for it is more usual and more socially acceptable to express liking; there is evidence that the perception of dislike by others is substantially less accurate than the perception of liking (Tagiuri, 1958).

GROUP COHESION AND SPLITTING

Group cohesion is the term used for 'the resultant of all the forces acting on all the members to remain in the group' (Cartwright and Zander, 1960). In practice, it is often measured as the ratio of in-group to out-group sociometric choices, i.e. the patterning of interpersonal attraction. It is clearly a phenomenon related to interpersonal attraction, in fact to such an extent that Lott and Lott (1965) entitled a review article 'Group cohesiveness as interpersonal attraction'. It is possible that in some situations attraction for the members of a group would be different in quality from attraction to the group as a whole; one might like one's friends but not all together. In such a case, despite a high number of in-group sociometric choices, the group might break up, indicating that cohesiveness is low. In practice, however, it seems likely that group cohesiveness, as defined by the cumulative desire of the individuals to remain in the group, will be very similar to the cumulative attraction by the individuals towards the other individuals within the group.

While group cohesion is closely related to interpersonal attraction, people may nevertheless remain members of a group even though they do not like its members because of high extrinsic rewards thus gained, or because that is the only way of getting a necessary task completed. However, if attraction between some of the group members is higher than between others, one may observe subgroups forming, and even competition between subgroups. The formation of such coalitions may be particularly liable to happen in multiperson teleconferences, where the configuration of the terminals naturally splits the group into subgroups at different locations. Whether splitting according to location is sufficient to produce sociometric or other splits is a matter to which we will return later in this chapter.

INTERVIEW STUDIES OF MEDIUM AND PERSONAL RELATIONS

Several hypothetical effects of medium of communication on interpersonal processes have been advanced in the last few pages. What evidence is there in previous work that suggests that experimental research in this area will be worthwhile?

Several of the studies of teleconference systems in everyday use have thrown up comments from the users on their feelings about the effects of teleconference systems upon their relationship with the others. The comment that opened this chapter is a particularly vivid example. One study (Short, 1973b) which asked 144 users of audio, video and face-to-face to give their comments on the various media, collected the following replies (frequency of occurrence of comment or similar, in brackets):

'The picture helps if you don't know the other' (6 times).
'I didn't get to know the other as well by video as face-to-face' (twice).
'The video is satisfactory if one knows the other person' (3 times).
'Noting facial expressions is an important guide to the other's feelings' (6 times).
'Without the visual channel one cannot detect sincerity, it is therefore easier to dissimulate' (5 times).
'In the telecommunications conditions there is less social chat as a warm-up' (4 times).
'The video allows more personal contact/awareness of the other person' (9 times).
'In the audio condition it is more difficult to project one's personality' (once).

'The video did not transmit the warmth and personality of the other' (twice).
'In the telecommunications conditions (particularly audio) there is a loss of rapport' (3 times).
'Video is useful whenever the trustworthiness of the other is in doubt' (once).
'I was self-conscious in the video condition' (3 times).

While most of these respondents have emphasized the positive aspects of the visual information, in that it allows them a greater feeling of social contact, allows them to perceive the other's personality or trustworthiness, and helps them in the difficult process of forming a relationship with a stranger, there are disadvantages. The last comment in the above list suggests one disadvantage which is expanded upon by a user of the Bell Canada teleconference system as follows:

'The advantage of audio conferencing is that we wouldn't have to sit up straight, stare at the camera and look presentable when we speak: we could take it easy. Also there would not be the fear of the camera suddenly focussing on you when you are not ready . . . that is embarrassing'.

This self-consciousness may have much to do with the formality and lack of personal contact engendered by all telecommunications systems. Video systems particularly are often seen as intrusive, an aspect which will be discussed later (Chapter 9).

Comments about the effect of the teleconference medium upon subgroup formation have been obtained. For instance, one user of a conference television system at the Department of the Environment, UK, had the following comment to make:

'. . . if he had come over here, we wouldn't have got the same impression that it was us and him; it would just have beeen a sort of cosy chat. And this, I suppose, is inevitable; so long as you have got two locations, you are bound to have two sides'.

Another user of the system said:

'Around a table we are five or six; we feel on equal terms. Over the TV we felt the four of us were against him'.

Clearly there is enough 'soft' evidence that interpersonal processes are affected by communications media for it to be worth pursuing with more systematic data.

METHODOLOGICAL PROBLEMS OF EARLY
EXPERIMENTAL STUDIES

A number of studies have compared the effects of the various communications channels on the impressions formed by judges. Such studies have all used one-way communications only, the 'message' has been recorded on film or tape so that the stimulus presented is identical for all subjects apart from the manipulations in the medium used. The validity of such a procedure will be discussed later.

Geidt (1955) had judges rate the personalities of psychiatric patients from a silent film, written transcript, sound track only or complete audio-visual film and found that while accuracy increased across the first three media, there was no difference in accuracy (in terms of predicting self-rating of personality, and sentence completions) between the media that interest us here: the sound track and the complete film. A study by English and Jelenevsky (1971) had trained judges rate films of psychotherapists for empathy, and found that inter-rater agreement (there was no external criterion for accuracy) was about the same for audio-only, visual-only and full audio-visual presentation. Maier and Thurber (1968) asked for judgements of honesty and dishonesty regarding transcripts, audio-tapes or live acting by role-playing students who were telling either the truth or lies according to an experimental design unknown to the judges. The accuracy of perception of lying was found to be similar for the groups using the first two media, but was significantly lower for those who saw the face-to-face interaction. There was a non-significant trend for the latter to be the most confident in the accuracy of their judgements. This result is somewhat surprising in view of Ekman and Friesen's (1969) finding that non-verbal cues, particularly from the leg and trunk area, can be used in the detection of lying.

Finally, Berman, Shulman and Marwit (1975) compared the decoding of affect from audio-only, video-only and full audio-video. They found that the decoding of the 'warmth' or 'coldness' of the target person was least consistent for audio-only, and equally good with video and audio-video. Six different encoders (i.e. actors on the tapes) were used, and a significant interaction between medium and individual coder was found; that is, some produced primarily visual cues, others primarily audio cues. One can speculate whether similar differences amongst decoders (the judges) could be identified.

These studies suggest that the addition of visual information allows relatively little, if any, improvement in the *accuracy* of person perception. It is still possible that while adding nothing of use in forming accurate judgements, the visual channel might lead to overall more favourable evaluation. However, the only relevant study (Byrne and Clore, 1966) which compared the written medium, audio-only and full audio-video films, found no significant effect. The actual content of the stimulus material was in this case only responses to a series of attitudinal items.

All these studies are inadequate for our present interest because they used one-way non-interactive situations. While this method of presentation has its advantages (primarily that it allows perfect control over the content, so that the experimenter can be sure that the auditory information is the same on the audio-only tape and the audio-visual film) it has serious disadvantages for our purposes. Firstly, no face-to-face condition can be included, so one is essentially comparing remote communications systems. Secondly, one cannot be sure of the representativeness of the behaviour shown as the stimulus. A single piece of behaviour, often specially acted for the purpose, is used in all the above experiments. One has only to accept the very reasonable hypothesis that visual information does not have an exactly equivalent importance in every situation, being of vital importance in some situations and totally redundant in others, to see that generalization from experiments of the above type is virtually impossible. While having high internal validity, such studies are of very low external validity. Finally there is the possibility that the very fact that the situation is not interactive may make the judge dependent on a different set of cues from those which he would use in interactive conversation.

Thus it would be hasty to conclude from these studies that medium of communication has no effect on impression formation or interpersonal attraction. In view of the several demonstrations of the importance of non-verbal behaviour in influencing these processes (e.g. Kendon and Cook, 1969, Patterson and Sechrest, 1970, Mehrabian, 1968) it is still appropriate to study the effects of differences of media in two-way interactive situations.

Apart from the work of the Communications Studies Group, two such studies have already been completed, though not published. The first study was by LaPlante (1971) at the University of Windsor. Subjects played a Prisoner's Dilemma game with a confederate. At three points during the game the confederate gave a short communication, face-to-face, by closed-circuit television, by telephone or by a written message. The situation was somewhere between one-way and two-way, since the confederate responses were preprogrammed and, in the latter three media, pre-recorded, although they were dependent on the responses of the subject. In addition, the subject was not informed that the messages had been recorded, and thus may have felt it to be a two-way interactive situation. As well as varying in communication medium, the messages were either friendly or unfriendly according to the predetermined experimental design.

After the 20 Prisoner's Dilemma trials, the subjects rated their impressions of the confederate (who they thought was also a subject) on a series of twenty-five rating scales. On most of these scales there was no effect of communications medium, but on one factor extracted by factor analysis (a 'pleasantness/friendliness' factor with 'pleasant-unpleasant', 'friendly-unfriendly', 'admirable-contemptible', 'altruistic-egotistic', 'unselfish-selfish', and 'good-bad' loading) a communications medium by message content interaction was found, this being due to the following mean scores.

'Friendliness' factor scores from LaPlante's (1971) ratings of the other person

Message content	Medium of communication			
	face-to-face	television	telephone	written
Friendly	1.02	0.80	0.46	0.34
Unfriendly	−0.93	−0.96	−0.70	−0.03

(N.B. Positive scores indicate that the mean tends towards the 'friendly' pole of the factor).

This effect is particularly interesting, since it corresponds exactly with what would be predicted from a knowledge of the importance of non-verbal cues in transmitting cues to friendliness or unfriendliness (see Chapter 4). With the friendly message, the most non-verbally rich medium, face-to-face, leads to the most favourable evaluations, with the other media leading to less favourable but still positive evaluations in descending order according to the number of non-verbal cues they transmit. With the unfriendly message, however, the order is exactly reversed. The more non-verbally rich media lead to the least favourable evaluations, with the descending order being perfect apart from the reversal between face-to-face and television. The difference according to the type of message is very small for the written mode, is larger for the telephone, even larger for the television and largest for face-to-face. This result is somewhat reminiscent of that of Ellsworth and Carlsmith (1968), who found that in a face-to-face interaction in which a confederate evaluated the subject favourably or unfavourably, liking for the confederate was greater if he maintained eye-gaze than if he looked away in the favourable evaluation condition, but greater if he avoided gaze in the unfavourable evaluation condition. Gaze seemed to act to intensify the evaluation, and the recipient responded in kind. In LaPlante's experiment, it seems as if the non-verbally rich media may similarly act as intensifiers of the predominant emotion being transmitted.

The second experiment was carried out by Klemmer and Stocker (1971) at Bell Laboratories. The media compared in this case were the Picturephone and an audio-only system with voice switching. They reasoned that the effects of communications medium might be strongest in relatively undefined situations, in which concentration upon an overt task would not dominate the interaction, and interpersonal communication might come more to the fore. In addition, they hypothesized that effects of medium would be most marked in interactions between strangers. Each subject had two ten-minute conversations, one over each medium, and the situation was fully interactive, the only constraint being a suggested topic. After the conversations, the subjects rated their partners on eight rating scales (only one of which, 'friendly–unfriendly', was clearly evaluative). The first subexperiment of 35 subjects showed a single difference in ratings between the media: people met via the Picturephone were considered more submissive than those met via the audio system. However, the second subexperiment of 24 subjects failed to confirm this difference, and found no other effects of communications medium.

These experiments are somewhat equivocal. LaPlante's experiment shows an effect of communications medium, but is methodologically somewhat less germane than Klemmer and Stocker's experiment which failed to find any such effect. However, the latter failure may have been due to the omission of a face-to-face condition, leaving a somewhat narrow range of media. In order to discover more about the effects of communications medium in this area, a series of experiments were carried out. We will discuss first those which deal with the accuracy of person perception via the different media, next those which deal with evaluative biases produced by meeting people via different media, and lastly with those investigating coalition formation in small groups.

THE EFFECTS OF MEDIUM ON THE ACCURACY OF PERSON PERCEPTION

Reid (1970) used a similar paradigm to the Maier and Thurber (1968) experiment summarized previously. Groups of three subjects took part; one being designated the speaker, and the other two the listeners. During the first five minutes of the session, the speaker talked about his school and college days, and during the second five minutes he described the furniture of his own home. Each five-minute period was broken down into thirty-second portions, separated by a buzzer, and the speaker was asked to lie or to tell the truth during the thirty-second segments according to a prearranged random sequence unknown to the listeners. One listener was face-to-face with the speaker, the other was at the end of an audio link; with the change of topic after five minutes, they changed places.

Each of the 16 listeners had a maximum correct score of 10

face-to-face and 10 over the audio circuit; actual correct judgements were 96 (59.9%) face-to-face and 94 (58.7%) over audio, clearly virtually identical. The listeners were also asked to rate their confidence in their judgements on the same three-point scale, 'very confident', 'fairly confident' and 'not at all confident': again it was found that there was higher confidence over face-to-face (clearly unjustified) but this was not quite strong enough to reach statistical significance.

These results suggest that, although medium of communication does not affect the accuracy of person perception, participants in the interaction believe that it does, in that they are somewhat more confident of their judgements face-to-face. However, Krauss (personal communication) has carried out an experiment using an interactive situation, which suggests that participants may be correct in believing that medium affects the ability to detect lying, but they are wrong as to which is the best medium! His preliminary results, like those from the Maier and Thurber (1968) experiment, suggest that face-to-face may be *worse* than audio for this kind of task.

A second experiment by Reid (1970) provided further evidence of the possibility of an irrational confidence in judgements made face-to-face. This experiment was a simulated interview in which a confederate was interviewed by 22 civil servants, who were told that they were to assess him for the award of a travel scholarship. Eleven of the civil servants interviewed him face-to-face and eleven interviewed him via the telephone. The confederate was free to act in any way he saw fit providing he kept within the role provided; this is obviously a weak point in the experiment since the confederate was almost certainly aware of the experimental hypotheses, and was certainly aware of which experimental condition he was in.

After the interview, the interviewer rated the interviewee on a series of 14-point scales, and also rated their confidence as to the accuracy of their judgements on these various scales as 'very confident', 'fairly confident' or 'not at all confident'. None of these rating scales showed a significant effect of communications medium, although there were strong trends for the confederate to be judged as more 'serious', 'mature' and 'responsible' after the telephone conversation than after the face-to-face conversation. A significant difference was found, however, in the degree of confidence with which the subjects made their judgements (as assessed by subsidiary 'confidence of judgement' scales). Face-to-face interviewers were found to express significantly higher confidence in their judgements than the telephone interviewers (p less than 0.02).

Although no differences in accuracy according to the medium used were found, the differences in confidence could have equally important practical implications. If interviewers cannot be confident in their telephone judgements, they will tend to avoid using the medium, even though it may have allowed them to make equally accurate judgements with great savings in time and money.

In view of the interesting results, but unsatisfactory methods of the interview experiment by Reid, this was repeated by Young (1974a). As before it was a selection interview situation, though it was somewhat more open-ended in that the interviewees were being given vocational guidance, with the general aim of finding if there would be suitable positions for them in some part of the Civil Service. There were 18 interviewers, all being experienced professional interviewers on refresher courses at the Central Youth Employment Executive; the 18 interviewees were university students. Both groups are thus representative of the groups to which we would wish to generalize the results (i.e. they were, or were likely to be, interviewers or interviewees in everyday life), and in both cases the participants were naive to the experimental hypotheses. Each interviewer had three ten-minute interviews with three different interviewees, each interview being conducted over a different medium of communication (one face-to-face, one via closed-circuit television and one via a loudspeaking audio system). After each interview, the interviewer rated the interviewee on 12 seven-point scales such as 'kind', 'rational', 'confident' and 'trustworthy', and for each judgement rated his confidence on a 'confidence' scale. At the end of the three conversations, the interviewer ranked all three of the interviewees on the same scales.

The interviewees were similarly asked to fill in scales giving their impression of the interviewers (on six scales) and the interviews (on six scales). They also ranked the three interviewers on the same six scales, and finally gave their opinions of their own personality on the twelve scales that the interviewers had judged them on.

This experimental design not only has a high degree of both internal and external validity, it allows measurement of the three basic dimensions of interpersonal judgement: accuracy, confidence and evaluative bias. Accuracy was calculated by taking the difference between the interviewer's perception of the interviewee's personality (as rated on the twelve 7-point scales) and the interviewee's perception of their own personality (on the same scales), with a suitable correction being incorporated to remove elevation and stereotype accuracy errors (Cronbach, 1955). Such a measure does assume that the interviewees' perceptions of their own personality is valid, which may not be necessarily so; further experiments using behavioural post-diction could add useful information.

Confidence was assessed by averaging the confidence judgements across all the scales filled out by the interviewers. Finally, bias in mean scores could be taken by averaging the ratings for all interviews via a particular medium.

Results were similar to those of the Reid (1970) experiments, in that confidence in judgements was slightly lower over the audio systems, though the mean (6.05 on a 9-point scale) was not significantly different from the confidence over video (mean 6.44) or face-to-face (mean 6.48). This is the same trend as was noticed in previous experiments (the two Reid experiments and Maier and Thurber, 1968). The accuracy of judgements was very similar over the three media, the mean error on Cronbach adjusted accuracy scores being 1.60 face-to-face, 1.67 video and 1.66 audio. Although accuracy is slightly higher face-to-face as expected, this effect does not approach statistical significance (which could be, in part, due to the fact that the interviewers were hardly accurate at all, apart from stereotype accuracy, over any of the media!)

The ratings and rankings *are* significantly biased by communications medium. The interviewers' ratings of the interviewees showed only one significant effect; the interviewees met over the video system were seen as more 'predictable' than those met over the other two systems. The rankings, however, showed more significant differences between the media (further discussion of differences between the two methods will follow). The face-to-face interviewees were considered less 'broadminded', less 'rational', than the telecommunications interviewees, while the audio interviewees were considered more 'dominant' than the interviewees over the other two media. Interviewees' judgements of interviewers and of interviews were not effected by medium of communication.

These results are not easy to interpret. Our Social Presence hypothesis would have predicted effects on other scales, particularly 'sociable' and 'formal' which were not affected by communications medium in this experiment. The confidence effect has failed to reappear, though one could argue that the effect on the 'predictable' scale is an indication that judges are less certain of the other, and less confident in predicting the other's behaviour.

MEDIA-INDUCED EVALUATIVE BIASES

Although there have been consistent failures to find effects of medium of communication on the accuracy of assessment of the other person's opinions, the experiments have repeatedly found indications of evaluative biases induced by the medium of communication. A series of experiments have been conducted to investigate these effects.

In all the experiments on person perception discussed hitherto, the interactors have had sharply different roles. Williams (1975a) investigated the effects of medium on the formation of evaluative feelings between equals. One hundred and forty-four civil servants took part. Individuals were paired in such a way that level of acquaintance was low (ranging from complete strangers to slight acquaintances). Each individual had two fifteen-minute conversations, each with a different conversation partner, and each with a different medium of communications (two out of face-to-face, the handset telephone and closed-circuit television). During these conversations, one of two tasks was carried out; one task being a free discussion on the 'Problems of Modern Life', the other being the so-called 'Priorities' task, in which each individual filled in a pre-conversation questionnaire on which he indicated his opinion as to the four most important problems of modern life, and was then instructed to ' . . . come to a mutual decision with your partner as to which are the three best items from the eight which you and he put on the "Problems of Modern Life" questionnaire'. These two tasks clearly differ on several dimensions. In particular they differed in the pleasantness of the interaction induced, since in the 'Priorities' condition, disagreement is virtually ensured, which presumably would frequently lead to a less pleasant interaction than the easygoing chatting of the 'Free Discussion'.

After both conversations were finished, participants filled in a questionnaire to give their opinion of the two conversations, and the two conversation partners. The scales on this questionnaire were in forced-choice form, so that respondents had to choose 'Which of the two conversations (people) did you find the more pleasant (polite, agreeable, formal, etc.)?' This form was adopted in preference to the more usual semantic differential type of rating scale, since it was felt that the use of the latter scale for rating people may mitigate against identifying differences: many respondents use only the most favourable ends of the scales (points 6 or 7 on a 7-point scale), and the resulting decrease in the range of scores makes the identification of differences caused by experimental manipulations less likely. The phenomenon is not unlike the well-known 'social desirability' set (Edwards, 1957) and is amenable to the same solution, the use of forced-choice scales. If the experimental manipulation has any consistent effect upon the feelings of the respondents, choices should not be random, and significant effects should appear.

The rating scales were factor analysed (oblique rotations) and three factors were identified for the 'conversation scales' and three for the 'person scales'. These were labelled 'conversation evaluation' (not impersonal, pleasant, agreeable), 'conversation interest' (interesting, not pointless, not unsatisfactory) and 'conversation argumentativeness' (not polite, argumentative, bad-tempered) for the conversation scales, and 'person evaluation' (not formal, friendly, sociable), 'person intelligence' (intelligent, successful, not boring) and 'person domineeringness (domineering, unreasonable) for the person scales.

An intercorrelation of these factors showed an important relationship. Using the method of Wrigley and Neuhaus (Harman, 1960) it was found that the correlation between 'conversation evaluation' and 'person evaluation' was +0.55, the correlation between 'conversation interestingness' and 'person intelligence' was +0.67, and the correlation between 'conversation argumentativeness' and 'person domineeringness' was +0.62. Correlations between other pairs of factors were considerably lower. It seems that the conversation and the person were not being evaluated totally independently which supports the earlier hypothesis that the pleasantness of the situation, which is influenced by the medium of communication, directly influences judgements of the pleasantness of the other person in the situation.

The two 'evaluation' factors correspond most closely, in terms of their constituent scales, with the Social Presence factor discussed at length in Chapter 5. It is therefore on these that we would expect the strongest media effects. The factor scores for individuals were extracted and denormalized (this latter process is necessary since the factor analysis programme adjusts all factor scores so as to have zero mean, but deviation from zero is the indicator of media preferences in this case). The mean scores for the three paired comparisons of media (one-third of the subjects used each pair) are shown in Table 8.1.

The significant effects (and most of the non-significant trends) are in the direction of the most non-verbally-rich medium, face-to-face, leading to more positive evaluations than closed-circuit television, which in turn leads to more positive evaluations than the telephone. As expected, the effects are concentrated in the evaluative factors. Analyses of variance with task and order of media as variables were also carried out for each of the subgroups (who had used different media pairs) and several significant effects of task appeared. In particular, there were indications of an effect of task type: while in the free-discussion condition, the pattern of medium preference was the same as for the experiment as a whole (i.e. face-to-face conversations and people preferred to closed-circuit television ones which were in turn preferred to audio ones), in the Priorities condition, the pattern was somewhat different. In the latter case, the closed-circuit television conversation and person are generally preferred to both face-to-face and telephone conversations and people, with the latter two not differing significantly.

This interaction between medium of communication and task is difficult to explain by means of any simple hypothesis as to the positive or negative effect of non-verbal cues of affect upon evaluative preferences. There are no non-verbal cues which are unique to closed-circuit television; that is, any cues transmitted by television will also be transmitted face-to-face, and possibily even by telephone. Therefore, a theory based solely on naive extrapolation of the functions of non-verbal cues (see Chapter 5) could not explain the finding that closed-circuit television leads to more favourable evaluations than either of the other media. Nor is Laplante's (1971) finding a sufficient parallel; one would expect that with a pleasant task face-to-face would lead to stronger preferences, with an unpleasant task the telephone would lead to stronger preferences, but an

Table 8.1 Means of denormalized factor scores on media preferences (positive scores indicate first-named medium chosen)

		Conversation factors				Person factors	
		Evaluation	Interest	Argumenta-tive	Evaluation	Intelligence	Domineering
Face-to-face v. telephone	Mean	+0.30	+0.14	+0.01	+0.04	+0.08	+0.12
	t	1.95*	<1	<1	<1	<1	<1
Face-to-face v. CCTV	Mean	+0.40	+0.01	+0.06	+0.03	+0.23	−0.01
	t	2.71**	<1	<1	<1	1.55	<1
CCTV v. telephone	Mean	+0.65	+0.00	+0.08	+0.32	−0.01	+0.12
	t	4.39***	<1	<1	2.29**	<1	<1

N.B. * indicates p <0.10, ** indicates p <0.05, *** indicates p <0.01. Standard deviation is about 1.0 in all cases.

intermediate task would only lead to no clear preferences, whatever the medium. A more complex approach is needed.

One such explanation can be derived from our Social Presence hypothesis, and the relationship of Social Presence to Argyle and Dean's (1965) intimacy concept. In Chapter 5, we suggested that the Social Presence of the medium was one variable that could contribute to intimacy, together with the other variables from the Argyle and Dean model, i.e. proximity, eye-contact, smiling and conversation topic. One can summarize, for our present purposes, the essential aspects of the 'Intimacy Equilibrium Model' as follows:

(1) Intimacy is influenced by proximity, eye-contact, smiling, conversation topic (and, we would add, communications medium).
(2) Intimacy can be too low or too high.
(3) When intimacy deviates from the optimum, the parties of the conversation will try to alter their behaviour to return intimacy to that optimum.
(4) If behaviour cannot be so altered, the non-optimal state of intimacy is found to be unpleasant.

Applying this to the results from the experiment just described, we can see that two influences on intimacy were varied: the communications medium (with face-to-face the most intimate, closed-circuit television intermediate and telephone the least intimate) and the topic of conversation (with, presumably, the argumentative 'Priorities' task being the more intimate and the easy-going 'Free Discussion' less intimate). However, several of the other cues that could have been used by the participants to adjust intimacy towards the optimum were unavailable (none available over the telephone, smiling only over the closed-circuit television). Accordingly, it was likely that in many of the conversations, intimacy remained non-optimal and effects were observed in terms of ratings of the pleasantness of the conversations. Thus for the less intimate task, 'Free Discussion', the medium giving the highest Social Presence, face-to-face, leads to the most favourable evaluations, and the lowest in Social Presence, the telephone, leads to the least favourable. For the more intimate task, 'Priorities', closed-circuit television leads to more favourable evaluations, while conversations via the media of higher and lower Social Presence, face-to-face and telephone, are seen as relatively unpleasant compared to video communication (the former too intimate, the latter not intimate enough). This would suggest that with tasks of very high intimacy, perhaps very embarrassing, personal or conflictful ones, the medium lowest in Social Presence, the telephone, would lead to more favourable evaluations than either of the other media. LaPlante's

(1971) unfriendly condition seems to have been such a situation, and similar effects were also found in one of the negotiation experiments (Short, 1972b). Anecdotal responses from telecommunications users included mention of this effect with highly intimate tasks.

Although this hypothesis is interesting in that it may allow us to tie in the 'Intimacy Equilibrium' theory with the concept of Social Presence developed in Chapter 5, caution is necessary. Hitherto it is only a *post hoc* hypothesis evolved on the basis of a single experiment. Further testing would clearly be useful.

Accordingly, a further experiment was conducted (Williams, 1972) with these purposes: (1) to confirm the effect of medium of communication on interpersonal evaluation on a new subject population and with new media, (2) to investigate further the relationship between task, medium and interpersonal evaluation, (3) to test whether level of acquaintance, which had been kept low in all previous experiments, does in fact modify the relationship between medium of communication and interpersonal evaluation, (4) to explore the effects of individual differences on the effects of medium of communication on interpersonal evaluation, and evaluation of the medium and the conversation.

Two media were used, a videophone and the same system with the vision off (here referred to as 'audio only'). Each participant (there were 96) used both media, having one ten-minute conversation with a different person via each system. For half the subjects, the conversation partners were complete strangers, while for the other half the other person was a friend (one contact person was asked to bring three friends to the experiment). The subjects were engineers, housewives and students, and were thus of both sexes. The individual difference measure selected was the Thing–Person questionnaire devised by Little (1971). This questionnaire consists of a series of questions relating to the respondents' interest in interacting with people (e.g. 'gain a reputation for giving good advice on personal problems' and 'make the first attempt to get to know a new neighbour') or with things (e.g. 'do sky-diving' and 'build a stereo set or home radio'). These dimensions were felt intuitively to be important in this context since a medium of communication is a 'thing' which allows varying amounts of interpersonal contact with other 'people'. Face-to-face and, to a lesser extent, a video system, give higher Social Presence and a better impression of the other person as a person, and thus might be especially popular with people having an orientation towards other people rather than towards things.

The final independent variable in this experiment was the task. One third of the subjects had a 'Free Discussion', another third did the 'Priorities' task (as in the first experiment) while the rest did a new task, a 'Persuasion' task. Subjects first chose four out of a list of

44 problems of modern life as the most important and were then told to discuss their choice with the other person, with whom they would disagree, and that their task was to 'persuade the other person that your list is correct and his incorrect'. This task bears some similarity to those discussed in Chapter 7. It was intended to introduce a somewhat less pleasant, more competitive atmosphere, and thus to cause the medium lowest in Social Presence, the audio, to lead to the most positive evaluations of the other.

After both their conversations, the subjects filled out an opinion questionnaire, indicating their feelings about the media, the conversations and the other persons on forced-choice scales as before. Eight of the scales referred to the media, eight to the conversations and eight to the other people. Media differences were evident in the results: five media scales, seven conversation scales and five person scales, showed significant biases in the choices according to the medium used. Factor analysis was used to simplify the results; two factors being extracted for the media scales, 'medium efficiency' (efficient, useful, reliable) and 'medium simplicity' (simple, private, easy to use); two for the conversations, 'conversation interest' (not boring, meaningful, enjoyable) and 'conversation cooperativeness' (not quarrelsome, cooperative), and finally three for the person ratings, 'person evaluation' (trustworthy, sympathetic, sensible), 'person formality' (formal) and 'person confidence' (confident, intelligent, sincere). As in the previous experiment, ratings of the medium, of the conversation and of the person were clearly not independent: for example, 'medium efficiency' correlated with 'conversation interest', $r = 0.51$ and 'conversation cooperativeness' correlated with 'person evaluation', $r = 0.68$. Factor scores for each individual were extracted and denormalized as before, with the results shown below in Table 8.2.

Table 8.2 Means for denormalized factor scores on 7 factors

	Mean	t	p
Medium (efficiency)	+0.885	8.68	<0.001
Medium (simplicity)	−0.284	2.78	<0.01
Conversation (interest)	+0.648	6.35	<0.001
Conversation (cooperativeness)	+0.218	2.14	<0.05
Person (evaluation)	+0.388	3.80	<0.001
Person (formality)	+0.235	2.30	<0.05
Person (confidence)	+0.164	1.61	not sig.

N.B. All probabilities are for two-tailed tests. Positive scores indicate that the videophone was chosen more frequently on that factor, negative scores indicate that the audio medium was chosen more frequently. Standard deviation is about 1.0 in all cases.

The effects of the medium of communication upon choices between media, conversations and persons are all strong, the only one on which it did not reach significance being the 'person confidence' factor. In most cases, the direction of the effect is for the videophone to lead to more favourable evaluations (more efficient medium, more interesting conversation, more positively evaluated person).

In order to assess the importance of the various independent variables, (level of acquaintance and task) on these factor scores, two-way analyses of variance were carried out for each of the seven sets of factor scores. The results of these analyses were generally negative with no consistent significant main effects. This result is surprising and interesting. It suggests that the basic difference between the media that was detected (*viz.*, Table 8.2) is remarkably robust, appearing whatever the task and whatever the level of acquaintance. The lack of influence of acquaintance is counterintuitive, and suggests that even between friends medium of communication can significantly affect the impression formed. The finding that task did not affect evaluations is counter to the previously discussed indications that task was an important moderator variable in the relationship between communications medium and personal preferences. A detailed look at the results for the two previously used tasks, the Free Discussion and Priorities tasks, suggested that, although effects did not achieve significance, even for these two, they were in the same direction as previously noted (the Free Discussions led to more favourable evaluations of the videophone medium, conversation and person than did the Priorities task). It is thus possible that the task effect did not appear because the exclusion of a face-to-face condition reduced the range of media to the point where effects become too weak to be observed reliably.

In contrast, effects were noted with the 'Thing–Person orientation' score (i.e. the person orientation score minus the thing orientation score) which correlated positively with no less than five of the sets of factor scores, 'medium simplicity' $r = +0.34$, 'conversation interest' $r = +0.19$, 'conversation cooperativeness' $r = 0.19$, 'person evaluation' $r = +0.17$ and 'person confidence' $r = +0.26$, all significant to at least the level of $p < 0.05$. All these correlations are positive, showing that those who were relatively more oriented towards people rather than things evaluated the videophone medium, conversation and person more favourably than the audio. The direction of the effect is as hypothesized, and is the first support for the intuitively reasonable idea that there will be individual differences between people in their reactions towards media. More detailed data on the effects of individual differences in the use of communication media would be a useful output from future experimental work.

METAPERCEPTIONS

The study of metaperceptions is relatively recent, having first been developed by Laing, Phillipson and Lee (1966). In brief, if a normal perception is what A thinks of B, then a metaperception is what A thinks B thinks of A, i.e. a measure of understanding. Laing *et al.* (1966) go even further, and study meta-metaperceptions (i.e. what A thinks B thinks A thinks of B, or the extent of realization of understanding or misunderstanding). These processes may be especially important during person perception over person-to-person communications media, since they depend crucially on two-way social interchange. Furthermore, if the medium produces distortion in communication, it may be most easily detectable for metaperception, where correct perception depends on correct transmission two or three times across the medium (i.e. if the perception is incorrect due to distortion, then the metaperception is very likely to be incorrect as well, but the metaperception could also be incorrect even if the original perception was not). Metastatements may also tend to be concentrated in the non-verbal channel, in that it is rude to say 'I am bored' but it may be possible to convey the same message non-verbally without offence. Metaperceptions which depend on metastatements will thus be especially prone to influence by communications medium.

There are two lines of research of relevance. The first has dealt with 'understanding' and 'feelings of being understood' at a global level. The second has tried to measure more directly the accuracy of metaperceptions.

Weston and Kristen (1973) had groups of six students discuss their courses face-to-face, or over audio-video or audio-only teleconference links. Each of the sixteen groups had three discussion sessions, always using the same medium. Amongst the effects of medium they found were significant effects on a series of scales gauging uncertainty. Out of the 27 scales, 12 showed a significant ($p < 0.05$) main effect of medium (audio and audio-video only) and of these several related to metaperceptions of the other, particularly:

(a) I had quite a bit of trouble knowing how the people at the other end were reacting to the things I said.
(b) When those at the other end were speaking, I never got the feeling that they were speaking directly to me.
(c) I (didn't) clearly understand the positions taken by people at the other end.
(d) I was sometimes uncertain whether the people at the other end were listening.
(e) It was sometimes hard to react to things said at the other end because it was hard to interpret what was meant.

134

(f) I felt that the two ends talked past each other quite a bit because all of us were confused about what was going on at each other's end.

In all cases the video came out more favourably than the audio. Clearly, whatever the objective performance of the groups, they felt confused and lacking in understanding of, and by, the others in the audio condition. This was further emphasized by two other questions on the questionnaire. Subjects were asked firstly to 'Indicate, as well as you can, whether or not each of the other people seemed to agree with you': the rated degree of perceived agreement was significantly lower for those at the far end of an audio link than for all the other groups. The second question asked them to 'Indicate . . . whether . . . people seemed to understand the implication of what you said, regardless of whether or not they seemed to agree'. Again, those at the far end of an audio link were rated as showing less understanding than others who had been face-to-face or at the end of a video link.

Young (1975) found a similar result in a three-person mixed-media game. When subjects were asked, 'How well did they understand your views, in regards to agreeing or disagreeing with them?', those at the other end of audio links were rated as showing less understanding.

However, when Young (1946b) took measures of the actual accuracy of understanding, no significant effect of medium was found. Pairs of people interacted by telephone or face-to-face, and after the interaction filled in various scales. Understanding was calculated by comparing A's rating of B on a series of adjectival scales, with B's rating, on the same scales, of how he felt A saw him. Perception of understanding could be calculated similarly. Although accuracy was generally higher than chance, no difference between the media was observed on either of these measures.

We thus have results on metaperception similar to those on simple perception. In both cases, the perception of personality (or perception of understanding) seems in actuality to be accurate at a constant level whatever the medium. However, the subject's confidence in his perception or personality (or perception of understanding) is influenced by medium, being lower after audio-only conversations.

GROUP PROCESSES: COALITIONS IN SMALL GROUPS

It is not possible to generalize directly from the behaviour of pairs of individuals to processes in larger groups, since several other psychological phenomena, such as leadership, clique formation and conformity are only realized in groups of three or more individuals.

From the practical point of view, group meetings seem to be at least as frequent as meetings between pairs of individuals (Goddard, 1971, found that 25% of government and business meetings were between groups of more than two persons, while Collins, 1972, obtained a figure of 32% for the same statistic). Furthermore, the larger the meeting, the more man-hours there are per meeting-hour, so that the number of man-hours expended is even greater in the larger meetings (82% of man hours spent in multi-person meetings, 18% in two-person meetings [Goddard, 1971] though this may be an overestimate due to the sampling method used).

In a group, interpersonal attraction can become differentiated, so that apart from liking for the group as a whole (group cohesion), each member will have evaluative preferences between the individuals in the group. This is the basis for clique formation and if, in addition, there is some opportunity for the 'joint use of resources to determine the outcome of a decision in a mixed motive situation . . .' (Gamson, 1964) then coalition formation can occur. Since positive effects of medium of communication upon interpersonal attraction have been observed in the experiments previously described, it seems logical to pursue this effect into the realm of groups.

Accordingly, an experiment (Williams, 1973) was set up in which 48 three-man groups were faced with a mixed motive situation. The groups communicated with two of the individuals face-to-face and the third at the end of a telecommunications link (audio only for half the groups, closed-circuit television for the other half). Each group had a 15-minute conversation, during which they role-played a situation specified in the experimental instructions. The instructions told the participants that they were to play the parts of three departmental managers of a small department store. The store had been overcome by a financial crisis, and it was necessary for one departmental manager to give an employee the sack, but it was not yet decided which department was to be the loser. This was the task of the three 'managers'. Apart from these overall instructions, each participant received individual instructions as to the great potential for his 'department' and the hardships which would be encountered by his 'employees' were they to be fired, and was encouraged to argue strongly against the redundancy being made in his department. This is thus a three-person zero-sum game, in which one participant must be voted down by the other two, though on the surface it appears more complex than similar games used elsewhere.

After the conversation and the vote, all participants filled out forced-choice rating scales of the type previously described. It was hypothesized that participants' opinions of the group members at the remote location would be less favourable than opinions of the face-to-face members. In addition, it was hypothesized that in the telecommunications conditions the vote as to which 'department' should suffer the redundancy would more frequently go against the remote participant, with the two face-to-face members of the group 'ganging up' against him.

The latter hypothesis was not supported by the results. Chance expectation was that the remote participant would be voted down in one third of the groups, i.e. in 16 out of the 48. The actual finding was that this chance expectation was not even exceeded, with only 13 of the remote participants being voted down. There is thus a slight (non-significant) tendency in the reverse direction; the remote participant is more successful than would be expected by chance. This finding is equally true whichever telecommunications medium was used; the remote participant was voted down 7 times (chance expectation 8) in the audio condition and 6 times (chance 8) in the closed-circuit television condition.

The rating scales also failed to show any strong effects. Some of the scales distinguished between the remote and face-to-face participants to the $p < 0.10$ level, but none to a stronger level. Discussions with the subjects suggested that the experimental manipulation was working *too* well. The mixed motive nature of the task was clear, and the 'two against one' situation produced by the distribution of the participants between the rooms was obvious to all. One participant, isolated from the other two, remarked as soon as he could see them over the CCTV 'you are ganging up on me, aren't you?' Several others remarked afterwards that they had such feelings during the conversations. Such clear perception of the experimental manipulation can have various effects depending on the motivations of the participants: in this case, it seemed to produce compensation. Thus the isolated subject, fearing at once that he would be voted down, may have become more aggressive and active in order to forestall the danger. The two subjects in the other room, perceiving his plight, may have leaned over backwards to avoid voting him down: several participants mentioned explicitly after the experiment that that was the prime motivation for their voting.

These *post hoc* hypotheses, while speculative, did suggest that it might be premature to dismiss the possibility of effects of medium on coalition formation. A further experiment (Williams, 1975c) was designed, using four-man groups (to avoid the problem of the obviously isolated group member). Forty-five such groups of four office workers took part, 15 groups communicating face-to-face, 15 via closed-circuit television (two people at each node) and 15 via a loudspeaking audio system. The participants were asked to generate ideas about travelling in Britain with 'brainstorming' type instructions. Each idea, to be noted by the secretary of the group (one of the subjects), had to have a proposer and a seconder, and in addition anyone who wished could have their name noted as a dissenter. Apart from the difference in atmosphere, this modification allowed a series of votes, one for each idea generated, and thus resembled a more typical group meeting where multiple decisions are made.

Although there were no clear experimental hypotheses as to the effects of medium of communication on the generation of ideas, it was possible to check for such effects in this experiment (considering the findings of Dunnette, Campbell and Jaastad, 1963, that face-to-face groups produce on average less ideas than the same number of isolated individuals, positive results might be expected). However, medium of communication had no significant effect on the number, quality or originality of ideas generated.

The subgroup formation hypothesis, however, was confirmed. With two people at each telecommunications node (or on each side of the table in the face-to-face condition) one would expect the proposer and seconder to come from the same node (or side) only one time in three (there are six possible pairs from four individuals, only two pairs comprising individuals from the same node). The number of such occurrences, however, exceeded chance expectation as shown below in Table 8.3.

Table 8.3 Distribution of proposers and seconders of ideas for the three communications media

Medium	Proposer and seconder on same side	Proposer and seconder on opposite sides	Chi square	Significance
Face-to-face	92 (91)	181 (182)	0.01	Not sig.
Video	126 (107)	195 (214)	5.06	$p < 0.05$
Audio	119 (99⅓)	179 (198⅔)	5.86	$p < 0.02$

N.B. Chance expectation in brackets.

For both telecommunications conditions, subjects at the same node supported each other more than they supported either of the individuals at the other node. As mentioned previously, dissenters from ideas were also noted by the secretary; are the patterns of dissent similarly affected? Again we can compare the pattern of dissenters being on the opposite side from proposed and seconder, with chance expectation. The results of the comparison are shown in Table 8.4.

Again a significant effect appears, but in this case it is only the audio system that produces a pattern deviating markedly from chance; both video and face-to-face produce chance patterns of dissent.

The participants' evaluations were analysed as before (see Table 8.5). Strong media effects on interpersonal evaluation are found for

Table 8.4 Distribution of dissenters to ideas for the three communications media

Medium	Dissenter on opposite side to proposer and seconder	Dissenter on same side as proposer or seconder	Chi square	Significance
Face-to-face	28 (25)	47 (50)	0.54	Not sig.
Video	20 (18⅓)	35 (36⅔)	0.24	Not sig.
Audio	40 (24⅔)	34 (49⅓)	14.27	$p < 0.001$

N.B. Chance expectations in brackets.

Table 8.5 Mean factor scores of the three media conditions on each of the five factors

Factor	Video	Audio
Factor 1 'Activity' (talkative, not quiet, not withdrawn)	−0.008	0.157
Factor 2 'Intelligence' (not boring, intelligent, alert)	0.002	−0.318***
Factor 3 'Argumentative' (inflexible, argumentative, unreasonable)	0.136	0.251*
Factor 4 'Sincerity' (sincere, trustworthy, sensible)	−0.118	−0.337****
Factor 5 'Emotionality' (emotional, not impartial, personal)	0.062	0.054

N.B. Standard deviation about 1.0 in all cases. Positive scores indicate that the person at the same end of the communication medium (i.e. who was face-to-face) was rated higher on that factor.
* indicates p less than 0.10, ** indicates p less than 0.05, *** indicates p less than 0.02, **** indicates p less than 0.01.

the audio groups, effects in the video condition are weaker and non-significant.

This experiment thus demonstrates that in a group situation, even one which is not overtly competitive, there is the possibility of the individuals' patterns of assent and dissent, and thus, in many situations, the actual group decision, being affected by the medium of communications which they are using; the intervening variable in this relationship quite likely being the interpersonal attraction between the individuals. On the assumption that a decision that is more swayed by the medium used is correspondingly less swayed by the logic of the case or the validity of the ideas, this effect could be taken as detrimental to the quality of the group product.

OVERVIEW

It may seem somewhat premature to generalize on the basis of the experiments to hand. Some of the media effects have, at present, only been demonstrated in a single experiment. However, one can make some tentative conclusions:

(i) Medium of communication does affect evaluative ratings of the conversation and conversation partner, with marked differences between face-to-face and audio systems, but much less difference between face-to-face and video.

(ii) Despite commonsense hypotheses to the contrary, level of acquaintance has not been shown to be a modifier of this effect. This lack of relationship may be due to limitations in the extent to which acquaintance was manipulated; one could speculate that differences would be found when comparing pairs who had never had any visual contact with each other, with pairs who had had varying degrees of visual communication.

(iii) Task carried out during the interaction has been shown to be a modifier of the effect of medium on evaluation in one experiment, though this was not subsequently confirmed.

(iv) Telecommunications systems can, by separating the group into subgroups, affect the lines along which coalitions will form.

(v) Accuracy of perception of the other (either the perception of lying or of the other's personality) has not been shown to be affected by medium of communication. Judges' confidence in this accuracy may be affected, however.

No doubt further research may extend, modify or even overthrow these conclusions. Tentative though these conclusions are, these experiments as a group do suggest that this area of interpersonal relations is affected by the medium of communication used. This corresponds to the opinions of users: in the next chapter Figure 9.2 indicates that 'getting to know a stranger' is felt as the least appropriate activity for telecommunications of all those rated by the users.

9

The Decision to Telecommunicate

In the previous chapters we have been concerned with how well different communications media can handle the range of person-to-person interactions which we observe in the normal face-to-face mode. We have examined evidence taken largely from the laboratory, where the effects of media on task performance, satisfaction and perceptions of the other person, have been studied under controlled conditions. We have hypothesized that the effects we have observed can be related to a variable we call the Social Presence of the communications medium. All of this we did whilst considering a 'captive' subject. We have not so far considered the possibility of the people we are studying refusing to use the communications medium we have provided for the task, but insisting, instead, on doing the task face-to-face. In real life, of course, the individual has a choice. He can conduct his business face-to-face, by a telecommunication medium, by letter or not at all if he so chooses.

In the present chapter we shall consider some of the factors which influence the decision of which communications medium is selected. Some of the evidence will be experimental, some primarily anecdotal.

THE COFFEE AND BISCUITS PROBLEM

'Over the T.V. we felt the four of us were against him. For example, we had arranged for coffee or tea to be served at our end of this first or second meeting, and he didn't have any. We sat there drinking our coffee and passing the biscuits around and he looked increasingly glum.' (User of a two-way television system installed for the Civil Service.)

One of the problems associated with telecommunications is that there is a very obvious barrier between the two parties communicating, no matter how 'transparent' that barrier may be. It will never be possible, no matter how sophisticated the system, to offer the other chap a cup of tea or a biscuit. So a whole new etiquette has to be developed. Is it polite to drink coffee when the other person has none? Should the two parties make sure before they hold the meeting that they agree on whether they are going to have refreshments or not?

The coffee and biscuits problem is just one example of a more general problem of *formality*. The chats at the beginning and end of the meeting, the break for lunch and the drinks in the bar, are all lost. An attempt is made to overcome this problem to some extent in some systems, such as the Confravision system, by providing an anteroom where the conference participants can hold informal chats before and after the meeting. This is at best a partial solution, because the chats are very obviously restricted to the people within each party. In a face-to-face meeting, some of the most valuable chats are between people from different parties, perhaps meeting for the first time. It is in these chats that new contacts are made with long-term, and perhaps ill-defined, goals in mind. It is here that 'behind the scenes' bargaining takes place, coalitions are formed, and perhaps the outcome of the meeting determined before it has even begun.

It is not simply the presence of the barrier itself which makes a telecommunications system formal. The seating arrangements often contribute to this. This is especially true of television systems, where, in order to be 'on camera', the individuals at each end must sit close to one another, often in a straight line. Users of such systems sometimes complain they feel like they are being 'lined up in the dock'. Apart from this effect on the individual, such a situation is potentially divisive. As one user commented, 'I don't think you want to have them all sitting lined up like a row of monkeys, side by side. It's not really the way to do business. Let's have a round table and make it clear that we're all in this together rather than on opposite sides.' Such comments reflect the importance of the seating arrangement in teleconferencing. It is often overlooked or else overrriden by the technical difficulties associated with having the individual participants arranged in any configuration other than a straight, or at best curved, line. Yet, it is not surprising that it is considered important by users, in view of the research by Sommer (1965) and others on seating arrangements preferred for different types of interactions. Sommer was able to demonstrate that the seating arrangement chosen by the individuals interacting in his experiments reflected the purpose of their interactions (e.g. conversation, cooperation, competition). It is not surprising, therefore, that users of teleconference systems often express concern about the impression given by the typical arrangement in which each party is lined up facing the other party. In Sommer's (1965) experiment, this arrangement was often chosen by dyads in which the two individuals were competing with each other, and never by dyads in which the individuals were cooperating. This could be an important factor contributing to the 'divisive' nature of telecommunications. That such effects can actually occur is demonstrated by the experiment on coalition formation described in Chapter 8.

In the Remote Meeting Table audio conference system, the six individuals at each location sit around a circular table. On the table, between the seating positions, are six loudspeakers representing the six people in the remote studio. This arrangement gives the impression that the members of the two parties are seated in alternation around the table.

The greater formality of the telecommunications meeting need not be construed as entirely a disadvantage. One executive of a large American bank, after using a stereophonic audio conference system for the first time, commented that, 'It would normally have taken us an hour to get through what we did in half an hour today without all the irrelevant chat that usually gets in the way of the real business'. This shortening effect has been demonstrated in an experiment by Craig and Jull (1974) in which two groups of managers had alternate meetings face-to-face and via an audio teleconference system. In both groups, the face-to-face meetings were about 40% longer than the teleconference meetings. Although the reduction in chat-time is a favoured explanation, an alternative is that since these were a series of meetings, business for which a telecommunications system was felt to be inappropriate was being held over to the next face-to-face meeting. Another aspect of this concentration upon work matters to the exclusion of social matters in teleconferences is that they are found more tiring. One user of the Bell Canada Conference television system said, 'I, for one, would not like to be involved with the thing for an entire day. The longest is an entire morning, three and a half hours .... it is a little easier face-to-face.' Of 190 users of that system, most disagreed with the statement 'One has to concentrate less than in a face-to-face meeting', but agreed with 'Using the system tends to make meetings shorter.'

Although it has been shown in the previous chapters that telecommunication can be useful in performing many work tasks, the omission of social chat may have deleterious consequences. There is a tradition of 'putting in an appearance' every so often just to remind people that one is still alive and functioning and, perhaps more important, monitoring what is being done. Thus, the busy executive who spends an hour travelling to a branch office for a committee meeting each week may feel it advantageous to spend a little time when he gets there just looking in various offices, 'passing the time of day', chatting a while, gently reminding his subordinates without mentioning it explicitly that he is keeping an eye on them. The formality of the telecommunications meeting, which *may* improve the efficiency of the meeting itself by cutting out the irrelevant chat, may also be a hindrance if it also cuts out the informal, chance meetings which precede and follow the major event. This would depend upon the extent to which face-to-face interaction is replaced by telecommunications. If the replacement is only partial, the residual face-to-face contacts may leave enough room for the important social contacts which contribute to efficient management.

This may seem far away from the 'coffee and biscuits problem' with which we began, but all the things we have discussed have an element in common: they reflect the fact that, no matter how elegant the telecommunications system is, the two parties are still in different places and this precludes certain types of activities. An important question which the telecommunications user must come to grips with is how to reorganize his activities so that all his business is completed via the various media with adequate efficiency. One can speculate that there is, for any person or job, an ideal 'communications diet', comprising various proportions of written, face-to-face and tele-communication. An increase in one component may result in all sorts of adjustments, in the amounts of the other components and in the mix and sequencing of the three. It is very difficult to examine this effect in the laboratory because one cannot readily simulate the total context in which meetings normally occur. Part of that context is the social chat between well-acquainted colleagues.

THE TRAVEL PROBLEM

Travel is always a problem, which telecommunications can help to solve. However, the travel time saved by telecommunicating is not always saved equally by both parties. In a face-to-face meeting there is always the question of who is inconvenienced by having to travel. Sometimes the question is resolved by both parties travelling to meet, in which case a congenial location such as a restaurant is often chosen. In the case of very large conferences it is not uncommon for the company to pay the expenses of its employees to travel and stay at a hotel to be wined and dined and generally to mix business with pleasure. In the case of a teleconference between two small groups of individuals, it is often the case that both parties must travel to a studio. There are exceptions to this, namely when the conference system is relatively simple and the terminal (e.g. speakerphone or video telephone) is in the user's own office. But in cases where each party must travel to a studio, the distance may not be negligible. For example, businessmen using a centralized conference facility system may have to spend half-an-hour travelling across town to get to the studio. In this type of situation, several interesting factors of a social psychological nature influence whether the meeting is actually held by telecommunications or by the traditional face-to-face mode.

One of the major factors is the status position of the two parties. As one user of a television conference system remarked, 'And so often, you see, our need to speak to people there, is with people who are somewhat more senior than ourselves. It's not very easy to ask the Minister to come down and talk in the television room, or his Parliamentary Secretary, or even Deputy Secretary.' This user is saying, in effect, that we also need to consider a rule of etiquette: that the less senior individuals should be prepared to put themselves out for their more senior counterparts. (This is often the more economic arrangement when travelling is involved because the time lost travelling is worth more for the more senior people.) A similar relationship occurs when people from different organizations meet. Usually one party feels that they are gaining more by the relationship, either because they are gaining free advice, or because they are being paid generously. In such a case it is normal for the party who is gaining more to repay this by travelling to the meeting. It is thus difficult for them to ask another favour of the other party: 'Will *you* travel to the studio in order to save *me* travelling effort?' Such a request will often seem unreasonable unless the saving of travel time to the face-to-face meeting is enormous compared to the travel to the teleconference studio.

Another factor is the number of people who would travel. It is normal etiquette for the smaller party to travel to the larger. Of course, this sometimes conflicts with the status obligation rules. There must be a balance point at which these two rules cancel each other out. We have certainly discovered cases in which a single, relatively high-status, individual has telecommunicated on a regular basis with a group of four or five lower-status people. In this type of situation, the 'size' rule says the single individual should travel to meet the other four or five individuals. The 'status' rule says the group of four or five should travel. The result sometimes seems to be that neither side travels but the meeting is held instead by telecommunications.

The situation in which a group of several low-status individuals telecommunicates with a single high-status individual is usually quite complicated. Not only do we need to consider the rules of etiquette governing who should travel, we also need to take into account a feeling expressed by one user in this way, 'In this slightly artificial situation of one chap there and half a dozen chaps here it tended to be a bit like an interview sort of arrangement, whereas, if he'd come over here, we wouldn't have got the same impression that it was us and him; it would just have been a sort of cosy chat.' In cases in which the lone person is the most senior member of the group, it must be very disconcerting to find himself 'being interviewed' by his subordinates.

A further factor we need to be aware of is again related to status. It is the distinction between the person who calls the meeting and those who respond by attending. Although, in theory, each individual who is asked to attend could express a wish that the meeting be held by telecommunications, it rarely works out this way in practice. As one user explained, 'They usually arrange the meeting, ask somebody from here to go, and we've got to make the best way we can; and if we can't do it then they carry on without us.' In such situations, the individual has little choice. He feels that any request to hold the meeting by telecommunications could be construed as a reluctance to put himself out for his superiors and would reflect badly on himself.

THE IMPORTANCE OF ACQUAINTANCE

'I would not be happy conducting my affairs on the telephone if I didn't know who the other man was and something about him. I think this is a very real danger of not merely the Civil Service but office life generally. People—it amazes me—get on to Christian name terms with people they've never set eyes on. And it happens an awful lot, you know. I don't want to sound pious, but I just don't like that way of conducting business; I like to know who the other man is. So I try not to conduct business by 'phone until I've seen the other man and made my number with him.' (Civil servant, interviewed by Christie, 1973b.)

In this context we really need to distinguish between two Acquaintance Hypotheses as follows. The first states that the choice of the communications medium selected for any given meeting is influenced by the degree to which the individuals who intend to interact are familiar with one another. The second states that the effects of the communications medium upon task performance are modified by the degree to which the individuals interacting are familiar with one another.

The first hypothesis, relating to the choice of communications medium, is supported by a great deal of anecdotal evidence and by a questionnaire study conducted for the American New Rural Society Project (Christie, 1973a). In this study, twenty business executives selected to be representative of the middle and upper management levels of several different American businesses were given a demonstration of audio-only conferencing, and were then asked to say under what circumstances they felt it *essential* to be able to see the people one is talking to. They were given the following examples and asked to check as many as they felt applied:

(A) routine conferences with people you meet regularly;
(B) non-routine conferences with people you know well;
(C) conferences where you will meet new people with whom you will need to confer frequently; and
(D) conferences where there will be people you have not met before but who will be there for some reason unconnected with your own work.

146

Only one person checked (A), one checked (B), seventeen checked (C) and fifteen checked (D). The binomial test shows that each of the observed numbers differs significantly from the chance expectation of ten ($p < 0.05$ in all cases) indicating significant agreement between the respondents. It is concluded that the group as a whole considered a visual channel to be essential only for cases in which the conferees have not met previously.

INSTRUCTIONS

Please consider the following hypothetical situation.

READ *ALL* THE POINTS CAREFULLY and be sure you understand each of them before answering the questions in the accompanying booklet.

1. Your office is at X.

2. You and two of your colleagues have a meeting scheduled with three people at Y.

3. This will be the first time the three of you will have met the other people.

4. The meeting you have scheduled is an important one. It will involve you and your two colleagues negotiating with the three people at Y. There will need to be a considerable amount of bargaining, persuasion and compromise if a satisfactory outcome is to be achieved. It is likely that personal conflicts will become apparent during the meeting and these will need to be resolved if the meeting is to be a success.

5. It would be agreeable to everyone involved in the meeting if it were held by telecommunications rather than by you and your colleagues travelling to Y. However, the decision is left for you, yourself, to make.

6. If you were to choose to hold the meeting by telecommunications, neither your party nor the other party would be involved in any travel at all because it happens that each party (at X and Y) is normally located right next door to a telecommunications studio forming part of a national network.

7. If you were to choose not to hold the meeting by telecommunications, you and your two colleagues would have to do some travelling. However, you could schedule the meeting for a time of day which would allow it to be held without the necessity for spending a night away from home. The time taken up in travelling (door to door) would be four hours *in each direction.*

8. The telecommunication system available is exactly like the audio-video conference system you have just used.

PLEASE RE-READ THE ITEMS ABOVE CAREFULLY BEFORE YOU ANSWER THE QUESTIONS IN THE ACCOMPANYING BOOKLET.

Figure 9.1 Example of the hypothetical meetings described to subjects in the study by Christie and Holloway (see text)

A more detailed experiment testing this same hypothesis was carried out by Christie and Holloway (1975). One hundred and four individuals from the management levels of business and government participated in the study. Each subject took part in a five- or six-person simulated business meeting using one of five teleconference systems.

These systems included three being developed by a consortium of the Scandinavian telecommunications authorities (one having manual switching, one having voice switching and one having headphones), a microphone and speaker system without any form of switching and a closed-circuit television system. After the half-hour meeting each subject filled in a questionnaire, which posed the hypothetical meeting shown in Figure 9.1. There were in fact 16 versions of this hypothetical meeting, varying the acquaintance specified (in the alternative version, paragraph 3 read 'The six of you have held several meetings during the last year and you feel you know each other very well'), the nature of the meeting task (in the alternative version, paragraph 4, sentences 2 and 3 read 'It will involve you and your two colleagues exchanging information with the three people at Y. There will need to be a considerable amount of asking and answering questions if a satisfactory outcome is to be achieved.') and the length of travelling time specified (in three alternative versions, paragraph 7 had half-an-hour, one hour or two hours instead of four hours). After each subject had read his particular version, he made his choice of whether he would travel or use the teleconference system that he had just experienced. Analysis of these choices showed the effects of:

the meeting task ('negotiation' gives more travel choices, $p < 0.0005$); the level of acquaintance ('strangers' gives more travel choices, $p < 0.025$); the travel time (shorter time gives more travel choices, $p < 0.05$).

However, which medium of telecommunication had been experienced had no effect upon the travel/telecommunicate choices.

It seems, then, that the first hypothesis delineated earlier, that the choice between face-to-face and some kind of telecommunications system is affected by the degree of acquaintance of the participants, is largely true. Can the same be said of the second hypothesis, that the effects of the communications medium upon task performance are modified to the degree of acquaintance of the participants.

Two experiments by Williams (1972, 1973) tested the hypothesis that degree of acquaintance can affect the impact of the medium on the outcome of the meeting. In neither case did degree of acquaintance influence the relationship between medium of communication and evaluative judgements of the other. The absence of laboratory evidence is in striking contrast with the confidence many users evidently have in their implicit hypothesis. It may be that level of acquaintance impacts on aspects of real-life tasks which cannot be adequately captured in the laboratory.

(a) Given that level of acquaintance is, in practice an important variable, what is the function relating the level of acquaintance to the acquaintance effect? That is, does the modifying effect of acquaintance become continuously greater as acquaintance varies or is there a 'quantal leap' between 'not acquainted at all' and 'acquainted to any degree'. If the function is continuous, what are the values of its parameters?

(b) Is it the number of meetings which is important or the total amount of time spent meeting? That is, does a three-hour meeting result in the same increment in acquaintance level as three one-hour meetings?

(c) To what extent is the degree of acquaintance resulting from any given meeting dependent upon the nature of the meeting? For example, is a two-hour cocktail party worth more or less than a two-hour business meeting?

(d) To what extent is the degree of acquaintance resulting from any given meeting dependent upon the communications medium used for the meeting? For example, is a three-hour audio-only meeting 'worth as much' as a three-hour face-to-face meeting?

One interesting anecdote, which suggests the answer to this last question was noted in a study conducted by Christie (1973c). As part of this study, a group of state planners at Hartford, Connecticut, held a meeting with a group of regional planners in Willimantic, a town some thirty miles distant. Only one of the five regional planners had met any of the state planners before. The two groups had been told that for the purposes of the experiment they would use a television link for the first half of their hour-long meeting, and an audio-only system for the second half of the meeting. However, upon arriving at the studios, they were informed that circumstances dictated that this procedure should be reversed, i.e. the first half of the meeting would be held in the audio mode, and the second half of the meeting in the television mode. This was greeted with dismay by the participants. One commented, 'That's going to make it very difficult'. This dismay was not related to any difficulties in showing diagrams, for the conferees could do this throughout their meeting. It appeared to be due to the feeling that it was important to be able to see the people in the other studio. Nevertheless, the meeting apparently progressed satisfactorily. At the half-way point, when the television was switched on, a very surprising and somewhat amusing thing happened. The person speaking stopped in mid-sentence, and everyone introduced himself to the others just as if they had never met before, though, in fact, they had been conducting business together for a full half-hour.

THE IMPORTANCE OF MEETING TASK

The experiment by Christie and Holloway (1975) mentioned earlier showed that the meeting task described (either negotiation or

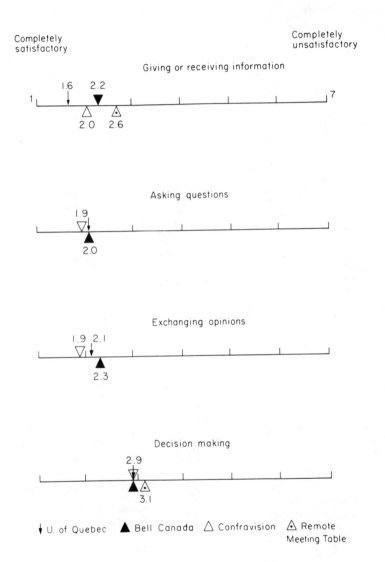

Figure 9.2 Responses of users of four teleconference systems (Confravision, the Remote Meeting Table, the Bell Canada Conference Television system and the University of Quebec audio conference system) to the question: 'How satisfactory do you think you would find the teleconference for the following activities?'

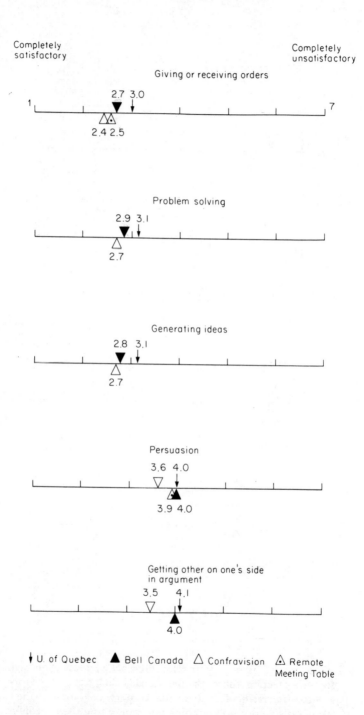

Completely
satisfactory

Completely
unsatisfactory

Giving or receiving orders

2.7 3.0

1

7

2.4 2.5

Problem solving

2.9 3.1

2.7

Generating ideas

2.8 3.1

2.7

Persuasion

3.6 4.0

3.9 4.0

Getting other on one's side
in argument

3.5 4.1

4.0

↓ U. of Quebec   ▲ Bell Canada   △ Confravision   ⚠ Remote
Meeting Table

Completely
satisfactory

Completely
unsatisfactory

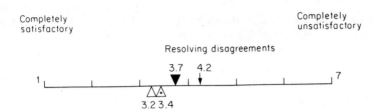

Resolving disagreements

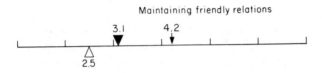

Maintaining friendly relations

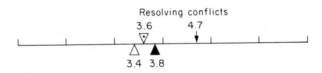

Resolving conflicts

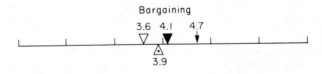

Bargaining

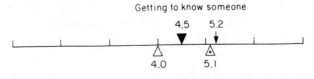

Getting to know someone

information exchange) had a marked effect upon the decision to telecommunicate or travel. Compared to the effect of meeting task, the influence of the nature of the telecommunications medium offered, even if they were as different as closed-circuit television and manually switched audio, was of negligible importance.

This finding has now been confirmed in the less carefully controlled, but more realistic environment of field studies. 193 users of Confravision (an inter-city closed-circuit television system run by the United Kingdom Post Office), 190 users of the Bell Canada Conference Television system (a similar system in eastern Canada), 140 users of the Remote Meeting Table (an audio-only system with speaker identification in use in the British Civil Service) and 186 users of the University of Quebec audio conference system (which connects up to 7 loudspeaking telephones together) were all asked the same question—'How satisfactory do you think you would find the teleconference system (that you have just used) for the various activities listed below?'. The replies for those scales which were used in all three surveys are shown in Figure 9.2 from Thomas and Williams (1975). This confirms that the task involved makes a very large difference. The two extremes, 'giving and receiving information' at the satisfactory end and 'getting to know someone' are rated as 2.0 to 2.5 scale points different on the three systems: a vastly significant (in the statistical sense) difference with these numbers. Clearly meeting task does affect how satisfactory teleconferencing is felt to be. On the other hand, the system used seems to make relatively little difference. Admittedly, this is not a true experimental comparison, since the users of the systems differ in nationality, occupation and many other characteristics as well as the system they are using. Nevertheless, the small size of the differences between the systems again suggests that the nature of the telecommunications system used is relatively trivial compared with the task variable.

One possible criticism of the data presented in Figure 9.2 is that the question related to the satisfactoriness of the communications system, rather than the actual decision to telecommunicate or travel. However, Champness (1973) in his study of the Confravision system asked questions on both the satisfactoriness of the teleconference system and the decision to travel or telecommunicate for the same list of meeting tasks. A very high correlation between the resultant ordering of tasks on the two types of question was noted.

AUDIO-ORIENTED VERSUS VISUAL-ORIENTED GROUPS

The effectiveness of a teleconference as compared with a face-to-face meeting seems to depend upon how 'visual' the meeting is. In general, the more emphasis there is on the visual channel, the less successful the meeting. This applies even when a television conference system is used. Consider the following comments made by a member of a group of civil servants who tried to use a television system to discuss plans for the new highways in London: 'Now, we tried showing maps on the television and, unfortunately, of course, unless the print you are using is something like half an inch in height, it doesn't come over no matter how much you use the zoom lens. The other drawback was, and don't think for one moment that I'm advocating colour television, but if you are using a map or plan, something of that nature, normally colour has a very real significance. And colour doesn't come through on a black and white definition television, so when you hold up some sort of plan or map to show the man at the other end, apart from the size problem, he's not getting it in colour and, therefore, really, the thing was, from that angle, hopeless.'

For such a complex visually oriented meeting, face-to-face is clearly necessary, rather than any of the existing teleconference systems. On the other hand, some meetings are so audio-oriented and straightforward that an audio system is all that is necessary.

It would seem that the type of meeting which requires and can be handled by a television conference system is one in which vision is important but is not the primary communication. A good example of such a meeting was provided by the Connecticut Department of Motor Vehicles in the New Rural Society study. The Department used the Hartford–Willimantic link for an hour-long meeting between the head office in Hartford and a unit in Willimantic. A dozen different topics were discussed successfully during the meeting. Simple visual displays, e.g. a new style of number plate, were used at various times to help make a point, but at no time were the displays essential to the progress of the meeting. Some small forms which were too detailed to be shown on the television system were sent by facsimile during the course of the meeting. The delay which this involved was not crucial because it was not essential that everyone see the forms immediately. It was helpful to see them, but the fact that some participants saw them only after they had been described and commented upon was not disturbing.

Although we are suggesting that a visual telecommunications link may not be necessary for certain types of meetings (specifically, non-person oriented, audio-oriented meetings), there is reason to suspect that people will still prefer to have a visual link under many circumstances. In the Hartford–Willimantic experiment, all the participants had a chance to experience two types of systems. One was a two-way television system. Another was a sophisticated two-way audio-only system. In both systems the participants could show each other graphics, but they could see each other only in the two-way television system. Only five percent of the participants said they would not be interested in having free access to the television system, whereas forty percent said they would not be interested in having free access to the audio-only system. Participants commented that, 'Lack of visual contact detracted from effectiveness of program', and 'I find it difficult to talk to a speaker—much prefer to look at someone'.

Perhaps our most cautious conclusion should be that for meetings which are extremely person-oriented or where documents are important, a visual channel is probably necessary, and for other types of meetings it is desirable if cost is not an important consideration.

ACCESSIBILITY AND OTHER FACTORS

The factors we have discussed do not form a comprehensive list of those which affect the decision to telecommunicate.

Security, for example, can be a problem for certain groups of people who need to be cautious about guarding against the possibility of information falling into the wrong hands. As one civil servant remarked, 'I remember being stopped on one occasion at least because I was reminded that the link was not secure.'

Champness (1972a) first drew attention to this factor when he had users rate telecommunications systems on various semantic differential scales. Although this study was conducted in the laboratory, so that all users knew that the experimenters were listening and tape-recording the conversation, ratings on the public–private scale were significantly different according to medium of communication. The closed-circuit television conversations were rated as less private then either the audio or face-to-face conversations. Another study (Champness, 1972c) used three-person groups rating media on similar semantic differentials. A privacy factor, including 'private–public', 'secure–insecure', and 'safe–unsafe' was discovered, and both audio-only and video media were rated as significantly less private than face-to-face (although all were under laboratory conditions).

The privacy factor has been found to be of importance in field studies of attitudes. In two studies of video systems, the Confravision study (Champness, 1973) and the Bell Canada Conference Television study (Williams and Holloway, 1974) users were asked to agree or disagree with statements such as:

'The system enables one to feel that the meeting is being held in private'.
'I would tend to avoid using it if I were going to discuss anything which I didn't want to end up in the wrong hands'.

The two teleconference systems gave somewhat different ratings, with the Bell Canada system being rated as less private. Williams and Holloway (1974) speculated that:-

'. . . it seems at least possible that this difference is due to the greater stress that the Confravision promotional literature places upon privacy, or the obtrusiveness of the technician's monitoring space in some of the Canadian studios. . . . Where the conference room is accessible to 'strangers' or technicians, apprehension about the privacy of meetings will probably increase. The actual location for the teleconference room within a building might thus affect attitudes towards the security of the system, and greater reassurance for users of the confidentiality of their meetings might boost confidence in the system.'

A second factor is ease of accessibility. One of the great advantages of teleconferencing over face-to-face communication is its convenience. Yet this can easily be destroyed by making it difficult for the user to gain access to the communication system. The point is obvious. Yet so often in real world applications equipment is kept locked up 'for security' or installed in some out of the way place because all the more convenient locations are being used for other purposes. Champness (1972a) noted this for facsimile machines with a Civil Service department. Usage seemed to be considerably discouraged by instructions from central office that the machine '. . . should be located in a locked room . . . strict control of keys . . . no operation without prior permission from Departmental Head or Security Officer . . . immobilised during the silent hours . . . by placing (the machine) in a security container'. One can only wonder what the usage of ordinary telephones would be if they were subjected to similar security requirements!

Not only security arrangements but also sheer distance can be a disincentive to use of a telecommunications system. To quote from the Champness (1972a) study again:

'He (a civil servant) had used the instrument (a loudspeaking telephone) on his desk, until someone "realised that it should have gone into a conference room". He was very strongly in favour of the machine, having used it in its "executive" capacity with great success, often with two or three assistants his end. After it was removed, and put into an empty office *next to his*, with an intervening door to his office, he hardly used it at all.'

Studies of face-to-face communication in large organizations have shown distance to be a very important factor. Allen and Fusfeld (1974), analysing the rate of face-to-face contact between research staff in a large research laboratory found that the rate of contact between those who had no formal links in the organizational hierarchy, fell off exponentially with distance, being four times higher at 2 metres than at 20 metres. If office workers are so reluctant to travel a few yards to talk to someone face-to-face, it is hardly surprising that they will be very reluctant to travel similar or greater distances to use a telecommunications system. Some systems, such as the audio teleconferencing system in the University of Quebec take account of this fact, and have a studio on every floor of the building. It is not merely fortuitous that this system is one of the most popular and well used systems there is. On the other hand, some systems have been designed with only one studio *per city*. The designers of such systems must not be too surprised if they fail to attract many users from distant parts of the city.

A lesson which must be learned by all who hope to improve an organization's communications by using telecommunications systems of any kind is that these systems must be made easily accessible by users if they are to yield the benefit hoped for.

The factors we have chosen to discuss seem to us, in the present state of our ignorance, to be the most interesting ones, but future research may show otherwise. We believe that testable hypotheses can be drawn from what we have said and that those hypotheses which are supported by research will form an important part of the social psychology of telecommunications.

10

Conclusions and Implications

SENSITIVITY TO MEDIUM OF COMMUNICATION

From the preceding chapters, it is apparent that the outcome of meetings can be significantly affected by the medium of communications used: face-to-face meetings show several significant differences from meetings held over telecommunications systems, and in some cases the type of telecommunications system, whether it is audio only or full audio-video, can have a significant effect upon the meeting. Some tasks are more sensitive than others: in particular those meetings involving conflict between the participants (e.g. attitude change or negotiation situations) or involving the formation of impressions of strangers or slight acquaintances.

Considering the wealth of previous studies demonstrating the importance of non-verbal communication (many of which are discussed in Chapter 4), one could be surprised that more media effects have not been identified. Eye-contact, for example, is considered to be important in communicating friendship, attraction, aggression and attentiveness. With such a wide range of functions, all of which have been demonstrated in experiments dealing with the face-to-face situation, one would expect that media which remove or disrupt eye-contact would seriously affect the progress and the outcome of the interaction. Audio-only media eliminate a number of other cues besides eye-contact: facial expression, gesture, posture, proximity and physical appearance. Audio-video media include some of these channels, but seriously distort the transmission of both eye-contact and proximity. Yet in many situations, such as problem-solving interactions, the omission of this multitude of non-verbal cues seems to have little effect upon the outcome of the task. Does this mean that the significance of non-verbal communication has been exaggerated?

We would suggest that non-verbal communication only has effects on the outcomes of mediated interactions to the extent that it determines feelings of Social Presence. Social Presence is a phenomenological variable more complex than the relatively simple variations in, say, amount of gaze. It is affected not simply by the transmission of single non-verbal cues, but by whole constellations of cues which affect the 'apparent distance' of the other. In turn, it is more useful than any simple knowledge of the functions of non-verbal cues in predicting which tasks would be affected by medium of communication, and which would be unaffected.

The importance of personal relationships in the various tasks could be used to explain, and even to predict, the occurrence of effects of communications media on the outcome of tasks. For example, it is generally agreed that information transmission and cooperative problem solving are activities in which interpersonal relationships are relatively unimportant; they are activities for which man–computer interaction is quite feasible. Since personal relationships are unimportant, it matters little whether interactors treat the other as a person or as an impersonal information source, and the Social Presence provided by the medium is not likely to influence the outcome of the task. It thus seems relatively unsurprising that no effects of medium of communication on the outcome of problem solving or information transmission were found (see Chapter 6). On the other hand, nearly everyone would agree that bargaining, persuasion, coalition formation and getting to know a stranger are activities which could only really be carried out with another person; it seems ludicrous to even conceive of trying to persuade a computer that its opinions are wrong. Similarly, one would not form coalitions with machines, or try to get to know them on a personal basis. It is thus critically important for the outcome of such tasks that the other person is treated as a person, rather than as an impersonal object; and the Social Presence afforded by the medium will, by affecting the extent to which the other is treated as a person, influence the outcome of the task.

The one correlation between a personality measure and media differences which was discovered, the correlation between person-orientation and liking for the visual medium, and the person met via that medium, can also be fitted into the same model. Although weak, this correlation seemed to show that people who were clearly oriented towards other people rather than towards things, were more favourable to the medium with higher Social Presence and thus towards the people met via such a medium, who, according to the theory developed in Chapter 5, must seem more like people rather than inanimate bodies.

In the light of this approach it would seem to be worthwhile to reassess the value of the various media. The original proponents of the use of visual media were of the opinion that the transmission of facial expressions and gestures via the television picture would make a closed-circuit television interaction very similar to a face-to-face one. Certainly, an approach based merely upon the non-verbal cues transmitted would suggest that there is a greater similarity between closed-circuit television and face-to-face, than between closed-circuit television and an audio-only connection. However, even a full-colour life-size three-dimensional motion-picture transmission of the complete body of the distant person by some futuristic television system, although a complete replication of the face-to-face situation in its reproduction of non-verbal and verbal cues, would not, according to the Social Presence approach, be exactly the same as face-to-face contact as long as the interactors were aware that they were separated. The knowledge of physical separation might suffice to make the telecommunicated interaction more like other telecommunicated interactions, rather than like face-to-face. Certainly, a consideration of the results in Chapters 7 and 8 suggests that it is as frequent for the two telecommunications media, audio-only and video, to be alike and different from face-to-face in terms of behavioural effects, as for the two visual media to be alike and different from the audio-only medium.

DIFFERENCES BETWEEN ONE-WAY MEDIA AND TWO-WAY MEDIA: METHODOLOGICAL IMPLICATIONS

The distinction between one-way media such as radio or television and two-way media such as the telephone or interactive closed-circuit television has often been insufficiently considered. At the most basic level, that of the design of equipment and studios, the critical experiments to determine the ideal picture size or quality have often been conducted in non-interactive situations where judges have merely looked at a still photograph or a self-view instead of interacting over the system (e.g. Duncanson and Williams, 1973, Snyder, 1974). The same dangerous simplification has been evident right through to experiments on bargaining (where subjects play against controlled strategies) or problem solving (where one subject is designated as the 'information source').

Most previous research comparing communications media has sprung from a primary interest in mass media and this has reinforced the tendency to study one-way media for reasons of simplicity and control. The most substantial single body of research on the comparative effectiveness of different media has been conducted in the educational context (see for example Allen, 1971, Chu and Schramm, 1967). Differences between face-to-face communication and the other media have generally been found to be small; a result which is not unexpected owing to the fact that the face-to-face communication has often been for essentially non-interactive tasks.

Despite the seeming similarity of the media comparisons (audio versus video versus face-to-face) the findings from non-interactive situations cannot be extrapolated to the kind of interactive situations with which we have been concerned. Middlebrook (1974), for example, in discussing the effect of channel of communication upon opinion change states that 'in general face-to-face communication is the most persuasive' (p.166). This conclusion, based on evidence from one-way communication situations, is clearly at variance with the experimental results obtained in experiments using two-way situations (see Chapter 7). The opportunity to reply to the distant person and the awareness that the other person will respond are probably of greater importance than the difference between visual and non-visual media. It is these 'interactive' aspects that must be captured in any adequate theories of social interaction. It is here that we feel that the concept of Social Presence may prove useful.

Medium of communication is a fundamental variable whose manipulation can be a powerful research tool shedding light on many aspects of interpersonal communication. But, however much such experiments add to the body of empirical knowledge, or even to psychological theory, the work is only significant in so far as it has a bearing on the solution of real world problems. We shall therefore return now to some of the major issues identified in Chapter 3.

Many of the problems are so wide that even a large programme of experiments, field trials and surveys can never hope to resolve all the issues. On some points we are in a position to be reasonably confident in our conclusions, and although extrapolation therefrom may lack scientific rigour, we trust that it may nonetheless represent a significant contribution to informed debate on the role of telecommunications in tomorrow's world.

SUBSTITUTION POTENTIAL AMONGST BUSINESS MEETINGS

For a variety of economic and social reasons there has recently been a growing interest in the possibility of the decentralization of offices from the larger conurbations (see Goldmark, 1972a, Hardman, 1973). Perhaps the major obstacle to the achievement of this goal arises from doubts about the possible inefficiency due to the greater difficulty of having face-to-face communication. It was this basic query that motivated much of the work discussed in the preceding chapters: to what extent can a meeting over a telephone link substitute for a face-to-face meeting?

As one might expect, the answer depends on the type of task. There are many tasks whose outcomes are not affected by variation in the medium of communication and which are therefore quite transferable to even such a simple system as the telephone. There are, however, significant groups of tasks (those necessitating interaction and in which the personal relationships of the participants are a major determinant of the outcome) where the outcome is different when different media are used.

This in itself does not mean that the task can not be done over a telecommunications link: one can not ignore the possibility that the telecommunications option might actually be more effective than face-to-face conversation—that is to say that the outcome after a telephone conversation might be more satisfactory than after a face-to-face conversation (see Chapter 7). The use of the word effectiveness, however, can represent a misleading oversimplification, as we mentioned in Chapter 5.

Where the meeting has a single purpose which is either fulfilled or not (e.g. information exchange) there is no problem, but typically there may be more than one goal, and the goals may be incompatible. The simplest example of this is in the fact that individuals probably have different private goals (getting to know one another, making a good showing in front of the boss, getting the issue settled quickly) which may be irrelevant to, or even incompatible with, the fulfilment of the group goal (deciding on the best site for a new chemical plant). Individual interests too can conflict: in a negotiation situation, for example, a good result for one side is likely to be at the expense of the other. How can one say which medium is best in these situations? It depends entirely on one's viewpoint.

In practice, these tasks whose outcomes are affected by which medium of communication is used, are the very tasks for which the users perceive media other than face-to-face as less satisfactory (See Chapter 9). Thus, despite the fact that a telecommunications meeting might objectively be more effective, the users are likely simply to follow the tradition of centuries and meet face-to-face. Despite uncertainty about the normative position, one can predict with reasonable confidence that substitution of teleconference meetings for face-to-face meetings will only occur for those activities which are not affected by the medium.

We have now arrived at the point where the various streams of research can be combined to give us an initial estimate of the extent to which business meetings at present taking place face-to-face could be transferred to telecommunications media. Before so doing, however, we must briefly re-emphasize the various limitations and reservations which must be applied to the type and mode allocation process, which were discussed more fully in Chapter 3:

(a) The allocation process can only deal with existing meetings (i.e. substitution demand), whereas, for all we know, generated demand may be many times greater.
(b) The nature of the meetings is assumed to be constant, even under the impact of new media.
(c) The people responsible for the decision to use telecommunications are assumed to be 'rational economic men' in that they will use the cheapest medium which is as effective as face-to-face.
(d) The meeting task is assumed to be the major factor affecting the relative effectiveness of the telecommunicated meeting as compared to a comparable face-to-face meeting.

Given these caveats, we can make our allocation decisions. This is a subjective activity. Although certain of the types of meeting identified by DACOM appeared to correspond well with distinctions commonly used in social psychology, many of them either bore no such relationship or appeared to be a mixture of processes. In some cases, therefore, the results of the laboratory work are difficult to apply, at least until the tasks used in the laboratory correspond more closely to the task types actually observed in the field.

Nonetheless, in some cases the results were clear and by making conservative assumptions for the other types, one can come out with a sort of 'best guess' as to which types of meeting could or could not be transferred to telecommunications. Williams (1974) applied this process to come out with his 'best guess' which was as in Table 10.1.

Table 10.1 Type allocation indications for individual scales: an interim answer

	Fairly definitely	Tentatively
Allocated to face-to-face	Inspection of fixed objects	Conflict Negotiation Disciplinary interview (Presentation of report)
Allocated to video	Forming impressions of others	Giving information to keep people in the picture
Allocated to audio	Problem solving Information seeking Policy decision making	(Delegation of work) Discussion of ideas

N.B. 'presentation of report' and 'delegation of work' have been put in brackets to indicate that the degree of tentativeness of the allocations in these cases are such as to make the allocations virtual guesswork. It might be fairer to split such groups between media (one third of such meetings to each medium), or to come to a decision according to the other scales that these two cluster with in any particular analysis.

Clearly many of these allocations could be argued over. However such argument is probably fruitless until more experimental results can be aduced in favour of or against present allocations.

The next stage is to weight these allocations according to the frequency of the types of meetings found by Connell (1974) (see Chapter 3). Most of the clusters identified by Connell contain mixtures of the basic functions and activities allocated to media in Table 10.1 above. In allocating his clusters, it is best to take a conservative view, and allocate a cluster to the most 'communications rich' alternative suggested by any of the constituent scales, with the sole limitation that two or more 'definite' allocations can outweigh one tentative one (because one might wish to reinterpret the tentatively allocated scale in view of what it is clustering with). Using this admittedly arbitrary technique on that data, we get the results shown in Table 10.2.

163

Table 10.2 Type allocations for Connell's (1974) meeting clusters

Allocated to face-to-face	Cluster B	10.1%
	Cluster F	4.6%
	Cluster G	6.3%
	Total	21.0% of meetings
Allocated to video	Cluster C	9.1%
	Cluster D	8.7%
	Cluster I	8.3%
	Total	26.1% of meetings
Allocated to audio	Cluster A	6.9%
	Cluster E	10.6%
	Cluster K	9.0%
	Cluster J	15.5%
	Total	42.0% of meetings
Unallocated (because they were unclustered, see Chapter 3)	The remainder	10.9% of meetings

For key to clusters see page 41

These exact percentages should not be taken too seriously, but rather considered to be a demonstration of the allocation procedure. Apart from the limitations of the type allocation model as a whole, and the arbitrariness of the allocation procedures used here, the experimental output is still not complete enough, particularly in the critical area of 'keeping people in the picture', which affects all the allocations to video. In addition, of course, these percentages will be affected by all the mode allocation factors, some of which will be discussed later.

However, other type allocation procedures using the same basic data, but different allocation decisions, arrive at broadly similar conclusions as in Table 10.3.

Table 10.3 Connell's (1974) type allocation results

Allocated to face-to-face	30.4% of meetings
Allocated to video	2.9% of meetings
Allocated to audio	38.1% of meetings
No allocation possible	28.6% of meetings

Other allocation procedures have been used, but all have had similar results; we may thus conclude:

'*On the basis of meeting task alone*, a majority of meetings seem capable of transfer from the face-to-face medium in which they now take place to a telecommunications medium, and for those meetings which can be so transferred, a majority seem transferrable to an audio-only medium, a minority require a full audio-video medium.'

Subsequent evidence may show that this is an overoptimistic estimate of the substitution potential of telecommunication. Such evidence is not likely to come from improved surveys, but rather from laboratory experiments. In order to show that a type of meeting can be satisfactorily transferred from face-to-face to telecommunications, it is necessary to demonstrate, by experiment, that there is no effect of medium of communication on outcome. Trying to prove such a negative effect is logically impossible: there is always a possibility, however remote, that poor experimental design, inadequate measures or extraneous variables have hidden an important media effect, which will then be demonstrated by the next experiment. This argument suggests that future experimentation will gradually whittle away the proportion of meetings which can be satisfactorily allocated to telecommunications.

On the other hand, there is an argument that suggests that the estimates are actually underestimates of the potential for the use of telecommunications. Hitherto, we have referred solely to the issue of direct substitution of travel for telecommunication for individual meetings; this may result in a conservative estimate of the potential for substitution. As indicated above, individual meetings will typically have more than one purpose; some of these activities can be done by telecommunication, others cannot. It would however be inappropriate to rule out substitution for all meetings with any component which could not be done by telephone since rearrangement of the agenda between meetings may well be possible, thus allowing substitution of a greater percentage of the total meetings.

MODE ALLOCATION DECISIONS

The introduction of the mode allocation factors will tend to decrease the percentages of meetings allocated to the telecommunications media. For example, although the differences in objective effectiveness are small, attitudes to video systems are generally more favourable than attitudes to audio systems. This is particularly true in respect of the critical dimensions of feelings of Social Presence (viz., Chapter 5). It could be argued that in many situations it is the *feeling* of having got to know someone that is more important than actually having got to know them. Perceived effectiveness might well be more important than objective effectiveness. On all these counts, video systems score more favourably than audio systems, though sometimes the differences are not as large as one might expect (viz., Figure 9.2). This would tend to decrease the expected demand for audio, and correspondingly increase the demand for video. On the other hand, face-to-face meetings are usually considered more satisfactory than video meetings, so, to the extent that attitudes have an influence on choice of decisions, the percentage of meetings taking place by video would be reduced, and that face-to-face correspondingly increased.

Despite the fact that favourable attitudes are generally found in field studies of operating video systems (e.g. Bell's Picturephone, the Post Office's Confravision and several in-houses systems reported by Collins, 1974) few systems actually experience the use which these evaluations would appear to suggest. This could well be due to the inertial effects discussed in Chapter 2, and one could optimistically hope that usage will pick up with time. At least initially, however, one would have to reduce correspondingly the proportion of meetings which one would expect to take place by telecommunications. In order to explain this low initial usage, interviewees sometimes point to design features such as the impossibility of holding meetings between more than two places simultaneously, but, in general it is details of the practice of the system (location, etc.) which weigh most heavily. With such favourable evaluations of the systems (both perceived and objective), it is probably a waste of resources to conduct detailed investigations of systems design (although we would hope that the type of work reported earlier would shed light on these matters). The effort would be more usefully deployed in detailed consideration of the practical difficulties manifested in field trials.

The cost of the use of the systems is another very important mode allocation factor which would reduce the expected proportion of meetings transferred to telecommunications. Cost studies indicate that, as a substitute for face-to-face contact, video systems are very seldom justified at any reasonable valuation of the participants' time (Cook, 1975, Dickson and Bowers, 1973). Furthermore, it seems likely from casual discussion with the users of teleconference systems that at least some of them are not prepared to cost the value of time saved; a teleconference system has to be justified in terms of travel costs saved only, and if it cannot be so, it is rejected as too expensive.

In defence of high-cost video systems, one could point out that they have very real advantages over face-to-face meetings. There is the possibility of arranging meetings at short notice, avoidance of the fatigue of travelling, and the possibility of bringing in extra colleagues or additional material at the last minute. However, these advantages apply equally to narrow-band audio conference systems (perhaps with some graphics capability). The very same cost studies indicate that, at all reasonable valuations of peoples' time, audio teleconference systems are cost-effective compared to travel for face-to-face contact. The introduction of cost factors into our allocation decisions will thus markedly decrease the allocation to video, in favour of face-to-face, but will leave the allocations to audio conferencing untouched.

As travel costs rise the cost balance can be expected to shift even further in favour of the teleconference alternative: video may become rational from the cost point of view. The reasons for this shift are various. On the one hand, transportation is becoming more expensive in real terms as two of its major inputs, energy and labour, increase in relative cost. On the other hand, technical advances in telecommunications are proceeding very rapidly, with new switching systems and new transmission technologies (e.g. waveguides, fibre optics) considered by some to be capable of reducing costs by an order of magnitude.

However, video will always remain more expensive than audio, if only because it uses a greater bandwidth in transmission. Whatever the system, the bandwidth required to transmit one video signal would transmit a hundred or more audio signals. In addition, video facilities require cameras, television screens and, of course, a complete audio link in parallel. Considering this large cost differential, we doubt that in general the additional effectiveness of a video system is sufficient to justify the increased costs.

GENERATION EFFECTS

While the mode allocation factors are likely to reduce the amount of usage of telecommunications below that shown in Table 10.2, one must stress the other side of the coin: the possibility of generation effects. The meetings transferred from face-to-face may be only a small part of the overall use of telecommunications. There are likely to be examples where the availability of the telecommunications options makes possible alternatives not previously open. Several examples of this effect can be cited. In the University of Quebec, telecommunications have been used to bring specialist post-graduate teaching to places where it would otherwise be unobtainable; this has allowed advanced students to work in places they would not otherwise have been prepared to live (because of the absence of teaching). Even where effectiveness per interaction is low, the telecommunications option may nonetheless be more effective in the end; a Bell System publicity leaflet entitled 'Phonepower' points out how the use of a telephone can enable a salesman to make 30 'visits' a day instead of three. Even if he is only one-quarter as persuasive over the telephone as he is face-to-face, he could still do more than twice as much business in the day. This type of generation effect may mean that objective effectiveness is only a relatively minor factor in the consideration of the overall effectiveness and impact of new forms of telecommunication.

Nobody knows the relative importance of the generation effects and the substitution effects. Field studies have identified generation effects but we do not yet have any objective measurements of the relative magnitude of substitution and generation effects. There is not yet a sufficient depth of experience to make any general statements, since the magnitude of this effect will vary considerably from situation to situation. One can only note that generation effects exhibit positive feedback and become more probable the more far reaching the existing upheaval in one's communication behaviour.

In summary, while mode allocation factors, particularly present high costs and inertia, may prevent the high levels of use predicted from the type allocation process from being reached for some time, in the longer term, even these high levels may be exceeded as generation effects stimulate demand.

THE EFFECTS OF EXPERIENCE

Closely related to generation effects are the learning effects as an individual, or even a whole organization, comes to use a new communications medium more effectively.

These learning effects could be of several types:

(1) Individuals learn to communicate more smoothly over new media.
(2) Individuals learn to determine more accurately which communications media are effective for which meetings.
(3) Small groups learn how to organize themselves, perhaps by special chairmanship arrangements, to use new media more effectively.
(4) Organizations learn more about the capabilities of new telecommunications devices, perhaps by innovations diffusing from organization to organization.
(5) Organizations learn how to reorganize their internal structure and work flows so as to use the new telecommunications possibilities more effectively.

Some of these types of learning would produce the 'generation' effects that we discussed earlier.

Despite the obvious importance of these learning effects, very little empirical research has yet been carried out. Two experiments at Carleton University (Weston and Kristen, 1973, Strickland et al., 1975) have studied small groups of students who had a series of meetings face-to-face or over a telecommunications medium. However, neither demonstrated strong learning effects at either the group or the individual level, in part because that was not the prime concern of the experiments. In addition, in the latter experiment, the students were initially unacquainted, so that comparing the first with the last meeting confounds acquaintance and experience with the medium. Other studies (e.g. Williams and Holloway, 1974) have measured attitudes towards the medium, and compared multi-time users and one-time users, with largely negative results. This method is, however, unsound, since the two groups may differ in other than experience: for instance, the multi-time users may have been much more enthusiastic about telecommunications right from the start.

The fact that we know little about the effects of experience with new telecommunications media does not invalidate the results from experiments where only a single usage was studied, such as those described in the previous chapters. As mentioned above, present evidence, admittedly somewhat sparse and unsatisfactory, is that experience does not have major and widespread effects. This may be due to the fact that some aspects of social behaviour are not under much conscious control, and are not easily adapted or modified. Furthermore, one could argue that the initial experience is a particularly crucial one, since it determines whether the person will continue to use that telecommunications system, or give up in disgust.

However, it remains indisputable that the effects of experience of new telecommunications media on individuals and organizations is an area where further research effort is important and necessary. This is one of the outstanding directions for extension of the research previously described. Eventually, greater knowledge on the problems of communicating via various media, and on the effects of experience, may allow special 'social skills' training systems which will ease the initial problems that users experience.

FUTURE RESEARCH DIRECTIONS

Although it is almost a cliché to conclude a discussion of research completed by saying, 'Clearly further research work in this area is necessary' we will nonetheless take a little space to point to some of the more promising directions for future research.

One limitation of most of the psychological experiments previously described is that the participants have been equals. The medium of communication has also been 'equal', in that transmission of the various channels (audio, video, etc) has been the same in the two directions. However, asymmetric situations arouse several interesting research issues, as well as dealing with situations that occur, or are likely to occur, in real life. Researchable aspects include:

(a) Interactions between superiors and subordinates over telecommunications, comparing them with peer interactions. Such
interactions seem more common than peer interactions: Westrum
(1972) found that amongst his sample of business managers, 71%
had at least one face-to-face contact per day with superiors and
84% had such contacts with subordinates, but only 63% had such a
high rate of contact with peers. Apart from being more frequent,
superior–subordinate interactions are likely to involve different
kinds of task, and perhaps the exercise or denial of power.
Milgram's (1965) experiments, which were described in Chapter 6,
showed that the 'experimenter' could less easily extract obedience
from the subject if he was communicating with him from the other

end of a telephone link than if he was face-to-face. Will physical separation result in actual, or perceived, loss of power for the superior?

(b) Surveillance may seem a dirty word, and certainly some of the least acceptable uses of telecommunications are for such purposes (viz., Orwell's Nineteen Eighty-four). However, it is normal in many offices for superiors to have visual contact with their subordinates, so that they can check occasionally whether they are present and working. A disadvantage of working from home (see next section) is that such unobtrusive surveillance will no longer be possible, and telecommunications alternatives would be seen as an intrusion of privacy. This may not result in the employees having any more freedom; it may simply prevent management acceptance of working from home. It would thus be worth investigating whether there are acceptable forms of telecommunicated surveillance (e.g. if surveillance is mutual, both parties able to watch the other).

(c) Some proposals for asymmetric media, such as full audio-video in one direction, audio only in the other, have been put forward, (e.g. the NYU-Reading Consortium, 1974). It would be interesting to know whether such asymmetry produces corresponding leadership and dominance relationships.

On a different tack, it is clear that our knowledge about the outcomes of telecommunicated meetings is not matched by equally detailed knowledge of the communication process via different media. Some initial studies have identified media differences in, for example, the speech content of telephone and face-to-face meetings (Wilson and Williams, 1975), but other reasonable hypotheses regarding media differences in communication processes have not been confirmed (Cook and Lalljee, 1972). While knowledge of outcome differences may be sufficient to allow the 'allocation' of meetings to one medium or another, only by understanding the processes will we be able to develop theory which can adequately explain the differences between the media in all possible circumstances. Processes that could be studied include the non-verbal and verbal message flow, changes in the perceptions of the other during the interaction, and the differentiation of roles, such as leadership, in groups.

These, then, are some possible future directions for psychological research. Has the present research shed any light on the likely future application of telecommunications?

THE FUTURE?

It is hard to foresee anything other than a continued boom in telecommunications use for both residential and business purposes. Direct costs favour telecommunications over travel; energy-saving considerations again favour the telecommunications alternative (Dickson and Bowers, 1973, Pye, Tyler and Cartwright, 1974). Telecommunication is also favoured by its lesser demands on resources and materials, and its virtual freedom from the noise and air pollution and intrusive effects on the urban environment associated with transport. These considerations seem to suggest that the 'energy crisis', the 'pollution crisis' and the 'crisis in the cities' may combine to enforce greater use of telecommunications, with scant respect for doubts regarding the effectiveness or acceptability of these systems.

With this conspiracy of circumstances, and considering the favourability of the task outcome and attitudinal results for telecommunications systems (see Chapters 6 to 9), many of the more exotic possibilities mentioned in Chapter 1 may not be so far off. The following paragraphs summarize the current situation concerning some potential applications which, in the light of the work on media effectiveness, do seem to be realistic possibilities.

(a) Working at Home

Moves towards the decentralization of offices from the cities can already be observed: over the period 1963 to 1970 the Location of Offices bureau recorded moves from London by 878 firms. It seems likely that such trends will continue, and in some American cities there is already anxiety that offices, like home-owners and industry, are fleeing to the suburbs or exurbs, leaving the central city to die.

At a more extreme level, there have been proposals that rather than commute to the central business district, the businessman should go instead to a neighbourhood work centre equipped with all the latest in telecommunications equipment. From the previous discussion, it can be seen that no one telecommunications device can meet all communications needs: even with a combination of video-conferencing, audioconferencing, facsimile and telex, some travelling would still be necessary for those meetings allocated to face-to-face in Table 10.2. The sharing of equipment in a neighbourhood work centre seems a more reasonable possibility than working from home and has been canvassed by various writers (Healy, 1968, Wise, 1971, Cassidy, 1969, Young, 1971, Libby, 1969). This latter would probably be unfeasible for most workers who presently have a substantial number of face-to-face meetings with colleagues, since only if video systems were installed in the home could enough of their meetings be transferred from face-to-face to make it worthwhile, and, for the present, video systems are unrealistically expensive for home installation.

Summarizing the results of four Delphi Studies in this area, Day (1973) concluded that the consensus of expert opinion was that these work-styles would be common by the end of the century. Our results support the feasibility of the use of telecommunications for a large percentage of the identifiable communication events occurring in the course of business activity. However the realization of the benefits of remote working hinges on hitherto unresolved uncertainties concerning the significance of less clearly identifiable functions such as supervision, the organizational implictions of remote working, and, above all, the attitudes of the staff (see Glover, 1974, for an introductory discussion to the last issue).

The supposed benefits of remote working include improvements in the quality of life through reduction in time wasted travelling, and the greater efficiency in the use of office space and travel facilities. The implications, if remote working were adopted on a large scale, would touch on everything from dwelling design, through commuting and leisure patterns, to major planning decisions and regional development issues. There is then the question of what effects such upheavals might have on social and subcultural structures. Above all, there is the issue of whether or not these developments are desirable, for there is always the danger that the main impact of decentralization may be misfortune, not for those who leave, but for those who have no option but to remain behind.

(b) Education at a Distance

Another much canvassed application is the possibility of education with greatly decreased contact between teacher and pupil. Teaching is principally an activity of information exchange and one might therefore expect that telecommunications could be an effective alternative to the traditional classroom. It is thus no surprise to discover that in reviewing 18 experiences of teaching by telephone in North America, Rao and Hicks (1972) conclude that students learn as much *or more* in telephone classes as in face-to-face discussion. There is good evidence too that learning from television is at least as effective as conventional face-to-face instruction (Chu and Schramm, 1967). With news of teacher shortages an everyday event, what are the factors that are limiting this application?

Conventional broadcasting applications in this field are limited by scarcity of air-space (forcing transmission at inconvenient times) and the absence of any possibility of interaction with the teacher. 'Hard-wire' technology such as the telephone or a cable TV network can overcome both problems, but both can be expensive in the context of limited educational budgets. Teacher attitudes have been in the past (and seem likely to continue to be) an important barrier to increased use of a technology whose principal attraction for the administrator may be that it can partially replace teachers. Recent reviews (e.g. Howarth, 1974) have thus been pessimistic about the application of new telecommunications by existing educational institutions. The real significance of the new technology lies in its promise of extending education to the non-traditional students: those who for a variety of reasons could not or would not attend existing institutions. The institutional problems are by-passed when one is dealing with the non-traditional student; cost-effectiveness comparison with face-to-face instruction is irrelevant if face-to-face is not a feasible alternative.

The Open University in Britain has been pioneering the use of the telephone for seminars and other teaching purposes since many Open University students would come under the heading of 'non-traditional' students. In Canada, the University of Quebec has exploited telephone tutorial sessions to permit research staff to work in remote locations where they would otherwise not have been prepared to work owing to the lack of supervision.

Pilot studies on the acceptability of these systems for tutors and students have been conducted: Holloway and Hammond (1975) assessed reactions to telephone teaching in the Open University. Their results suggested that telephone teaching was an acceptable method, and that the impersonality involved was not important since the teaching was essentially an impersonal activity. However, in many educational settings, graphic material is an important aspect of the course, and one could argue that telephone applications are only scratching the surface and the full potential of telecommunications in education will only materialize when an extensive network of cable television systems allows programmes including visual material to be delivered to the majority of homes. An alternative possibility is that cheap graphics systems which use the telephone lines, and, perhaps, the domestic television as a display, will be developed at a cost that most households can afford.

(c) Remote Medical Diagnosis

Another application much cited by the propagandists of the new telecommunications technology concerns the field of health care. Thus for example the 1971 report of the National Academy of Engineering lists among two dozen 'applications of communications technology for urban improvement' four in the field of health care. In the last ten years at least 24 telemedicine projects have been instituted or planned in the United States or Canada; all have the general goal of delivering health care to as many persons as effectively possible. The applications include conventional teleconferences and educational applications (both inside and outside the medical professions), but the distinctive application is remote medical diagnosis. In the right circumstances this can allow for more efficient use of specialists' time through the increased use of less experienced or para-professional staff and improvements in either the speed or scale of the delivery of health services to remote or inaccessible areas. Anywhere where the distribution of health care is perceived to be a major problem, the scope for the use of telemedecine is enormous, but unfortunately the costs are often no less considerable.

The growing literature on this subject is summarized in recent reviews by Park (1974), Reich (1974) and Bashur, Armstrong and Youssef (1975): the preliminary conclusions are encouraging in that diagnosis by television has proved possible in a high proportion of cases, although there is still scope for much detailed work on this point. Studies of effectiveness have tended to suggest that visual tele-communications are seldom, in the present state of affairs, cost-effective. Telediagnosis represents an exception to this general rule: here the visual channel is more important than in business, since the doctors are frequently referring to visual material such as X-rays, cardiograms, the appearance of sores or cuts, and the general appearance and demeanour of the patient. Certainly, the assumption that a visual channel is necessary runs deep, since nearly all the telemedicine field experiments to date have used broadband video links, often with the addition of remote stethoscopes and other ancillary equipment.

It is thus disconcerting to find that the only controlled comparison of communications media for telediagnosis (Conrath et al., 1974) showed little difference between the media in outcome. Conrath et al. had 32 patients each interviewed four times by four different doctors. One interview was face-to-face, the others were by colour television, black-and-white television and an audio-only link. The patients in the telecommunications conditions were assisted by a nurse, and did, of course, know that they were taking part in an experiment.

Diagnosis of critical ailments (i.e. those which could seriously affect the patient's health) was equally effective via any of the media, varying from 69% diagnosed correctly over colour TV to 85% correct over black-and-white TV, with audio and face-to-face intermediate. Secondary diagnosis (other minor ailments) was more effective face-to-face (62% correct diagnosis) than over any of the telecommuni-cations media, which did not differ between themselves (between 34% and 42% correct diagnosis).

We must therefore conclude that while the prospects for telemedicine look promising, the case for concentrating on video is not proven. Certainly, this study throws doubt on the value of expensive prestige projects in the field of telemedicine (for example, the transatlantic medical consultation that occurred in September 1973 over a television link between Montreal and Lyon). Although many of the projects may be proved beneficial, the type of cost-effectiveness study which would allow a meaningful assessment of the future scope for telemedicine has been notably absent.

IN CONCLUSION

Despite the evident effectiveness of substituting telecommunications for many regular activities in the fields of business, education and health care, none but extremists would suggest complete substitution, for there remains something unique about the social contact achieved in a face-to-face meeting. Even in the most successful applications, regular continuing face-to-face contacts have proved indispensable. With the additional safeguard of extreme costliness, one need have little fear of the nightmare situations, beloved of fiction writers, brought about by excessive use of telecommunications (see for example E. M. Forster's 'The Machine Stops'). Nonetheless such allegories are serious and, before closing this discussion, it is appropriate to take a little space to provoke further discussion of the role of research into the applications and impacts of telecommunications.

An ever increasing proportion of man's activities both at work and leisure are concerned with the communication and processing of information. Many western societies are indeed reaching a stage at which more people are engaged in information processing activities than in productive enterprise (Parker, 1975). With increasing pressures to make use of the increased range of remote alternatives, analysis of the means of communication will become an ever more salient topic for all social scientists.

But to what end? The obvious rationale is that improvements in communication can contribute to many of the problems of today. Thus for example the Sloan Commission (1971) wrote 'The problem of the inner city will not be solved by communication alone, but communication may be brought to play a most significant part. If cable technology proves indeed to be the heart of the communications revolution, its impacts upon society's most urgent needs might be enormous.' So far so good, but there is an erroneous assumption which often follows to the effect that more communication is inherently desirable. Recently, however, writers such as Meier (1973) and Toffler (1970) have drawn attention to the fact that the accelerating rate of interaction in society can prove too much for certain individuals. They stress the importance of the converse issues, privacy and the need for provision of a facility for opting out of what can be viewed as a communications flood. The goal of increased understanding of human communication stands but we must never lose sight of the fact that the same technology which ushers in the 'new rural society' can equally be a force for the progressive dehumanization of society and the basis for centralized systems of social control such as those caricatured in George Orwell's *Nineteen Eighty-Four*.

References

(Mimeographed Communications Studies Group papers are available from Post Office Telecommunications (TMk3.3.1.) Room 120, 2-12 Gresham Street, London EC2V 7AG.)

Albert, S. A., and Dabbs, J. M. (1970). 'Physical distance and persuasion, *J. Pers. Soc. Psychol.*, **15**, 265-70.

Allen, T. J., and Fusfeld, A. R. (1974). *Research Laboratory Architecture and the Structuring of Communications.* Mimeograph.

Allen, W. H. (1971). 'Instructional media research: Past, present and future', *Audio-Visual Communications Review*, **19**, 5-17.

Allport, F. H. (1920). 'The influence of the group upon association and thought', *J. Exp. Psychol.*, **3**, 159-82.

Amara, R., and Vallée, J. (1974). *Forum: A Computer Based System to Support Interaction among People.* Institute for the Future, Menlo Park.

Ansoff, H. I. (1965). *Corporate Strategy. An Analytic Approach to Business Policy for Growth and Expansion.* McGraw-Hill, New York.

Applbaum, R. L., et al. (1973). *Fundamental Concepts in Human Communication.* Harper and Row, New York.

Argyle, M. (1957). 'Social pressure in public and private situations', *J. Abn. Soc. Psychol.*, **54**, 172-5.

Argyle, M., and Dean, J. (1965). 'Eye contact, distance and affiliation', *Sociometry*, **28**, 289-304.

Argyle, M., Lalljee, M., and Cook, M. (1968). 'The effects of visibility on interaction in the dyad', *Human Relations*, **21**, 3-17.

Argyle, M. (1969). *Social Interaction.* Methuen, London.

Argyle, M., Salter, V., Nicholson, H., Williams, M., and Burgess, P. (1970). 'The communication of inferior and superior attitudes by verbal and nonverbal signals', *Brit. J. Soc. Clin. Psychol.*, **9**, 222-31.

Argyle, M., and McHenry, R. (1971). 'Do spectacles really affect judgements of intelligence?', *Brit. J. Soc. Slin. Psychol.*, **10**, 27-9.

Aronson, E., and Golden, B. W. (1962). 'The effect of relevant and irrelevant aspects of communicator credibility on opinion change', *J. Pers.*, **30**, 135-46.

Aronson, E. (1973). *The Social Animal.* Routledge and Kegan Paul, London.

Aronson, S. H. (1971). 'The sociology of the telephone', *Int. J. Comp. Sociol.*, **12**, 153-67.

Atkinson, J. W. (Ed.) (1958). *Motives in Fantasy, Action and Society.* Van Nostrand, New York.

Backman, C. W., and Secord, P. F. (1959). 'The effect of perceived liking on interpersonal attraction', *Human Relations*, **12**, 379-84.

Bales, R. F. (1955). 'How people interact in conferences', *Scientific American*, March, 3-7.

176

Barnlund, D. C. (1968). 'Introduction', in Barnlund, D. C. (Ed.) *Interpersonal Communication: Survey and Studies.* Houghton Mifflin Co., New York, pp. 3–14.

Bashur, R. I., Armstrong, P. A., and Youssef, Z. I. (1975). *Telemedicine: Explorations in the use of telecommunications in health care.* Thomas Springfield.

Bass, B. M. (1966). 'Effect on the subsequent performances of negotiators of studying the issues or planning strategies alone or in groups', *Psychol. Monog.,* 80, 1–31.

Bauer, R. A. (1965). *A Revised Model of Source Effect.* Presidential address to the division of consumer psychology, American Psychological Association annual conference, Chicago.

Bell System (1971). 'The Picturephone system'. Special issue of *Bell System Tech. J.,* 50, 219– 09.

Bergum, B. O., and Lehr, D. J. (1963). 'Effects of authoritarianism on vigilance performance', *J. applied Psychol.,* 47, 75–7.

Berman, H. J., Shulman, A. D., and Marwit, S. J. (1975). 'Comparison of multidimensional decoding of affect for audio, video and audio video recordings', *Sociometry,* 38.

Birdwhistell, R. L. (1952). *Introduction to Kinesics.* University of Louisville Press, Louisville.

Birdwhistell, R. L. (1968). 'Body behaviour and communication', in Sills, D. (Ed.) *International Encyclopedia of Social Science,* Vol. 3. McMillan, New York.

Birdwhistell, R. L. (1970). *Kinesics and Context.* University of Philadelphia Press, Philadelphia.

Blake, R. R., and Mouton, J. S. (1961). 'Competition, communication and conformity', in Berg, I. A. and Bass, B. M. (Eds.) *Conformity and Deviation.* Harper, New York.

Bonney, M. E. (1944). 'Relationships between social success, family size, socioeconomic home background and intelligence among school children in Grades III to V', *Sociometry,* 7, 26–39.

Brown, B., and Helmer, O. (1964). *Improving the Reliability of Estimates Obtained from a Consensus of Experts.* RAND report no. P-2986.

Brown, R. (1965). *Social Psychology.* MacMillan, New York.

Byrne, D., and Clore, G. L. (1966). 'Predicting interpersonal attraction toward strangers presented in three different stimulus modes', *Psychon. Sci.,* 4, 239–40.

Byrne, D. (1969). *Attitudes and Attraction in Advances in Experimental Social Psychology,* Vol 4 (Ed. Berkowitz, L.). Academic Press, New York.

Cantril, H., and Allport, G. W. (1935). *The Psychology of Radio.* Harper, New York.

Cartwright, D., and Zander, A. (1960). *Group dynamics: Research and Theory.* Harper and Row, New York.

Cassidy, W. D. (1969). 'Substitutes for transportation', *Transportation Research Forum,* 141–50.

Champness, B. G. (1970). 'Mutual glance and the significance of the look', *Advancement of Science,* March, 309–12.

Champness, B. G., and Reid, A. A. L. (1970). *The Efficiency of Information Transmission: A Preliminary Comparison Between Face-to-face Meetings and the Telephone.* Unpublished Communications Studies Group paper no. P/70240/CH.

Champness, B. G. (1971). *Bargaining at Bell Laboratories.* Unpublished Communications Studies Group paper no. E/71270/CH.

Champness, B. G., and Davies, M. F. (1971). *The Maier pilot experiment.* Unpublished Communications Studies Group paper no. E/71030/CH.

Champness, B. G. (1972a). *Attitudes Towards Person-person Communications Media.* Unpublished Communications Studies Group paper no. E/72011/CH.

Champness, B. G. (1972b). *The Perceived Adequacy of Four Communications Systems for a Variety of Tasks.* Unpublished Communications Studies Group paper no. E/72245/CH.

Champness, B. G. (1972c). *Feelings Towards Media in Group Situations.* Communications Studies Group paper no. E/72160/CH.

Champness, B. G. (1973). *The Assessment of User Reactions to Confravision: II. Analysis and Conclusions.* Unpublished Communications Studies Group paper no. E/73250/CH.

Chapanis, A. (1971). 'Prelude to 2001: Explorations in human communication', *Amer. Psychologist*, **26**, 949-61.

Chapanis, A., Ochsman, R., Parrish, R., and Weeks, G. (1972). 'Studies in interactive communication: I. The effects of four communication modes on the behaviour of teams during cooperative problem solving', *Hum. Fac.*, **14**, 487-509.

Cherry, C. (1957). *On Human Communication.* MIT Press, Cambridge, Mass.

Cherry, C. (1971). *World Communication: Threat or Promise?* Wiley, London.

Christie, B. (1972). *Report on series I experiments.* Unpublished paper from New Rural Society project, Fairfield University, Conn.

Christie, B. (1973a). 'Appendix M', in P. C. Goldmark *et al. The 1972/73 New Rural Society Project.* Research report available from Fairfield University, Connecticut.

Christie, B. (1973b). *An Evaluation of the Audio-video Conference System Installed in the Department of the Environment.* Unpublished Communications Studies Group paper no. W/73360/CR.

Christie, B. (1973c). 'Appendix N', in P. C. Goldmark *et al. The 1972/73 New Rural Society Project.* Research report available from Fairfield University, Connecticut.

Christie, B. (1974). *Semantic Differential Judgements of Communications Media and other Concepts: I. Differences between the media.* Unpublished Communications Studies Group paper no. E/74120/CR.

Christie, B., and Holloway, S. (1975). 'Factors affecting the use of telecommunications by management'. *J. Occup. Psychol.*, **48**, 3-9.

Chu, G. C., and Shramm, W. (1967). *Learning from TV: What the Research Says.* Institute for Communications Research, Standford University.

Coll, D. *et al.* (1974). *The Wired City Laboratory: Studies in Interactive Broadband Communications.* Carleton University, Ottawa.

Collins, H. (1972). *The Telecommunications Impact Model: Stages I and II.* Unpublished Communications Studies Group paper no. P/72356/CL.

Collins, H. (1974). *Business Telecommunications Applications: Field Trials of Television Conference Systems.* Post Office (Long Range Studies), Bulletin no. 5.

Connell, S. (1974). *The 1973 Office Communications Survey.* Communications Studies Group paper no. p/74067/CN.

Conrath, D. W. Buckingham, P., Dunn, E. V., and Swanson, J. N. (1974). *An*

Experimental Evaluation of Alternative Communication Systems As Used for Medical Diagnosis. 7th International Symposium on Human Factors in Telecommunications, Montreal.

Cook, A. (1975). *A More Detailed Comparison of the Costs of Travel and Telecommunications.* Communications Studies Group paper no. P/75008/CK.

√Cook, M. (1971). *Nonverbal Signalling in Social Interaction.* Unpublished Ph.D. thesis, Oxford University.

Cook, M., and Lalljee, M. (1972). 'Verbal substitutes for verbal signals in interaction', *Semiotica,* 6, 212–21.

Cowan, P. (1973). 'Moving information instead of mass: Transportation versus communication', in Gerbner, G., Gross, L. P., and Melody, W. H. (Eds.) *Communications Technology and Social Policy.* Wiley, New York.

Craig, J., and Jull, G. (1974). *Teleconferencing Studies: Behavioural Research and Technological Implications.* Paper read at 7th International Symposium on Human Factors in Telecommunications, Montreal.

Croft, R. G., Stimpson, D. V., Ross, W. L., Bray, R. M., and Breglio, V. J. (1969). 'Comparison of attitude changes elicited by live and videotape classroom presentations', *Audio-Visual Communications Review,* 17, 315–21.

Cronbach, L. J. (1955). 'Processes affecting scores on "Understanding of others" and "Assumed similarity" ', *Psychol. Bull.,* 52.

Daniels, V. (1967). 'Communication, incentive and structural variables in interpersonal exchange and negotiation', *J. Exp. Soc. Psychol.,* 3, 47–74.

Darwin, C. (1872). *The Expression of the Emotions in Man and Animals* John Murray, London.

Dashiell, J. F. (1935). 'Experimental studies of the influence of social situations on the behaviour of individual human adults', in Murchison, C. (Ed.) *Handbook of Social Psychology.* Clark University Press, Worcester, Mass.

Davies, M. A. (1971). *Communication Effectiveness as a Function of Mode.* Unpublished M.A. thesis, University of Waterloo.

Davies, M. F. (1971a). *Cooperative Problem Solving: An Exploratory Study.* Unpublished Communications Studies Group paper no. E/71159/DV.

Davies, M. F. (1971b). *Cooperative Problem Solving: A Follow-up Study.* Unpublished Communications Studies Group paper no. E/71252/DV.

Day, L. (1973). 'An assessment of travel/communications substitutability', *Futures.*

Deutsch, M., and Gerard, H. B. (1955). 'A study of normative and informational social influence upon individual judgement', *J. Abn. Soc. Psychol.,* 51, 629–36.

Deutsch, M. (1958). 'Trust and suspicion', *J. Conflict Resolution,* 2, 265–79.

Deutsch, M. (1960). 'The effect of motivational orientation upon trust and suspicion', *Human Relations,* 13, 123–39.

Deutsch, M., and Krauss, R. M. (1962). 'Studies of interpersonal bargaining', *J. Conflict. Resolution,* 4, 52–76.

Dickson, E., and Bowers, R. (1973). *The Videotelephone: A New Era in Telecommunications.* Report to the National Science Foundation from Cornell University.

Dittman, A. T. (1962). 'The relationship between body movements and moods in interviews', *J. Consulting. Psychol.,* 26, 480.

Dorris, J. W., Gentry, G. C., and Kelley, H. H. (1972). *The Effects on Bargaining of Problem Difficulty, Mode of Interaction, and Initial Orientation.* Unpublished paper of University of Massachusetts.

Douglas, A. (1957). 'The peaceful settlement of industrial and intergroup disputes', *J. Conflict. Resolution*, **1**, 69–81.

Druckman, D. (1968). 'Prenegotiation experience and dyadic conflict resolution in a bargaining solution', *J. exp. soc. Psychol.*, **4**, 367–83.

Druckman, D., and Zechmeister, K. (1970). 'Conflict of interest and value dissensus', *Human Relations*, **23**, 431–8.

Duncan, S. (1972). 'Some signals and rules for taking speaking turns in conversations', *J. Pers. Soc. Psychol.*, **23**, 283–92.

Duncanson, J. P., and Williams, A. D. (1973). 'Videoconferencing: Reactions of users', *Human Factors*, **15**, 471–85.

Dunnette, M. D., Campbell, J., and Jaastad, K. (1963). 'The effect of group participation on brainstorming effectiveness for two industrial samples', *J. Appl. Psychol.*, **47**, 30–7.

Edwards, A. L. (1957). *The Social Desirability Variable in Personality Assessment and Research*. Dryden Press, New York.

Ekman, P. (1965). 'Communication through nonverbal behaviour: A source of information about an interpersonal relationship', in Tomkins, S. S., and Izard, C. E. (Eds.) *Affect, Cognition and Personality*. Tavistock, London.

Ekman, P., and Friesen, W. V. (1969). 'Nonverbal leakage and clues to deception', *Psychiatry*, **32**, 88–105.

Ekman, P. (1971). 'Universals and cultural differences in facial expressions of emotion', in Cole, J. K. (Ed.) *Nebraska Symposium on Motivation*. University of Nebraska Press, Lincoln.

Elliot, F. R. (1937). 'Eye versus ear moulding opinion', *Public Opinion Quarterly*, **1**, 83–7.

Ellsworth, P. C., and Carlsmith, J. M. (1968). 'Effects of eye contact and verbal content on affective response to a dyadic interaction', *J. Pers. Soc. Psychol.*, **10**, 15–20.

English, R. W., and Jelenevsky, S. (1971). 'Counsellor behaviour as judged under audio, visual, and audiovisual communication conditions', *J. Counselling Psychol.*, **18**, 509–13.

Estabrook, G. G. (1930). 'A standardized hypnotic technique dictated to a victrola record', *Amer. J. Psychol.*, **42**, 115–6.

Etzioni, A. (1972). *MINERVA: A Study in Participatory Technology*. Unpublished paper of Center for Policy Research, Columbia University, New York.

Exline, R. V., Thibaut, J., Brannon, C., and Gumpert, P. (1961). 'Visual interaction in relation to Machiavellianism and an unethical act', *Amer. Psychologist*, **16**, 396.

Exline, R. V. (1963). 'Explorations in the process of person perception: Visual interaction in relation to competition, sex and need for affiliation', *J. Pers. Soc. Psychol.*, **31**, 1–20.

Exline, R. V., and Winter, L. C. (1965). 'Affective relations and mutual glances in dyads', in Tomkins, S. S., and Izard, C. E. (Eds.) *Affect, Cognition and Personality*. Springer, New York.

Exline, R. V., Gray, D., and Schuette, D. (1965). 'Visual behaviour in a dyad as affected by interview content and sex of respondent', *J. Pers. Soc. Psychol.*, **1**, 201–9.

Exline, R. V. (1971). 'Visual interaction: The glances of power and preference', in Cole, J. K. (Ed.) *Nebraska Symposium on Motivation*. University of Nebraska Press, Lincoln.

180

Festinger, L., Schachter, S., and Back, K. (1950). *Social Pressures in Informal Groups: A Study of Human Factors in Housing.* Harper and Row, New York.

Festinger, L., and Maccoby, N. (1964). 'On resistance to persuasive communications', *J. Abn. Soc. Psychol.,* **68,** 359–66.

Fishbein, M. (1965). 'Prediction of interpersonal preferences and group member satisfaction from estimated attitudes', *J. Pers. Soc. Psychol.,* **1,** 663–7.

Forster, E. M. (1947). 'The machine stops', in *Collected Short Stories of E. M. Forster.* Sidgewick and Jackson, London.

Frandsen, K. D. (1963). 'Effects of threat appeals and media of transmission', *Speech Monographs,* **30,** 101–4.

Frijda, N. H. (1968). 'Recognition of emotion', in Berkowitz, L. (Ed.) *Advances in Experimental Social Psychology.* Academic Press, New York.

Froman, L. A., and Cohen, M. D. (1969). 'Threats and bargaining efficiency', *Behavl. Sci.,* **14,** 147–53.

Gamson, W. A. (1964). 'Experimental Studies of Coalition Formation', in *Advances in Experimental Social Psychology,* vol. 1. Berkowitz, L. (Ed.). Academic Press, New York.

Geidt, F. H. (1955). 'Comparison of visual content and auditory cues in interviewing', *J. Consult. Psychol.,* **19,** 407–19.

Gerard, H. B. (1964). 'Conformity and commitment to the group', *J. Abn. Soc. Psychol.,* **68,** 209–11.

Glover, J. (1974). *Long Range Social Forecasts: Working from Home.* Post Office Long Range Intelligence bulletin no. 2.

Goddard, J. P. (1971). 'Office communications and office location: A review of current research', *Regional Studies,* **5,** 263–80.

Goldberg, G. N., Kiesler, C. A., and Collins, B. E. (1969). 'Visual behaviour and face-to-face distance interaction', *Sociometry,* **32,** 43–53.

Goldmark, P. C. (1972a). 'Tomorrow we will communicate to our jobs', *The Futurist,* April, 55–8.

Goldmark, P. C. (1972b). 'Communication and community', *Scientific American,* **227,** 142–50.

Gullahorn, J. T. (1952). 'Distance and friendship as factors in the gross interaction matrix', *Sociometry,* **15,** 123–34.

Hall, E. T. (1963). 'A system for the notation of proxemic behaviour', *Amer. Anthropologist,* **65,** 1003–26.

Halloran, J. (1970). *The Effects of Television.* Panther, London.

Hammond, K. R. (1965). 'New directions in research on conflict resolution', *J. Soc. Issues,* **21,** 44–6.

Hardman, H. (1973). *The Dispersal of Government Work from London.* Cmnd. 5322. Her Majesty's Stationery Office.

Harkness, R. C. (1973). 'Communication innovations, urban form and travel demand: Some hypotheses and a bibliography', *Transportation,* **2,** 153–93.

Harman, H. H. (1960). *Modern Factor Analysis.* University of Chicago Press, Chicago.

Haworth, J. E. (1972). 'Confravision', *The Post Office Elec. Eng. J.,* **64,** 220–4.

Healy, T. J. (1968). 'Transportation or communications: Some broad considerations', *IEEE Transactions in Communication Technology,* **Com-16.**

Heber, R. F., and Heber, M. E. (1957). 'The effect of group failure and success on social status', *J. Educ. Psychol.,* **48,** 129–34.

Heilbronn, M., and Libby, W. L. (1973). *Comparative Effects of Technological and Social Immediacy upon Performance and Perceptions during a Two-Person*

Game. Paper read at the Annual Convention of the American Psychological Association, Montreal.

Hess, E. H. (1965). 'Attitude and pupil size', *Scientific American*, **22**, 46–55.

Hillen, C. F. J. (1972). 'The face-to-face telephone', *Post Office Telecoms. J.*, **24**, 4–7.

Himmelweit, H., Oppenheim, A. N., and Vince, P. (1958). *Television and the Child.* Oxford University Press, Oxford.

Hockey, R. (1969). 'Noise and efficiency: the visual task', *New Scientist*, May, 244–6.

Holloway, S., and Hammond, S. (1975). *Tutoring by Telephone: A Case Study in the Open University.* Communications Studies Group paper no. P/75025/HL.

Hovland, C. I., Lumsdaine, A. A., and Sheffield, F. D. (1949). *Experiments on Mass Communication.* Princeton University Press, Princeton.

Hovland, C. I., Janis, I. L., and Kelley, H. H. (1953). *Communication and Persuasion.* Yale University, New Haven.

Howarth, T. (1974). *Education and Telecommunications, 1974–2000.* Council for Educational Technology.

Hsia, H. J. (1968). 'Output, error, equivocation and recalled information in auditory, visual and audio-visual processing with constraint and noise', *J. Communication.*

Hurwitz, J. I., Zander, A. F., and Hymovitch, B. (1960). 'Some effects of power on the relations among group members', in Cartwright, D., and Zander, A. (Eds.) *Group Dynamics; Research and Theory.* Harper and Row, New York.

Ives, H. E. (1927). 'Television', *Bell System Technical Journal*, **6**, 551–9.

Jaffe, J., and Feldstein, S. (1970). *Rhythms of Dialogue.* Academic Press, New York.

James, W. T. (1932). 'A study of the expression of bodily posture', *J. Genet. Psychol.*, **7**, 405–37.

Jones, M. V. (1971). *A Technology Assessment Methodology: Some Basic Propositions.* Mitre Corporation.

Kasl, S. V., and Mahl, G. F. (1965). 'The relationship of disturbances and hesitations in spontaneous speech to anxiety', *J. Pers. Soc. Psychol.*, **1**, 425–33.

Katz, E., and Lazarsfeld, P. F. (1955). *Personal Influence.* Free Press, Glencoe, Illinois.

Kelly, G. A. (1955). *The Psychology of Personal Constructs.* Norton, New York.

Kendall, P. (1960). *Medical Education as Social Process.* Paper read at Amer. Social Association, New York.

Kendon, A. (1967). 'Some functions of gaze direction in social interaction', *Acta Psychologica*, **26**, 1–47.

Kendon, A., and Cook, M. (1969). 'The consistency of gaze patterns in social interaction', *Brit. J. Psychol.*, **60**, 481–94.

Kleck, R. E., and Nuessle, W. (1968). 'Congruence between the indicative and communicative functions of eye contact in interpersonal relations', *Brit. J. Soc. Clin. Psychol.*, **7**, 241–6.

Kleinke, C. L., and Pohlen, P. D. (1971). 'Affective and emotional responses as a function of other person's gaze and cooperativeness in a two-person game', *J. Pers. Soc. Psychol.*, **17**, 308–13.

Klemmer, E. T., and Stocker, L. P. (1971). *Picturephone Versus Speakerphone for Conversation Between Strangers.* Unpublished company data.

Klemmer, E. T. (1974). *Some Current Questions Regarding Subscriber Services.*

Paper given at 7th International Symposium on Human Factors in Telecommunications, Montreal.

Kogan, N., and Wallach, M. A. (1967). 'Effects of physical separation of group members upon risk taking', *Human Relations*, **20**, 41–8.

Kollen, J. H., and Garwood, J. (1974). *The Replacement of Travel by Telecommunications*. Paper given at 18th International Congress of Applied Psychology, Montreal.

Komorita, S. S., and Brenner, A. R. (1968). 'Bargaining and concession making under bilateral monopoly', *J. Pers. Soc. Psychol.*, **9**, 15–20.

Krauss, R. M., and Deutsch, M. (1966). 'Communication in interpersonal bargaining', *J. Pers. Soc. Psychol.*, **4**, 572–7.

Kuusinen, J. (1969). 'Affective and denotative structures of personality ratings', *J. Pers. Soc. Psychol.*, **12**, 181–8.

Laing, R. D., Phillipson, H., and Lee, A. R. (1966). *Interpersonal Perception*. Tavistock, London.

Lamm, H. (1967). 'Will an observer advise higher risk taking after hearing a discussion of the decision problem', *J. Pers. Soc. Psychol.*, **6**, 467–71.

Laplante, D. (1971). *Communication, Friendliness, Trust and the Prisoners Dilemma*. M.A. thesis, University of Windsor.

Libby, W. L. (1969). *The End of the Trip to Work*. Ohio State University.

Little, B. R. (1971). *A Provisional Manual for the Thing–Person scale*. Unpublished paper of Department of Experimental Psychology, University of Oxford.

Loomis, J. L. (1959). 'Communication, the development of trust and cooperative behaviour', *Human Relations*, **12**, 305–15.

Lorr, M., and McNair, D. M. (1965). 'Expansion of the interpersonal behaviour circle', *J. Pers. Soc. Psychol.*, **2**, 813–30.

Lott, A. J., and Lott, B. E. (1965). 'Group cohesiveness as interpersonal attraction: a review of relationships with antecedent and consequent variables', *Psychol. Bull.*, **64**, 259–309.

Loveless, N. E., Brebner, J., and Hamilton, P. (1970). 'Bisensory presentation of information', *Psychol. Bull.*, **73**, 161–99.

Maddox, B. (1972). *Beyond Babel*. Deutsch, London.

Maier, N. R. F., and Thurber, J. A. (1968). 'Accuracy of judgements of deception when an interview is watched, heard and read', *Personnel Psychol.*, **21**, 23–30.

Management Science Center (1967). *A Model Study of the Escalation and deescalation of Conflict*. Unpublished paper of University of Pennsylvania.

Martin, J. (1971). *Future Developments in Telecommunications*. Prentice-Hall, Englewood Cliffs, N.J.

McBride, G., King, M. G., and James, J. W. (1965). 'Social proximity effects on galvanic skin responsiveness in adult humans', *J. Psychol.*, **61**, 153–7.

McClintock, C. G., Nuttin, J. M., and McNeel, S. P. (1970). 'Sociometric choice, visual presence, and game playing behaviour', *Behavl. Sci.*, **15**, 124–31.

McGuire, W. J. (1969). 'The nature of attitudes and attitude change', in Lindzey, G., and Aronson, E. (Eds.) *The Handbook of Social Psychology*, Vol. 3. Addison Wesley, Reading, Mass.

McLuhan, M. (1964). *Understanding Media*. Routledge and Kegan Paul, London.

Meadows, D. H., Meadows, D. L., Randers, J., and Behrens, W. W. (1972). *The Limits to Growth*. Universe Books, New York.

Mehrabian, A. (1968). 'Inference of attitudes from the posture, orientation and distance of a communicator', *J. Consult. Clin. Psychol.*, **32**, 296–308.

Mehrabian, A. (1971). *Silent Messages.* Wadsworth, Belmont.

Meier, R. L. (1962). *A Communications Theory of Urban Growth.* MIT Press, Boston, Mass.

Meier, R. L. (1973). 'Urban ecostructures in a cybernetic age: Responses to communications stress', in Gerbner, G., Gross, L. P., and Melody, W. H. (Eds.) *Communications Technology and Social Policy.* Wiley, New York.

Methesne, E. G. (1970). *Technological Change: Its Impact on Man and Society.* Harvard University Press, Cambridge.

Middlebrook, P. N. (1974). *Social Psychology and Modern Life.* Knopf, New York.

Milgram, S. (1965). 'Some conditions of obedience to authority', *Human Relations,* 18, 57–75.

Milgram, S. (1970). 'The experience of living in cities', *Science,* 13, 1461–8.

Miller, G. R., and Hewgill, M. A. (1964). 'The effects of variations in nonfluency on audience ratings of source credibility', *Quart. J. Speech,* 50, 36–44.

Miron, M. S. (1969). 'What is it that is being differentiated by the semantic differential? *J. Pers. Soc. Psychol.,* 12, 189–93.

Mitre (1972). 'TICCIT and beyond', *Mitre Matrix,* 5, 22–37.

Morgan, W. R., and Sawyer, J. (1967). 'Bargaining, expectations and the preference for equality over equity', *J. Pers. Soc. Psychol.,* 6, 139–49.

Morley, I. E., and Stephenson, G. M. (1969). 'Interpersonal and interparty exchange: a laboratory simulation of an industrial negotiation at the plant level', *Brit. J. Psychol.,* 60, 543–5.

Morley, I. E., and Stephenson, G. M. (1970). 'Formality in experimental negotiations: a validation study', *Brit. J. Psychol.,* 61, 383.

Morley, I. E. (1971). *Formality in Experimental Negotiations.* Paper read at British Psychological Society, Social Section Conference, Durham.

Moscovici, S., and Plon, M. (1966). 'Les situations colloques: observations theoretiques et experimentales', *Bulletin de Psychologie,* 247, 702–22.

Mouton, J. S., Blake, R. R., and Olmstead, J. A. (1956). 'The relationship between frequency of yielding and the disclosure of personal identity', *J. Pers.,* 24, 339–47.

Neufeld, R. J. (1970). 'Generalization of results beyond the experimental setting: Statistical versus logical considerations', *Percept and Motor Skills,* 31, 443–6.

Newcomb, T. M. (1961). *The Acquaintance Process.* Holt, Rinehart and Winston, New York.

Nichols, K. A., and Champness, B. G. (1971). 'Eye gaze and the GSR', *J. Exp. Soc. Psychol.,* 7, 623–6.

NYU-Reading Consortium (1974). *Experiment in Urban Telecommunications.* Proposal to National Science Foundation (Research Applied to National Needs).

Orwell, G. (1949). *Nineteen Eighty-four.* Secker and Warburg, London.

Osgood, C. E., Suci, G. J., and Tannenbaum, P. H. (1957). *The Measurement of Meaning.* University of Illinoise Press, Urbana.

Osgood, C. E. (1966). 'Dimensionality of the semantic space for communication via facial expression', *Scand. J. Psychol.,* 7, 1–30.

Park, B. (1974). *An Introduction to Telemedicine: Interactive Television for Delivery of Health Services.* Alternate Media Center, New York University.

Parker, E. B. (1975). *Social Implications of Computer/Telecommunications Systems,* Paper presented to OECD conference on Computer/Telecommunications systems. Paris, France.

Patterson, M. L. and Holmes, D. S. (1966). *Social interaction correlates of the MPI extraversion–introversion.* Paper read at the annual meeting of the American Psychological Association, New York.

Patterson, M. L. and Sechrest, L. B. (1970). 'Interpersonal distance and impression formation', *J. Pers.,* **38,** 161-6.

Patterson, M. L. (1973). 'Compensation in nonverbal immediacy behaviour: A review', *Sociometry,* **36,** 237-52.

Penner, L. A. and Hawkins, H. L. (1971). 'The effects of visual contact and aggressor identification on interpersonal aggression', *Psychon. Sci.,* **24,** 261-3.

Pessin, J. (1933). 'The comparative effects of social and mechanical stimulation on memorising', *Amer. J. Psychol.,* **45,** 263-70.

Popelka, G. R., and Berger, K. W. (1971). 'Gestures and visual speech reception'. *Amer. Annals of the Deaf,* 434-6.

Porter, E., Argyle, M., and Salter, V. (1970). 'What is signalled by proximity?', *Percept and Motor Skills,* **30,** 39-42.

Pye, R. (1972). *The Communications Factor in Dispersal: An Overview.* Communications Studies Group paper no. P/72272/PY.

Pye, R., Champness, B. C., Collins, H., and Connell, S. (1973). *The Description and Classification of Meetings.* Unpublished Communications Studies Group paper no. P/73160/PY.

Pye, R., Tyler, M., and Cartwright, B. (1974). 'Telecommunicate or travel?', *New Scientist,* September, 1974.

Rao, P. V., and Hicks B. L. (1972). 'Telephone based instructional systems', *Audio-Visual Instruction,* **4,** 18.

Raven, B. H. (1959). 'Social influence on opinions and the communication of related content', *J. Abn. Soc. Psychol.,* **58,** 119-28.

Reich, J. J. (1974). *Telemedicine: An Assessment of an Evolving Health Care Technology.* M.A. thesis, Washington University.

Reid, A. A. L. (1970). *Electronic Person–Person Communications.* Communications Studies Group paper no. P/70244/RD.

Reid, A. A. L. (1971). *The Telecommunications Impact Model.* Communications Studies Group paper no. P/71161/RD.

Rosenfeld, H. M. (1966). 'Instrumental affiliative functions of facial and gestural expressions', *J. Pers. Soc. Psychol.,* **4,** 65-72.

Rosenthal, R. (1967). 'Covert communication in the psychological experiment', *Psychol. Bull.,* **67,** 356-67.

Rowley, V., and Keller, E. D. (1962). 'Changes in children's verbal behaviour as a function of social approval and manifest anxiety', *J. Abn. Soc. Psychol.,* **65,** 53-7.

Ruesch, J. (1966). 'Nonverbal language and therapy', *Psychiatry,* **18,** 323-30.

Rutter, D., and Stephenson, G. M. (1974). *The Role of Visual Communication in Synchronising Conversation.* Paper read at British Psychological Society, Social Section, London.

Schacter, S., and Singer, J. E. (1962). 'Cognitive, social and physiological determinants of emotional state', *Psychol. Rev.,* **69,** 379-99.

Scheflen, A. E. (1965). *Stream and Structure of Communication Behaviour.* Eastern Pennsylvania Psychiatric Association, Commonwealth of Pennsylvania.

Schein, E. H. (1965). *Organizational Psychology.* Prentice-Hall, Inc., New Jersey.

Scherer, S. E., and Schiff, M. R. (1973). 'Perceived intimacy, physical distance and eye contact', *Perceptual and Motor Skills,* **36,** 835-41.

Scheritz, L., and Helmreich, R. (1973). 'Interactive effects of eye contact and verbal content on interpersonal attraction in dyads', *J. Pers. Soc. Psychol.*, **25**, 6-14.

Schlosberg, H. (1952). 'The description of facial expressions in terms of two dimensions', *J. Exp. Psychol.*, **44**, 229-37.

Schultz, D. P. (1969). 'The human subject in psychological research', *Psychol. Bull.*, **72**, 214-28.

Sensenig, J., Reed, T. E., and Miller, J. S. (1972). 'Cooperation in the Prisoner's Dilemma as a function of interpersonal distance', *Psychon. Sci.*, **26**, 105-6.

Shamo, G. W., and Meador, L. M. (1969). 'The effect of visual distraction upon recall and attitude change', *J. Communication*, **19**, 157-62.

Shapiro, J. G. (1968). 'Relationships between visual and auditory cues of therapeutic effectiveness', *J. Clin. Psychol.*, **24**, 236-9.

Shapiro, J. G., Foster, C. P., and Powell, T. (1968). 'Facial and bodily cues of genuineness, empathy and warmth', *J. Clin. Psychol.*, **24**, 233-6.

Sharp, M., and McClung, T. (1966). 'Effect of organization on the speaker's ethos', *Speech. Monog.*, **33**, 182-3.

Shaw, M. E. (1958). 'Some effects of irrelevant information on problem solving by small groups', *J. Soc. Psychol.*, **47**, 33-7.

Short, J. A. (1971a). *Bargaining and Negotiation—An Exploratory Study.* Unpublished Communications Studies Group paper no. E/71065/SH.

Short, J. (1971b). *Cooperation and Competition in an Experimental Bargaining Game Conducted over Two Media.* Unpublished Communications Studies Group paper no. E/71160/SH.

Short, J. A. (1972a). *Conflicts of Opinion and Medium of Communication.* Unpublished Communications Studies Group paper no. E/72001/SH.

Short, J. A. (1972b). *Medium of Communication and Consensus.* Unpublished Communications Studies Group paper no. E/72210/SH.

Short, J. A. (1972c). *Medium of Communication, Opinion Change and Solution of a Problem of Priorities.* Unpublished Communications Studies Group paper no. E/72245/SH.

Short, J. A. (1973a) *A Report on the Use of the Audio Conferencing Facility in the University of Quebec.* Communications Studies Group paper no. P/73161/SH.

Short, J. A. (1973b). *The Effects of Medium of Communication on Persuasion, Bargaining and Perceptions of the Other.* Unpublished Communications Studies Group paper no. E/73100/SH.

Short, J. A. (1974). 'Effect of medium of communication on experimental negotiation', *Human Relations*, **27**, 225-34.

Shulman, A. D., and Stone, M. (1970). *Expectation Confirmation-Disconfirmation as a Determinant of Interpersonal Behaviour: A Study of Loudness of Voice.* Presented at Southwestern Psychological Association meeting, St. Louis.

Simon, H. A. (1960). *The Shape of Automation for Men and Management.* Harper and Row, New York.

Sinaiko, H. W. (1963). *Teleconferncing: Preliminary Experiments.* Institute of Defence Analysis, Research and Engineering Support Division Research paper P 108.

Singer, J. E. (1964). 'The use of manipulative strategies: Machiavellianism and attractiveness', *Sociometry*, **27**, 128-150.

Sloan Commission on Cable Communications (1971). *On the Cable: The Television of Abundance.* McGraw-Hill, New York.

Smith, D. H. (1969). 'Communication and negotiation outcome', *J. Communication*, **19**, 248–56.

Smith, H. C. (1967). *Sensitivity to People.* McGraw–Hill, New York.

Smith, R. L., Richetto, G. M., and Zima, J. P. (1972). 'Organizational behaviour: an approach to human communication', in Budd, R.W., and Ruben, B. D. (Eds.) *Approaches to Human Communication.* Spartan Books, New York, 269–89.

Snyder, F. W., and Wiggins, N. (1970). 'Affective meaning systems: A multivariate approach', *Multivariate Behavioural Research*, **5**, 453–68.

Snyder, F. W. (1970). *Travel Patterns: Implications for New Communication Facilities.* Unpublished paper of Bell Laboratories.

Sommer, S. (1965). 'Further studies in small group ecology', *Sociometry*, **28**, 337–48.

Stapley, B. (1972). *Visual Enhancement of Telephone Conversations.* Unpublished Ph.D. thesis. Imperial College, University of London.

Stass, J. W., and Willis, F. N. (1967). 'Eye contact, pupil dilation and personal preference', *Psychon. Sci.*, **7**, 375–6.

Strickland, L. H., Guild, P. D., Barefoot, J. R., and Paterson, S. A. (1975). *Teleconferencing and Leadership Emergence.* Carleton University.

Strongman, K. T., and Champness, B. G. (1968). 'Dominance hierarchies and conflict in eye contact', *Acta Psychologica*, **28**, 376–86.

Swensson, R. G. (1967). 'Cooperation in the prisoner's dilemma game: I. The effects of asymmetrical payoff information and explicit communication', *Behavl. Sci.*, **12**, 314–22.

Tagiuri, R. (1958). 'Social preference and its perception', in Tagiuri, R., and Petrullo, L. (Eds.) *Person Perception and Interpersonal Behaviour.* Stanford University Press, Stanford.

Tagiuri, R. (1969). 'Person perception', In Lindzey, G., and Aronson, E. (Eds.) *Handbook of Social Psychology*, Volume 3. Addison-Wesley, Reading, Mass.

Tajfel, J. (1972). 'Experiments in a vacuum', in Israel, J., and Tajfel, H. (Eds.) *The Context of Social Psychology.* Academic Press, London.

Terhune, K. W. (1968). 'Motives, situation and interpersonal conflict within the Prisoner's Dilemma', *J. Pers. Soc. Psychol.*, **8**, monograph part 2.

Thomas, H., and Williams, E. (1975). *The University of Quebec Audio Conference System: An Analysis of Users' Attitudes.* Communications Studies Group paper no. P/75190/TH.

Thorngren, B. (1972). *Studier: Lokalisering.* Ekonomiska Forskningsinstitutet, Stockholm.

Thornton, G. R. (1944). 'The effect of wearing glasses on judgements of personality traits of people seen briefly', *J. Appl. Psychol.*, **28**, 203–7.

Toffler, A. (1970). *Future Schock.* Random House, New York.

Toussaint, J. H. (1960). 'A classified summary of listening 1950–59', *J. Communication*, **10**, 125–34.

Turoff, M. (1973). 'Human communication via data networks', *Computer Decisions*, 25–9.

United Nations (1971). *United Nations Statistical Review.*

Vine, I. (1970). 'Communication by facial visual signals', in Crook, J. K. (Ed.) *Social Behaviour in Animals and Man.* Academic Press, London.

Vinokur, A. (1971). 'Review and theoretical analysis of the effects of group processes upon individual and group decisions involving risk', *Psychol. Bull.*, **76**, 231–50.

Vitz, P. C., and Kite, W. R. (1970). 'Factors affecting conflict and negotiation within an alliance', *J. Exp. Soc. Psychol.*, **6**, 233-47.

Voissem, N. H., and Sistrunk, F. (1971). 'Communication schedule and cooperative game behaviour', *J. Pers. Soc. Psychol.*, **19**, 160-7.

Wall, V. D., and Boyd, J. A. (1971). 'Channel variation and attitude change', *J. Communication*, **21**, 363-7.

Wapner, S., and Alper, T. G. (1952). 'The effect of an audience on behaviour in a choice situation', *J. Abn. Soc. Psychol.*, **47**, 222-9.

Warner, K. E. (1974). 'The need for some innovative concepts of innovation: An examination of research on the diffusion of innovations', *Policy Sci.*, **5**, 433-51.

Warr, P. B., and Haycock, U. (1970). 'Scales for a British personality differential', *Brit. J. Soc. Clin. Psychol.*, **9**, 328-37.

Watson, O. M., and Graves, T. D. (1966). 'Quantitative research in proxemic behaviour', *Amer. Anthropologist*, **68**, 971-85.

Watts, W. A., and McGuire, W. J. (1964). 'Persistence of induced opinion change and retention of induced message content', *J. Abn. Soc. Psychol.*, **68**, 233-41.

Weston, J. R., and Kristen, C. (1973). *Teleconferencing: A Comparison of Attitudes, Uncertainty and Interpersonal Atmospheres in Mediated and Face-to-face Group Interaction*. Department of Communications, Canada.

Westrum, R. (1972). *Communications Systems and Social Change*. Unpublished Ph.D. thesis. University of Chicago.

White, R., and Lippitt, R. (1960). 'Leader behaviour and member reaction in three "social climates" ', in Cartwright, D., and Zander, A. (Eds.) *Group Dynamics: Research and Theory*. Harper and Row, New York.

Wichman, H. (1970). 'Effects of isolation and communication on cooperation in a two person game', *J. Pers. Soc. Psychol.*, **16**, 114-20.

Wiener, M., and Mehrabian, A. (1968). *Language within Language: Immediacy, a Channel in Verbal Communication*. Appleton-Century-Crofts, New York.

Wilke, W. H. (1934). 'An experimental analysis of speech: the radio and the printed page as a psychological device', *Arch. Psychol. (NY)*, **169**.

Williams, E. (1972). *Factors Influencing the Effect of Medium of Communication upon Preferences for Media, Conversations and Persons*. Unpublished Communications Studies Group paper no. E/72227/WL.

Williams, E. (1973). *Coalition Formation in Three-person Groups Communication via Telecommunications Media*. Unpublished Communications Studies Group paper no. E/73037/WL.

Williams, E. (1974). *A Summary of the Present State of Knowledge Regarding the Effectiveness of the Substitution of Face-to-face Meetings by Telecommunicated Meetings: Type Allocation Revisited*. Unpublished Communications Studies Group paper no. P/74294/WL.

Williams, E., and Holloway, S. (1974). *The Evaluation of Teleconferencing: Report of a Questionnaire Study of Users' Attitudes to the Bell Canada Conference Television System*. Unpublished Communications Studies Group paper no. P/74247/WL.

Williams, E. (1975a). 'Medium or message: Communications medium as a determinant of interpersonal evaluation', *Sociometry*, **38**, 119-30.

Williams, E. (1975b). *Speech Patterns During Mediated Communication Within Small Groups*. Unpublished Communications Studies Group paper no. E/75275/WL.

Williams, E. (1975c). 'Coalition formation over telecommunication media', *Europ. J. Soc. Psychol.*

Wilmott, P., and Young, M. (1957). *Family and Kinship in East London*. Kegan Paul, London.

Wilson, C., and Williams, E. (1975). *Watergate Words: A Naturalistic Study of Media and Communication*. Unpublished Communications Studies Group paper.

Winer, B. J. (1962). *Statistical Principles in Experimental Design*. McGraw-Hill, New York.

Wise, A. (1971), 'The impact of electronic communications on metropolitan form', *Ekistics*, **188**, 22–31.

Woodside, C., M. Cavers, J. K., and Buck, I. K. (1971). *Evaluation of a Video Addition to the Telephone for Engineering Conversations*. Unpublished company data.

Young, G. A. (1971). *Commuters—Stay Home*. AIAA Paper no. 71-490. Presented to Urban Technology Conference, New York.

Young, I. (1974a). *Telecommunicated Interviews: An Exploratory Study*. Unpublished Communications Studies Group paper no. E/74165/YN.

Young, I. (1974b). *Understanding the Other Person in Mediated Interactions*. Unpublished Communications Studies Group paper no. E/74266/YN.

Young, I. (1975). *A Three Party Mixed-Media Business Game: A Progress Report on Results to Date*. Unpublished Communications Studies Group paper no. E/75189/YN.

Zajonc, R. B., (1965). 'Social facilitation', *Science*, **149**, 269–74.

Zajonc, R. B., and Sales, S. M. (1966). 'Social facilitation of dominant and subordinate responses', *J. Exp. Soc. Psychol.*, **2**, 160-8.

Name Index

Subject Index